THE CHURCH
IN AN AGE
OF Secular
Mysticisms

THE *CHURCH*
IN AN AGE
OF Secular
Mysticisms

Why Spiritualities without God
Fail to Transform Us

Andrew Root

Baker Academic
a division of Baker Publishing Group
Grand Rapids, Michigan

© 2023 by Andrew Root

Published by Baker Academic
a division of Baker Publishing Group
Grand Rapids, Michigan
www.bakeracademic.com

Printed in the United States of America

Library of Congress Cataloging-in-Publication Control Number: 2023015035

ISBN 978-1-5409-6673-5 (paper)
ISBN 978-1-5409-6691-9 (casebound)

Baker Publishing Group publications use paper produced from sustainable forestry practices and post-consumer waste whenever possible.

23   24   25   26   27   28   29   7   6   5   4   3   2   1

To Dave Lose and Rolf Jacobson,
with gratitude for two decades
of friendship and conversation.
And hopefully several decades more
if we stop eating Idaho Nachos.

CONTENTS

PREFACE

It happens to me a lot. In committee meetings, I often say things that land with a thud. In group discussions, I come upon a big idea that, when shared, just seems odd. It's not the committee's fault. It's hard to have real estate in my head.

The origins of this final (I promise!) volume of the Ministry in a Secular Age series started one such time. In a committee meeting of faculty and staff at Luther Seminary, we were discussing evangelism and discipleship. Our conversations began moving toward transformation and spirituality. It struck me that people far outside the church, many who had walked away from the church, followed a pathway of transformation and spirituality. They were undeniably seeking to be transformed. All these people possessed some sense of spirituality—usually a spirituality without God—that delivered what they believed was transformation. I came to recognize that we would only understand what practices and visions of evangelism and discipleship were needed if we could front (to both affirm and deny) the many competing secular spiritualities of transformation that exist in our late-modern world. So I suggested we do so. The committee looked at me blankly.

The group had been tasked with creating some exercises to be used in classrooms to discuss evangelism and discipleship. I suggested that we read twenty or so memoirs and trace out the different pathways of transformation they articulate, particularly focusing on their views of the self. My sense was that memoirists had become our new mystics in late modernity. Memoirists offer routes of transformation, stories of conversion, steps into a spirituality. Interestingly, almost all of them articulate transformation without a living, acting God. The more I talked, the deeper the blank looks on the committee members' faces became. They started to tilt their heads like a dog confused by an odd sound. Recognizing the stare, I returned to where I'm most comfortable, my lonely home office, to dive into memoirs and type away. I wrote this book, completing the Ministry in a Secular Age series, as a way of explaining myself.

The objective of this final book is to delve into one understandable response to the claim that we live in a secular age. People often respond with, "If we are in a secular age, it also seems like a postsecular age. There are a lot of spiritualities all around us, aren't there?" Indeed. But those many spiritualities are actually evidence that we *are* living in a secular age. What Charles Taylor means by a secular age includes this proliferation of spiritualities. Organized and classic forms of religious belief and practice have been fragilized to such a point that a new space is open for all sorts of spiritualities to enter the scene. Our secular age is *not* void of spirituality but instead creates a buffet of many, many spiritualities. The secularizing forces we've discussed in the previous five volumes (particularly the first three) make all spiritualities equal, and therefore those spiritualities are dependent on individual use. We all search for our own unique way of being spiritual.

Even our views of transformation (what it means to be changed, to be made new, to find a new way of life, to discover the right path) are linked directly with our spiritualities. Interestingly, inside this secular age, mysticism broadly returns to our society. By "mysticism" I don't just mean an ecstatic experience bound inside an abbey or a monastery; I mean a form of spirituality that seeks to overcome our impediments, impossibilities, and even guilt. We find all sorts of these mysticisms on YouTube and Instagram. The difference in our late-modern age is that these mysticisms are without God (something those in the Middle Ages could not have imagined). These mystics without God, who offer their positions in memoirs, offer us pathways for transformation. My job below will be to lay out these pathways and why they are shaped thus. Before I can lay out these pathways and show their shape, I must first articulate our new conception of the self and how this conception brings spirituality back to the surface. I do so for descriptive purposes, but more so, I believe that the Christian pastor and ministry leader, if not careful, too often adopts these secular views of transformation embedded in our late-modern concepts of the self. What is problematic about these secular views of transformation is not only that they are mysticisms/spiritualities without God but more so that their views of the self become incongruent with the Christian faith. At the core of a transformation into Christ by the Spirit is a claim about how the self stands before God. The self comes before God in need, in confession. The secular mysticisms and their roads toward transformation do something quite different with the self. They apotheosize the self to such a point that the self is not only no longer in need of anything but is the very location of transcendence. The self becomes worshiped.

I don't mean this to sound so harsh. I actually find many of these secular spiritualities of transformation, these mystical memoirists, interesting and even helpful at points. But hidden under their articulations is a view of the self that I believe, if not uncovered, will wreak havoc on our formation into the life of the crucified Christ. If not examined, this view of the self will colonize our Christian views of transformation, further gutting pastoral identity. Focusing on confession and surrender is important because, unlike with secular mysticism, it moves the self outside itself, into an encounter (into yearning) for a living God who breaks in, arriving in the world. Louis Dupré, a historian of mysticism, says beautifully about Christian forms of the mystical life, "Thus while thinking only about God the Christian mystic teaches an important lesson about the self, namely, that the self is in its deepest nature more than itself. To move into myself means in the end to move beyond myself into what is 'higher' than the self or 'deeper' than the self."[1]

What is offered in this book continues the direction of my overall project. I offer a description of our contemporary moment through a cultural philosophy that has the *theologia crucis* (theology of the cross) as its bedrock. The *theologia crucis* is the cornerstone of a theological building that I hope those directly engaged in ministry can live within.

The shape of this final project matches the other five volumes. It first describes our situation, examining our cultural time and how these new spiritualities evolved in relation to the self. The self is a major focus in the first five chapters, clearing the ground for us to turn directly to these myriad memoirs and their pathways of transformation. If you find yourself anxious to get to memoirs, you can jump to chapter 6. But the importance of the first five chapters is to see how the mysticisms/spiritualities of memoirists are embedded in our late-modern view of the self. In these early chapters, I show particularly how and why guilt has returned with teeth in late modernity—something

---

1. Louis Dupré, *The Deeper Life: An Introduction to Christian Mysticism* (New York: Crossroad, 1981), 25.

very unexpected. In chapter 6, I begin creating a map of the spiritualities/
mysticisms of our secular age. I'm not shy in my appreciation for mysticism
without God, but I'm also not shy in saying that Protestantism particularly
needs to return to what I call a "Beyonder" way of being. A Beyonder way sees
transformation coming not through the inner genius of the self or the heroic
actions of the self but only through the confession and surrender of the self
to something beyond the self. I'll come to the process of mapping more than
a dozen memoirs, revealing their inner shape of transformation. In chapter 7,
I turn from description to theological construction, pulling out the *theologia
crucis* to shape a theology of transformation. This will start with a critical
chapter that uses the thought of philosopher Byung-Chul Han to show that
not all mysticisms (not all pathways to transformation) are equal. The final
three chapters show why the pathway of confession and surrender is most
helpful to the church and pastoral ministry.

This is the sixth and final book of what started as a three-volume series.
These final three volumes are not so much distinct volumes as deepening
companions to the first three volumes. The way they connect makes a kind
of mirror reflection. Volume 3, *The Congregation in a Secular Age*, is directly
connected to volume 4, *Churches and the Crisis of Decline*. Volume 2, *The
Pastor in a Secular Age*, is connected to volume 5, *The Church after Innovation*. And volume 6, this book, is connected to volume 1, *Faith Formation
in a Secular Age*. In volume 1, I discuss Taylor's articulation of authenticity,
showing how it has deeply affected our view of faith, then turning to Paul's
views of what it means to have faith and how faith itself is a movement into
(being *in*) Christ. I discuss a movement from humility to communion to deep
transformation. Here in volume 6, I move further into this transformation,
pushing more directly into the mystical dynamic. Building on my work with
Paul, I return to the mystical tradition of Christianity that supports the *theologia crucis*, placing all this in conversation with a certain reading of Luther
(I did something congruent in volume 1 as well, drawing from the Finnish
interpretation of Luther).

There are many to thank as this series comes to end. Particularly in their
help with this book I'd like to thank Erik Leafblad, Megan Clapp, Wes Ellis,
and Jon Wasson, who again read this whole book and offered important
feedback. My colleagues Justin Nickle and Lois Malcolm—two incredible
readers and theologians—offered important insights. My closest friends from
my Princeton days, Blair Bertrand and Jessicah Duckworth, deeply engaged

with this work; I'm thankful to them both for twenty years of conversations. I'd also like to thank Denise Carrell, a student at Princeton Theological Seminary, for helping me gather the memoirs. As usual Bob Hosack and Eric Salo, and all the folks at Baker, have been amazing to work with.

Again it is to Kara Root that I offer the biggest thanks. It is mainly to her and her ministry that I write, with the hope that my thoughts might be a small blessing to her. Her incredibly faithful ministry to her congregation and the persons in it will receive the last word in this book and therefore the series—which is only right!

READ BEFORE USING
(DON'T SKIP)

A very short user's guide is necessary for this book. Because this book concludes a long six-volume series, there are a lot of dimensions to this final book. In the pages to come I'll describe the many cultural forms of transformation, spirituality, and mysticism that have shockingly arrived in late modernity. I'll also offer my take on why many of these forms cannot bring us to the transformation we seek and why pastoral practice should avoid many of these secular mysticisms.

I build to this point by setting stone on top of stone to build an argument. Therefore, you should be aware that my goal in the first four chapters is to lay out how our view of the self has come to be. We cannot talk about spirituality and transformation without understanding our sense of the self. The first four chapters examine how the self became so important to us late-modern people and yet also has become burdened, unexpectedly, with guilt. It is quite odd that in a secular age when people can live without God, our views of the self have led us to seek spiritualities, even mysticisms, without God. All this work on examining the self leads us into thinking about the many ways we imagine that the self can be changed or transformed even in our secular age of immanence.

Chapters 5 and 6 are the heart of the project. Here I map our secular mysticisms. I show that the memoir and the memoirist is the mystic in our secular age. These memoirists have given us three pathways with eleven lanes for transformation. Two of these pathways have no need for a living God. The third pathway cannot be without a living God. Chapters 5 and 6 will sketch and diagram the shape of our secular spiritual world.

But not all of these mysticisms or spiritualities are equal. Therefore, starting in chapter 7, I begin to move from description into normative assertion. Drawing from philosopher Byung-Chul Han I show that the mysticisms/spiritualities without God cannot deliver, and they fall into many of the traps of the self laid out in chapters 1 through 4. In chapters 8 through 10 I delve into theological construction to articulate the shape of transformation/spirituality that occurs before God. This perspective claims a very different view of the self, one that I contend pastors and ministers must embrace to renew their practice of ministry in a secular age. In outline form:

Chapters 1–4. Provide an overview of the self and how late modernity gives us a much different view of what it means to be a self. These chapters show how we can so easily be spiritual but not religious.

Chapters 5–6. Map our secular spiritualities.

Chapter 7. Shows that not all spiritualities are equal.

Chapters 8–10. Provide a constructive theology for transformation and renewed conceptions of the self for a spirituality/mysticism before and with God.

1

<hr>

New Mystics without God

Closed World Structures and Memoirists

It's already dark when we land. The evening covers the beauty of the island like a veil. I can't hear it, but even from outside the airport I can smell the ocean. The alluring presence of the surrounding Pacific laps its aloha into my body. The thought of being surrounded by those blue waters bobbing, even on the Big Island in Hawaii, does something to me. As I await our luggage, I remind myself that we're standing in the middle of the Pacific, on top of a volcano oasis of tropical beauty plopped in the middle of the majestic belly of the great ocean. Nothing else is around us for almost a thousand miles.

We squeeze our luggage into an UberX and head to an Airbnb. I put the windows of the tattered Toyota all the way down, in part to escape the un-inviting personalness of the shared UberX. Sliding into an UberX is always a tad uncomfortable. It's like choosing to be locked alone with a stranger in their bedroom. You're forced to sit uncomfortably for thirty minutes with this stranger in one of their most intimate living spaces. In this UberX the heavy smell of Febreze seems to be doing its own veiling of cigarette smoke. This is one reason to put my head as close to the open window as I can. Not close enough to be mistaken for a golden retriever but more than adequate to feel the warm air on my face. With each mile the darkness becomes thicker, but the presence of the ocean more looming.

When we arrive, we can't tell. As the door swings open there is only the sweet smell of ocean air. The Airbnb is perfect: plain but not tattered. The time change makes it essential we find the bedrooms and call it a day. Kara and I find the master. We open the windows and hear the Pacific. But we can't see it. "It seems close," I say out loud as I fade into sleep.

The next morning, to our surprise, it's right outside our window, staring us right in the eye. The bluest blue of the Pacific is as far from our bed as first base is to home plate. The rocky shore radiates its beauty. The blue washes each black lava stone. Before I rise from the pillow on the first morning, I know what my whole vacation will consist of: nothing. I'll sit on a chair right below our bedroom, my feet in the ground, my eyes on the blue, and I'll just be. I'll stare at the Pacific as it stares back at me. The mutual gaze, I trust, will be transforming.

Yet, it's hard to just be. I've never been good at staring contests. Transformation, even inside the radiance of such beauty, is seemingly harder to come by than I assumed. To cope with my busy mind's aversion to being, I drag the dozen books I packed with me to my seat on the beach. I read for a living, so it feels like I'm cheating on my vacation. But I justify this by reminding myself that the books I packed are outliers. They don't fit into any specific research project. They're not for a class I'll be teaching. They're just fun—at least to my twisted mind. In my stack are a few historical biographies and even a popular history of the English Premier League (I'm a party animal!). I sit and read. I break eye contact with the Pacific blue, but its lapping rhythm still fills my ears. Its majestic aura of salt and breeze wrap around me. It's good. It's needed. It's a gift. But it's not quite the transformational moment I assumed it would be when I first awoke and caught eyes with the blue.

There's one book in my stack I've been putting off. It has two strikes against it. First, it was a gift. I really shouldn't write that, because the only thing I love more than books is free books. These words shouldn't dissuade anyone from gifting me a book or two. Yet, when someone gives me a book that I'm not immediately interested in, it becomes an assignment. Unfortunately, I'm the kind of person who feels compelled to do all his assignments. I try not to have books in my library that I haven't read. Thus, this book, which I didn't really want to read, was packed in my suitcase.

The second strike is the genre: memoir. For some reason, to my idea-opposed head a five-hundred-page historical biography on Beethoven is way more appealing than a memoir. I know, stupid. But this stupidity made Tara Westover's *Educated* the last book I read at the feet of the Pacific. It was the last but by far the best book of the stack.

Educated and Transformed

Westover tells the amazing story—with such crisp writing—about going from being a homeschooled (really, unschooled) mountain girl in Idaho to earning a Gates Cambridge University scholarship and eventually a PhD. Westover grew up in a very conservative Mormon family that isolated itself, for both religious and political reasons, from the rest of society. They did this most directly by refusing to allow the secular government to get its hands on their children, thereby corrupting them with its ideas and schools. In Westover's father's mind, the apocalypse was right around the corner. Therefore, what his children needed to know was not how to live in a society and get a job but how to survive in the end times.

The mountains and the family land became Westover's classroom. Her primary teacher was her father, with his manic survivalist ways. The picture Westover paints is captivating. The stories of life and the (un)education of her and her siblings is probing, sensitive, and insightful. By the middle of the book the reader can't help but ask how this person could end up at Cambridge or even write at all (let alone a book).

In part 2 of her book, a great transformation begins. It's the eve of Y2K. Westover's father is sure this is it. When the seconds turn us over to the year 2000 the apocalypse will commence. And he's more than ready! Westover, now in her teens, has tried a few times to persuade her father to allow her to go to school. But he'll have none of it. Why would he? As the clouds of apocalypse gather on the horizon, what could be more of a waste of time than school? But the storm never comes. The jammed gears of societal breakdown don't occur. In its place comes the depression. Westover's feverish father becomes now even more manic than usual.

He's so agitated that when Westover is in a car accident, severely injuring her neck, her father refuses to allow her to see a doctor or visit a hospital. Her brother Shawn becomes her advocate, heroically standing up to her father. But soon her heroic advocate becomes her abusing adversary. Shawn's own frustrated torture is physically released on Westover. Home is no longer safe, for multiple reasons. At just seventeen, without a day in school or even much interaction with the rest of society, Westover is on her own.

By chance Westover is told that if she scores high enough on the ACT, Brigham Young University will admit her. They have a program for children just like her, who stumble their way out of the mountains. She scores well enough and soon her first day (ever!) of school is in a university classroom at BYU. As though thawed from a glacier, Westover both appears and feels like a person from another era. She has none of the socialization or years of report cards to assure herself, in this very different world, that she can be educated.

The rest of the memoir proves not only that Westover can indeed be educated but that education itself can radically transform a life. The book has had such a wide reach because it reminds us of the power of education. Westover's memoir makes the claim that education itself is an engine of transformation. The book is a kind of humanist call back—a late-modern spin on the humanism coming out of the Renaissance. In the Late Renaissance, particularly through thinkers such as Erasmus, it was assumed that education, particularly learning to read and recite the classics, formed a soul. Echoing back to ancient times, humanist thinkers believed that to be educated was to be taught a new way of being. Education wasn't about future employment. It had little direct functional purpose. To be educated was to have your spirit transformed by sacred and trusted knowledge. This knowledge had as its source an inbreaking transcendence. It had a kind of metaphysical quality to it. The humanists were concerned with the human form, but they believed what made the human form was a rhetorical education that formed the soul (through the tongue).[1] Education allowed a person to enter a direct process of soul-shifting transformation. Westover concurs and testifies to how education transformed her.

Westover, of course, is not writing as a fifteenth- or sixteenth-century humanist. Rather, she writes as a late-modern academic. A strange one due to background, for sure, but a late-modern academic nevertheless.

Transformation in a Closed World Structure

Charles Taylor has taught us that our secular age is *not* without the possibility of belief, transcendence, and therefore deep forms of transformation. Nevertheless, inside this kind of secular age there are groups, collectives, and associations that nevertheless construct closed views of our world. These groups, collectives, and associations see belief in God, religious practice, and the thought of an inbreaking transcendence as misguided at best and pathological at worst. Taylor says such groups, collectives, and associations operate with a "closed world structure." There happen to be certain parts and segments

1. See Stephen Toulmin, *Cosmopolis: The Hidden Agenda of Modernity* (Chicago: University of Chicago Press, 1990).

(but not the whole) of Western modernity that have little to no openness to what the humanists thought was obvious: being transformed depended on a knowledge that had its source, at least partly, in something beyond (some kind of inbreaking transcendence). Taylor explains that these groups and peoples who presume a closed world structure are scattered across the whole of society. But where they can be found most consistently is in academia. Taylor believes that consistently, and somewhat ironically,[2] the academic world operates as a closed world structure, allergic to inbreaking transcendence.

Westover is too sanguine about how our pasts make us—too compassionate on those she's left in the mountains—to ferociously defend the closed world structure. She throws no shade on those who still believe in a living God. She makes no gestures toward adding another dead bolt to the door of the closed world structure (though she of all people could be forgiven for doing so). Yet her testimony to a great transformation wears few to no marks of the movement of an inbreaking personal God. She seems to have left such language in the mountains as she departs BYU for Cambridge and Harvard. Ultimately, there is no sense that what makes education transformational is that the knowledge itself is bound in the inbreaking being of God (or any other spiritual reality for that matter).

I make this observation not to disqualify or even minimize Westover's testimony to transformation. The intent is definitely *not* to say that her transformation doesn't count. Rather, it's the opposite. Whether you're reading *Educated* on a beach while being serenaded with lapping alohas or in a dentist office awaiting a root canal, the book can trigger a deep resonance. It is a true tale, an honest testimony, of transformation. It's beautiful. And yet, if we stop and think about it, acknowledging her transformation perplexes those of us who oversee and lead communities of faith and therefore are committed, to some degree, to a world where a living God breaks in, transforming the world and its persons.

In other words, if even inside a closed world structure (whether securely locked down as it is in academia or just relatively so) there are sure testimonies to transformation, why do we need openness to an inbreaking transcendence? Especially openness to the movements of a living God? If this is true, if lives can be transformed without God, why do we need God at all? If education saved Westover, what need is there for the saving God of Israel? Particularly, why is there a need for any church to exist, made up of persons who still yearn

2. This is ironic because before the Enlightenment, education and the university were built around the hidden knowledge of the transcendent.

for and believe it is necessary to witness to a transformation delivered freely and solely by the hand of the inbreaking God of the exodus? If transformation can happen outside of this—so far outside that it can happen inside closed world structures— what is a pastor or ministry leader doing at all?

The answer is reductive, flattening an entire vocation like a pancake. Not wanting to be confused as someone who is even tangentially similar to Westover's father, and acknowledging that those who are respected by the closed world structures don't talk of an inbreaking God (and don't even trust those who do), we often settle for religious management. Inside the concession to the closed world structure, the church and its leadership can only be about the management of institutional religion. Forget the stuff about inbreaking. The closed world structure heralds that if there is a place at all for those who still gather as believers, it is inside a privatized life segment called "religion." Religion is a segment, like a hobby or affiliation, that someone can choose as they wish. Why they would wish to choose it is hard to know for those committed to the closed world structure. But it's assumed to have something to do with nostalgia or an unfortunate proclivity to weak-mindedness.

Inside the closed world structure, belief can only be belief in a religion that loses the act of the inbreaking God and therefore has no way of testifying to how our being is transformed. The minister's job becomes ultimately and finally about managing religion. It is not testifying, contemplating, and leading the people into ways in which our finite beings participate in the inbreaking life of the infinite God. Inside the closed world structure, or even adjacent to it, the closed world structure can only offer tales of its own kind of transformation, and the pastor must settle for ossified religion. Church life and pastoral ministry become about something other than reflection, preparation, and direct participation in transformation.

Ironically, just when most mainline church leaders (sick of feeling embarrassed and cross-pressured with an uneasy doubt) stopped talking about transformation, those in the closed world structure, as well as those in many other parts of society in our secular age, began talking about it. For the last fifty years the publication of memoirs has proliferated. For the last decade or so memoir after memoir has told tale after tale of transformation. Almost all of those memoirists have found their transforming moments without the necessity of any inbreaking transcendence. In one way or another, they directly or indirectly claim that deep transformation—so deep it even touches on the mystical—*can* happen without an inbreaking God. Each claims a kind of salvation without a transcendent savior. As a matter of fact, the memoirists of the last decade and a half might be called *mystics without God*.[3] How this is possible, and what it looks like, will be my task in the chapters to come. My goal will not be simply to point out how one author or another uses the word "God" or doesn't. Rather, I hope-to sketch out the shape of transformation itself, seeking for the inner logic, the core dimensions of a transformational path that contends with the inbreaking of God. I will ask if it is possible for our secular age to affirm, and therefore return to, the mystical path of transformation that has its source in God.

Before going any further, though, we need a clear definition of "mystical." By "mystical" or "mysticism" I don't necessarily mean a call back to abbeys and monks, saints and the ecstatic. Rather, by "mystical" I mean a spirituality that seeks to overcome our impediments (even our guilt) by drawing us into a spiritual union. It just so happens that the object of this union—the very thing we seek to be united to that can overcome our impediments—has shifted from God to our self. Therefore, we'll need to focus in the early chapters on how the self has become so inflated in importance to us late-modern people seeking spiritual transformation.

I take up this task only to make a larger point: that pastoral identity is confused, and the ministry of the church is flattened, when we can no longer feel compelled to speak of transformation. As the body of Jesus Christ, we can speak of transformation only when we recover a sense of the inbreaking of God (revelation). As the failures of the last century of Protestantism in America have shown, speaking of God can deliver transformation only when it is the God who is God (and not a mascot to our denominational or political religion). It must be a God who is God. Paradoxically (or better, dialectically), it must be a God who cannot be known but whom we nevertheless encounter as inbreaking.

The ultimate task of this project is to map transformation inside our secular age. This mapping will take some time to build up to. We first need to explore how the self has become so important to us late-modern people. To

---

3. Mary Karr discusses the rise of the memoir in *The Art of Memoir* (New York: Harper, 2015). Karr moves further in the direction that I'm moving in, asserting that the memoirist is a kind of mystic. She says, "I once heard Don DeLillo quip that a fiction writer starts with meaning and then manufactures events to represent it; a memoirist starts with events, then derives meaning from them. In this, memoir purports to grow more organically from lived experience. When I asked a class of undergrads what they liked about memoir, I heard them echo the no-doubt-naïve sentiment that they drew hope from the mere fact of a writer living past a bad juncture to report on it. 'It's a miracle he even survived!' was written on many papers. The telling has some magic power for them, as it does for me" (xvii).

map secular transformations we'll need to see what the self has become in our time. After exploring in the first five chapters the state of the self and its spirituality, I'll turn to the mapping. I'll use as my primary source a handful of contemporary memoirs to explore the pathways of transformation (picking up this task directly in chap. 6). Historically it's been the mystics who've kept the path(s) of transformation before a society. They've beckoned societies to remember that human *beings* can be transformed and should seek transformation. The mystics have sought this transformation by attending to the self's needs, longings, and impediments. Surprisingly, but assuredly, such mystics have returned even inside our Protestant-birthed secular age, even in a culture where closed world structures with no room for transcendence per se are present and powerful. Even inside closed world structures, as Westover shows, the mystics of transformation have returned as memoirists, offering pathways of spiritual transformation. But it just so happens, as we'll explore, these are mystics without an inbreaking God.

These late-modern, secular age mystics, each with a quite different view of the self, present paths that are much different from ones that would be recognized by Anthony in Alexandria, Basil in Cappadocia, Cuthbert in northern England, or Meister Eckhart between the Rhineland and Paris. In the eighteenth century, Paris was the birthplace of a mysticism without an inbreaking transcendence. Paris is the place where the mystics of inbreaking transcendence, such as Eckhart, who once wandered the narrow streets of the Latin Quarter, were replaced by an antimysticism that birthed an all-new modern kind of mysticism.[4] By entering Paris, we can see this, and it will return us again to Westover.

---

4. It is hard to get a handle on what mysticism is. Rudolf Otto gives us some touchstones. He says, "Essentially Mysticism is the stressing to a very high degree, indeed the overstressing, of the non-rational or supra-rational elements in religion; and it is only intelligible when so understood. The various phases and factors of the non-rational may receive varying emphasis, and the type of Mysticism will differ accordingly as some or others fall into the background. What we have been analysing, however, is a feature that recurs in all forms of Mysticism everywhere, and it is nothing but the 'creature-consciousness' stressed to the utmost and to excess, the expression meaning, if we may repeat the contrast already made, not 'feeling of our createdness' but 'feeling of our creaturehood,' that is, the consciousness of the littleness of every creature in face of that which is above all creatures. . . . A characteristic common to all types of Mysticism is the Identification, in different degrees of completeness, of the personal self with the transcendent Reality. . . . 'Identification' alone, however, is not enough for Mysticism; it must be Identification with the Something that is at once absolutely supreme in power and reality and wholly non-rational." Otto, *The Idea of the Holy: An Inquiry into the Non-Rational Factor in the Idea of the Divine and Its Relation to the Rational* (n.p.: Pantianos Classics, 1917), 25.

2

When Dogs Bark during Paris Lockdown

Meet the Magnificent Jean-Jacques

This Airbnb is welcoming. It's small but far from tattered. As a matter of fact, it is darn stylish. But there is no view, no lights from Paris to catch your eye. The little apartment is on the ground floor inside a tiny courtyard. Beyond two large security doors is not so much the heart but the mind of Paris. The Sorbonne is just a few blocks away. The Pantheon, the Parisian intellectual and cultural hall of fame, is just up the street.

It feels like we've snuck into the great European city. Just weeks earlier, France started welcoming their first visitors since COVID-19 had shut the borders. When we arrive fully vaccinated, Paris is still on curfew. It will end the day before we leave. Our last evening is the first without restrictions. When the last evening comes, our dream of sitting on the Seine, taking in the scenes as the clock slides late into the night, meets our travel fatigue. The prospect of our looming early flight sends us back to the tiny courtyard just as dusk is descending on this early July evening.

To our bad luck, the Luxembourg metro station we need to use to get back to the airport is closed. To save us from disaster in the morning, I decide to scout out an alternate. I leave my family behind and enter the streets, moving toward the Latin Quarter. After finding the alternative metro station and making plans for breakfast, I walk back to the courtyard Airbnb. The energy on the streets is palpable. The closer I get to the Sorbonne, the more young people I see and the more energy I feel. I decide to walk up to the Pantheon. I want to take it in one more time before departure.

The dusk descending on the Pantheon is luminous. The light in Paris is always enchanting. As this evening light cascades against the domed building, I breathe in the moment. This incandescent light mixed with the buzz of the lifted curfew makes it feel like all of Paris is bursting with celebration. Or maybe it's just the young people. Around the Pantheon, they're everywhere. They're sitting in circles of twenty or so talking, drinking, laughing, and listening to music. Their music and wine make it clear they're here for the night.

Standing right in front of the Pantheon, pausing to take in its dusk-bathed beauty, I walk to the right. There are more than thirty, maybe fifty, young people sitting on benches around a statue. Some are even perched on the base of the statue. I can get close enough to see the plaque. Below the statue, on the base, it reads "Jean-Jacques Rousseau." I somehow knew it was him before I read the plaque. Jean-Jacques's presence still saturates this part of Paris 250 years after his death. His presence is not absent from these young people in their expressive celebration on the ground of this university of enlightenment.

There are few people more responsible for our conflicting and (at times) contradictory ways of being modern than Jean-Jacques Rousseau. Few people are more responsible than him for claiming that an individual can be transformed without any need for an inbreaking transcendence, or that without God there is indeed a way for a new kind of self to re-embrace the mystical.

When Dogs Bark *At* and *For* the Mystical

To be modern is to hold within us the dueling barking dogs of reason and expression. In the West, we have somehow built societies around conflicting commitments to firm rationality and to potent romantic expressivism. Sometimes we can balance these two commitments. Other times—like in the middle of a public health crisis—we struggle mightily as each dog barks violently at the other. We believe that truth is found in the numbers of a firmly ordered natural world. And yet we also contend that everyone has their own truth. That indeed some of our deepest truths—that we love, that we experience beauty in nature, that we yearn for freedom—can only be accessed by something in us that is beyond reason. Our societies and human lives are built around both the stiff numbers of reason and the incalculable inner feelings of expressing our true selves. Integrating these two commitments, when it is necessary, is often confusing, inconsistent, and frustrating. Just like Jean-Jacques Rousseau himself!

It was Jean-Jacques who kicked off this conflicting combination. He placed one dog of reason in the yard of our imagination with the other dog of inner expression. Rousseau knew they'd bark when first put together. But he hoped they'd eventually make good kennel mates.[1] Yet, Jean-Jacques's assumption never really came to fruition. Others with even more intellectual dexterity, such as Immanuel Kant (who had a picture of Jean-Jacques on his wall in Königsberg), tried with more success. To keep the analogy going, Kant was a master dog trainer. But even Kant couldn't get these dogs of reason and expression to completely cohabitate. Rather, these dogs have been barking at each other ever since—with fluctuating levels of fury.[2] But never have they cuddled up, forming a single pack with pups.

Yet, bringing these two dogs together, even in their animosity, birthed a new kind of modern mysticism through a new view of the self. The rational hound showed its teeth whenever mystery and claims of an inbreaking God were used as an explanation for anything in the world—Why does the sun rise? Why does a king have authority? Why are leaves green? Why do nobles deserve their standing? The dog of reason growled whenever it was assumed that human beings could be swept up into the absolute or find their consciousness transformed by deep spiritual meaning. The hound snapped its jaw when such explanations were offered for how a life could be transformed. It's an overstatement, but only slightly, to assert that the hound of reason was trained to guard against thinking it plausible that any transformation—whether in the natural world or in the self—had anything to do with transcendence.

It was assumed that the hound of reason had chased the mystical out of the West for good. John Locke and David Hume, like Max Weber after them, were tone-deaf to the mystical. It was a kind of music they couldn't hear and therefore didn't like. But the dog of reason's bark was worse than its bite. Soon another dog, a scrappy terrier, appeared, ushered into the yard by the

---

1. Isaiah Berlin in his book *The Magus of the North: J. G. Hamann and the Origins of Modern Irrationalism* (London: John Murray, 1993), 102–4, discusses what Johann Hamann thought of Rousseau. He articulates how Rousseau was seeking to bring together reason and expressivism.

2. Romantic and proto-Romantic thinkers on the other hand—particularly Johann Hamann and to a less degree Johann Herder—knew that these dogs could never be kenneled together. Hamann even thought it was an abomination to try. Hamann had a particular hate for the French Enlightenment. For more, see Berlin, *Magus of the North*, 22–30.

hand of Jean-Jacques himself. The terrier at first thought it might be friends with the hound. But soon the terrier was nose-to-nose with the hound, open jaw to open jaw, meeting one bark with another. These dogs would never be friends. The terrier of expressive romanticism growled back at the hound of reason. The terrier's barking began as a revolt against the loss of spiritual depth, at the refusal to give up on something like the mystical. Art and the novel were proof that a mysticism, wearing the garb of deep expressivism, could not and should not be chased completely from the yard of the West.[3] Now that the hound and terrier were barking, their teeth showing, a new kind of modern mysticism became necessary. A mysticism was needed that could live with the hound and his incessant barks of reason.

Jean-Jacques couldn't get these dogs to lie peacefully together, but in trying he, maybe unknowingly, inaugurated new forms of mysticism for a modern world, new pathways for transformation and a new view of the self. It may have been inadvertent, because Rousseau never would have said it like this, but the Germans of the next generations of the nineteenth century would

---

3. It would take until the German revolt of romanticism for this to come to be. It's seen particularly in Herder, Scheller, Schelling, and Hölderlin. But the novel was essential to Rousseau. Maurice Cranston says:

> Rousseau says he could read before he was three; the only books which served for reading lessons were the seventeenth-century French novels that had once belonged to his mother; to be nourished on such Literature at that impressionable age was responsible, he believed, for giving him a highly romanticized and sentimental vision of the world. The reading would go on throughout the night, so eager were father and son to get to the end of a story. "Sometimes my father, bearing the swallows of the morning, said shamefacedly: 'We must go to bed; I am more of a child than you are.'" From French novels Rousseau claimed that he acquired a precocious knowledge of human passions: when they had been read, he turned to more manly and serious literature—the books his mother had inherited from Pastor Bernard. "Le Sueur's *History of the Church and the Empire*, Bossuet's *Discourse on Universal History*, Plutarch's *Lives*, Nani's *History of Venice*, Ovid's *Metamorphoses*, La Bruyère, Fontenelle's *Worlds and Dialogue with Death*, and some plays by Moliere," Rousseau recalls, "were transported to my father's workshop; and I read them to him then while he worked." (Cranston, *Jean-Jacques: The Early Life and Work of Jean-Jacques Rousseau, 1712–1754* [Chicago: University of Chicago Press, 1982], 24)

John Ralston Saul explains further, "The novel was not a product or a creature of reason. It was the most irrational means of communication, subject to no stylistic order or ideological form. It was to intellectual order what animism is to religion—devoid of organized precedence or dependence on social structure. For the purposes of the novelist, everything was alive and therefore worthy of interest and doubt. At its best the novel became a vehicle for humanistic honesty. However, like democracy, it rose in tandem with the forces of reason. The endless specifics of reform made them allies to such a degree that the novel became the dominant linguistic form of the rational revolution." Saul, *Voltaire's Bastards: The Dictatorship of Reason in the West* (New York: Simon & Schuster, 1992), 537.

have, and they loved Jean-Jacques. These new forms and pathways, of course, stood outside the mysticism of the inbreaking transcendence of the wholly other God. Nevertheless, Rousseau's attempt at placing one dog with the other created a new space for a kind of mysticism without God, transformation without inbreaking transcendence.

Conflicting Confessions

Rousseau may never have successfully unified reason and expression, but his early try indelibly changed our world. Without Jean-Jacques, there would be no Tara Westover. Westover herself is a kind of American, late-modern Rousseau (we'll see how more fully in the sections below). Long before Westover, Jean-Jacques wrote personal protomemoirs that shaped all the Continent. It was a way of breaking the heavy hold of reason alone that dominated Paris. Rousseau even titled one of these late works *Confessions*, showing without subtlety that a new kind of transformation was coming from his pen. Rousseau's *Confessions* was a kind of affirmation, and yet also a sharp needle stabbed in the side, of the greatest protomemoir of Western history, Saint Augustine's *Confessions*.

Jean-Jacques never lacked confidence, which often spilled over into unwieldy (and fragile) hubris. (He was known to be easily offended, and Voltaire picked on him every chance he got.) Rousseau's unwieldy hubris led him to imagine that his *Confessions* was replacing Augustine's. In Jean-Jacques's mind, his *Confessions* would be hailed by the ages that would come after the reign of reason alone, bringing something mystical to reason, while Augustine's *Confessions* was for the passing ages of the ancient and medieval world. Jean-Jacques's *Confessions* was a new kind of mysticism for a new age, a new self. Augustine's sort of mysticism was too antiquated to continue: that self had passed away.[4]

---

4. Christopher Kelly contrasts the two confessions books, saying, "The narration of this seemingly trivial youthful indiscretion is in fact extremely important in that it is one of the passages of Rousseau's *Confessions* that invites direct comparison with a corresponding passage in Augustine's *Confessions*. In Book I of the latter Augustine tells the story of his own youthful theft of pears. In his story about theft, Augustine, like Rousseau, emphasizes that greed played no role. Also, like Rousseau, he indicates that pressure from his friends did play a part. Nonetheless, unlike Rousseau, Augustine attributes responsibility for his sin to no one but himself. Moreover, he explicitly claims that a sinful desire to harm someone else played a decisive role. In short, whereas Rousseau looks for an explanation in feelings misdirected by social forces outside himself, Augustine gives his example as an illustration of his own and humankind's

Jean-Jacques's *Confessions*, he imagined, would have to overcome Augustine's, because at the core the two *Confessions* books spoke of two starkly different experiences.[5] And, importantly for us, they spoke also of two understandings of transformation. In Augustine's *Confessions*, for instance, a transformation is recorded that is dependent completely and finally on an inbreaking transcendence. What transforms is *not* found necessarily inside of Augustine but outside of him, making its way deep into him. Augustine finds inside himself something that is not part of him. For Augustine, the inner life is the place where God moves, the place of transformation. Jean-Jacques can affirm, and even double down on, this focus on the inner life. But for Augustine this transformed inner life has its source in something far outside the inner life.

For Augustine, his inner life is transformed when he encounters the mystical experience of a child telling him to pick up and read. Augustine is transformed when picking up and reading Romans. The Word, which is outside of him, meets his inner life as an inbreaking. We could say that the mystical voice of the child and the Word of Romans transformed Augustine. This transformation clearly has its source in an inbreaking transcendence. The inbreaking transcendence reorders Augustine's inner life, transforming him forever. Augustine believes that without this something that is outside the inner life, the inner life, and therefore the whole person, is drowned in sin.

Not so much for Jean-Jacques. Rousseau can't follow that—the hound of instrumental reason barks too loud. The mystical tones of Augustine are in tune with the ideas of sin and the impossibility of the self to save itself. Jean-Jacques's new mystical emphasis is built around how the self, by attending more fully to itself, can remain the perfect self that it is by nature.

---

great propensity toward sin. In comparison with Augustine's explanation, Rousseau's certainly leans in the direction of absolving humans of responsibility for their own wicked actions. At the very least it suggests that a naturally good man should be pitied when unjust social institutions lead him astray." Kelly, "Rousseau's *Confessions*," in *The Cambridge Companion to Rousseau*, ed. Patrick Riley (London: Cambridge University Press, 2001), 314.

5. "On one of his walks to Vincennes to visit Diderot, Rousseau had an illusion which has been compared to the vision seen by St Paul on the road to Damascus. In the *Confessions*, he describes it fairly briskly. He explains that in order to moderate the pace of his walk, he had the idea of taking with him something to read on the road. 'Once I took the *Mercure de France* with me, and reading it while I walked, I came across the subject proposed by the Academy of Dijon as a prize essay for the following year: "Has the progress of the arts and sciences done more to corrupt or to purify morals?" When I read these words, I beheld another universe and became another man.' What he claimed to have seen in this flash of inspiration was that progress had not purified morals at all, but corrupted them disastrously." Cranston, *Jean-Jacques*, 228.

Rousseau, and with him almost all of Western late modernity, including my own children's school, believes the opposite of Augustine. Schools in late modernity tend to remind students, in so many words and actions, that their inner self—their inner feelings of their own self, if they can refuse the messages of haters and bullies outside the self—is truth. The inner life is completely pure, and the self is totally innocent and free from sin (a disgusting word anyway), without need of anything whatsoever that is outside itself.

Jean-Jacques thinks such an outlook is obvious. After all, where does reason itself come from? While reason describes the laws of nature, the breakthroughs in discovering these laws come *not* from a mysterious revelation outside the self but from the natural genius of the self. Isaac Newton describes motion through mathematics, but he comes to know such amazing things not necessarily from a revelation outside himself but from a calculating genius within.[6] Like reason and its methods of reflection, Rousseau's *Confessions* are uniquely directed toward the *nature* of the self. This focus on the nature of the self can solve the problems of the inner life by stripping away the gross mysteries of civilization to get to the bare natural self. The natural self in methodological reflection can find the laws of the universe, quantifying gravity and calculating the motion of planets, and in turn transform the self.

To Rousseau's surprise, though, even this reworked mysticism of the self makes the hound of reason bark. Jean-Jacques is surprised, because it's a mysticism built around what reason loves: nature and the natural. It's a mysticism rooted in humanity (not mystery and transcendence) and what can be observed by human knowers. (What is "natural" is what can be observed or known by human minds.) Jean-Jacques assumes this should appease the hound. The hound should, Jean-Jacques wrongly contends, smell the scent of a friend in the expressive natural mysticism he seeks. Modernity, particularly late modernity, has more than accepted this continued cacophony of snapping and howling. The dual barking of the hound of reason and the terrier of expression is the soundtrack to our modern life. Regardless of the continued dual barking, Rousseau deserves credit for bringing these two dogs together, convincing us that the barking is just a common and expected part of life.

6. Michael Polanyi challenges this very point in *Personal Knowledge: Towards a Post-Critical Philosophy* (Chicago: University of Chicago Press, 1962), but this argument comes some two hundred years after Rousseau.

Rousseau's Self-Made Self

When Jean-Jacques wrote his *Confessions*, he flipped our sense of the self on its head. In this flipped fashion, Rousseau asserts that what corrupts the inner life, suffocating the self in perdition, does not come from within the self. Corruption can only ever come from without. Whereas Augustine believes that the inner life is sinful and therefore an inbreaking from outside must reach into the inner life, Rousseau believes the exact opposite. The inner life is pure and innocent as it is. It is the outside inbreaking that corrupts it. Civilization, its culture and orders, inbreak, warp, and contaminate the inner life. The strictures of society corrupt the pure nature of the self, tying down the genius of the self. It is not, for Jean-Jacques, the nature of the self that is crooked, needing something outside of it to save it and bend it plumb.[7] If the self becomes crooked, for Rousseau, it is only because society in all its forms is askew.

Rousseau's contribution is to allow the rational problem-solving method of the Enlightenment to be directed onto the self and its inner life. He shows that, just as reason cares for the natural, expressions of the inner life too can be understood as expressions of reason. The inner life, the self, needs to be educated so it can be transformed. But the inner life must never be educated by something outside itself, never by something like the Spirit who overcomes sin and death with life. The inner life must be educated to embrace the natural goodness of the self and its expressions. This natural goodness of going deeper into the self for the sake of the self opens us to a new kind of expressive mysticism. The German Romantics seized upon this mysticism, pushing this expressive mysticism, bound in poetry, further into our imaginations. Their assumption was that the more the inner life can listen only to the genius of its pure, untainted self, the more it can be transformed.

The mystical path of Rousseau has taught us to listen only to the primitive natural goodness of the self. It is always there, down deep, untainted by civilization and other human collectives. For Rousseau, the new mystical way after reason needs nothing outside itself to be (Rousseau wouldn't called it "mystical," though his followers in Jena and Weimar did). The pursuit of this

---

7. This Kant didn't believe. Following the lead of his pietist upbringing, Kant still held that there was something crooked in humanity itself. Isaiah Berlin often quotes a phrase he attributes to Kant: "Out of the crooked timber of humanity no straight thing was ever made." Berlin, *The Crooked Timber of Humanity* (Princeton: Princeton University Press, 2013), 19.

new mystical way is a pathway deeper into the self. It is *not* a pathway into the mystery of God's unknowability and this unknowability's way of changing us into what we are not (into Christ, for instance).

Receiving something into you that is completely not you is exactly what Augustine and all the mystics of the Eastern church believed. The foreign reality of Christ himself, or of the host, or of the Word, comes into what the self is not, turning what the self cannot be into something new. The self is transformed mystically into Christ. The transformation never comes by the power of the self, which is too bound in sin and death. The self must receive, and commune with, something that the self is completely and fully not, the Spirit of the true God.

Instead, Rousseau contends—and with him almost all of late modernity, which shows how deeply Jean-Jacques is in our bloodstream—that the self is perfect and complete in its natural state. When my daughter Maisy was eleven years old, I put her to bed with an Augustinian-type prayer, saying, "God, bless Maisy, may you come to her and change her, meeting and making her new. Amen." When I finished, she looked up at me and said, "Daddy, why do I need to be changed? Aren't I perfect as I am?"

Good old Rousseau had his way with her imagination. Her schooling had educated her well. If Jean-Jacques had been sitting at the foot of her bed, he would have responded, "Hear, hear! You are right, you don't need to change; you are indeed perfect! What you need to learn is to never allow what is outside you in society to convince you otherwise." The route of transformation, the path to rework the inner life, is *not* to receive something from without but to get back to the perfect natural self. Transformation, for Jean-Jacques, comes not from the encounter with what is foreign and other to the self but by learning to accept the self by discarding all those bad messages received from outside the self—whether from society, your family, or the church.

Jean-Jacques knows all this because he's done it himself. His own transformation comes by the power of his own self to find and save his own self, by throwing off what corrupts the self, getting the self back to its pure and primitive state. Jean-Jacques is educated by the power of his self to escape the traps of society, by learning to embrace his natural state, by time and again leaving Paris for the untainted countryside. The mystical, then, is bound in the natural (not in the impossible otherness of God). Rousseau asserts that through a new kind of education (an education that, of course, only

Jean-Jacques has mastered) that puts reason and expression together, the powers of reason can change—or better, free—the self by the self.

Jean-Jacques is sure that his life is proof of all this. His *Confessions* reveals this ability. After all, he was born a vagabond in Geneva, transforming himself into a celebrated (maybe the greatest!) Parisian author. He has done this solely through the power of his own inner constitution. Even more than Voltaire and all the other French philosophers of the Enlightenment, Jean-Jacques is a self-made man. This is a sure sign, at least in Jean-Jacques's mind, that he is the true man of enlightenment. The Enlightenment made a strong case that esteem and prestige needed to be shifted from the blood of the highborn to the merit and accomplishments of the enlightened. Much to Voltaire's annoyance, no one was further from the highborn than Jean-Jacques, and therefore no one was more qualified to say that reason and self-education had made him than Jean-Jacques.

Jean-Jacques signed each of his books "Jean-Jacques Rousseau, a citizen of the Republic of Geneva." It signals that he is completely self-made, not only *not* highborn but *not even from Paris*. Yet now his books dominate Paris. What a performance of the self!

Rousseau's *Confessions* is a protomemoir of self-animated (as opposed to inbreaking) transformation. It is the confession of a self that turns deeply into itself, finding its natural state as pure and mystical transformation. Jean-Jacques's protomemoir is the first of many. In the twenty-first century, author after author has followed Jean-Jacques with memoirs of exactly this kind of transformation. We've already touched on Westover's *Educated*, and we'll explore some further examples in the chapters to follow (particularly chap. 6).

Educated onto Mystical Pathways

In more than one way, Tara Westover is the prodigy of Jean-Jacques Rousseau for the twenty-first century. She follows the trail Rousseau blazes for the genre of the memoir. Like Jean-Jacques, Westover highlights education and its place in freeing and transforming the self, giving a mystical quality to education. Both Rousseau and Westover, in their own way, are foreigners entering and conquering the modern world. Westover is hidden from society in the Idaho mountains. Jean-Jacques is no Parisian like Voltaire; he's a citizen of Geneva. His upbringing is as odd and ruptured as Westover's. She stumbles into BYU and makes good. Jean-Jacques stumbles his way into Paris and becomes a phenom—again, to Voltaire's jealousy. Their respective entering and conquering has a mystical overtone for both, even without direct attention to God. The inner transformation of the self, done by the self through education, is a transforming mysticism without God. Why else would Rousseau use the title *Confessions*?

Westover's memoir of educational transformation fits squarely next to Rousseau's renowned protomemoir, *Emile, or On Education. Emile*, perhaps even more so than *Confessions*, points in a mystical direction. Jean-Jacques's *Confessions* reveals that transformation can come through the inner-constituting genius of the self. But those are Jean-Jacques's confessions of how he educated himself. Not everyone can enact this self-education. Jean-Jacques knows he is a particularly talented performing self, acutely aware that he is special (the new St. Augustine of reason). But even inside this hubris, as a man of reason, Rousseau believes there must be some way to allow others to access at least a diluted form of this transformational power he has mastered. There must be some way to educate others onto this mystical path, thereby giving them the ability to hold on to their natural inner goodness. Because Jean-Jacques has mastered this, he can teach others. *Emile*, which precedes *Confessions*, is the story of how Rousseau teaches a boy named Emile to do so.

Emile, like Westover, is shaped by a whole new form of education, an education born straight out of the genius of Jean-Jacques's inner self. Westover and Emile, through Rousseau, are transformed by being educated. Yet, it's an education that doesn't rely on inbreaking, transcendent knowledge. The legacy of that knowledge, with its transcendent quality—which even humanists held to—is now forever broken. Knowledge after the Enlightenment is no longer connected to mystery. The mystical transformation of education is no longer bound in what is outside the self but rather in maintaining the self's inner nature. All knowledge is natural. It has no inbreaking, transcendent quality.

But there remains a lingering mysticism, a pathway to hold on to. Education can allow one to escape all false stories and strictures that restrict the self's expressive genius. Knowledge is now completely in nature because it is completely about freeing the self to find its natural state. Education becomes about helping students like Emile keep their innate inner and natural goodness. It's about helping them throw off the false education of a manic father in the mountains. Westover's father is a kind of false, counterfeit Rousseau. Westover's father wants his children to be free of society. Rousseau could agree with that. But Rousseau can't agree with the lack of reason. Westover's father takes his children away from society to the primitive purity of the mountains, but he does so for the sake of something other than finding your inner truest self (in complete opposition to Jean-Jacques). Particularly, her father's reason for doing so is to obey some outside force or reality. He escapes society for the sake of the apocalypse, not the purity of the self.

Westover's story shows us that in late modernity, oddly, the legacy of Rousseau has shifted from the primitive state of the woods and landed instead squarely in the university. It's no surprise today that Rousseau's statue in front of the Pantheon overlooks the Sorbonne. There still may be something, as Rousseau and Thoreau imagined, in the woods to get us back to our truest self. But ultimately, the Rousseauian education of the inner truest self has taken root inside the closed world structures of the university (and modern schools that prepare students for university). Academia and the university follow a Rousseauian, rather than Augustinian, confession. Westover testifies that she is educated onto this Rousseauian path of transformation, finding her truest self inside the closed world structure of the university.

The university of late modernity follows Jean-Jacques, who tells us how he heroically educated young Emile.[8] The university of today also heroically educates generations to find their true inner self (maybe that justifies the tuition cost!). Rousseau teaches Emile to be like Rousseau, a genius of the individual self. After *Emile* was published, parents all over Paris wanted their children educated just like Emile. They wanted the inner life of their children to be nurtured in its purest nature by someone as heroic as Jean-Jacques. The university—idealistically—now promises just this.

Westover is educated; Rousseau is the educator. Westover is Emile, and academia is her Rousseau. For both Westover and Emile, education transforms the self. Westover is freed from the corruption of the uneducated society of the mountains. Rousseau teaches Emile to find his inner genius, to transform himself by freeing his self to find the pure genius of his self. Rousseau is the ultimate heroic educator who frees the boy from what taints his inner goodness so he can embrace his goodness and be transformed by it.

Both Rousseau and Westover see the source and pathway of transformation as both internal and heroic. Because it's so deeply transformational, it is also mystical. It's a downright miracle that Westover is educated at Cambridge.

8. Unlike Westover, who so carefully relays what really happened as best she can, Jean-Jacques seems to make things up.

Rousseau himself is a wonder-working educator (miraculously not from Paris but Geneva). These mystical miracles are locked completely inside the immanence of the inner life, appearing to be heroic to everyone outside the inner life.

Thanks to Jean-Jacques, overtones of the mystical continue in modernity, particularly late modernity. But since Rousseau, these mystical overtones, which even the closed world structure of the university seeks, have been tethered to either (1) inner genius or (2) heroic action. Jean-Jacques can do both, but most people, as our examination of contemporary memoirs in chapter 6 will show, emphasize one or the other. As so many of these memoirs point to, there are two pathways to the mystical in our secular age. These two paths sometimes cross and sometimes run parallel. One path is marked "inner expressive genius." The other is marked "heroic action."

It appears that in late modernity these two paths are cleared and open. Transformation, as a kind of mysticism, happens on these two trails in late modernity, usually with little or no need for God. All of us, unless we flee for the mountains like Westover's father, are educated by Jean-Jacques in one way or another.

That said, there is a third pathway, one walked by Augustine and Meister Eckhart. While this pathway appears overgrown and hard to see, it is still available in late modernity. This third path is a mysticism (even in late modernity) that seeks encounter with an inbreaking transcendence. This mysticism contends that what transforms the self is completely foreign to the self, that the self in actuality has no constitution within to transform itself. This mysticism, unlike Jean-Jacques's, believes that the action of the heroic is rendered impossible and that the inner self needs something outside of it to save it. This third pathway of mysticism asserts that contemplation and passivity (confession and surrender) must replace inner expressive genius and heroic action. It's a pathway shaped by the cross.

"Holocene"

To my surprise, as dusk slides into darkness, and the dome of the Pantheon receives, like a gift, the last radiating light of this Parisian midsummer day, I hear the third pathway. It's ironically being broadcast right from the feet of Jean-Jacques. A beautiful rhythmic guitar echoes off the walls of the university of Enlightenment. The singer's lyrics seem to be a call back, but in the most modern of ways, to those like Thomas Aquinas, Bernard of Clairvaux, and

Meister Eckhart, who, long before Jean-Jacques, walked the narrow streets of the Latin Quarter seeking the third pathway of mysticism. The juxtaposition makes me smile: these young people released from curfew, sitting at Rousseau's feet, singing along with this song on their wireless speaker.

The song is Bon Iver's "Holocene." It's a catchy, beautiful, trance-like song, sung in high octave. The young people sip wine and guzzle beer as the guitar and high-pitched lyrics wash over them. It all creates an ambience to this first night of freedom. There is a kind of short, one-line chorus in the song. Maybe it has no more meaning than that it's the only part of this numinous song that repeats itself. But every time this one line comes, the young people sing together. They lift their glasses and shout right into Jean-Jacques's ears, "At once I knew I was *not* magnificent."

The song is too poetic to be clear about its meaning. But this one line— "At once I knew I was not magnificent"—repeats three times. It's the spine of the song. The song's other lines point to a pained and yet profound realization that the self cannot possess or even be what it seeks. "At once I knew I was not magnificent"—this confession bathes the listener in the yearning for something far outside the self to meet the self and transform the self.

Justin Vernon, the songwriter and singer, at the feet of Rousseau on this night, becomes the pained voice of Emile. I begin to imagine Vernon's words as a grown Emile's own words. "Holocene" could be imagined as Emile's pained response to Jean-Jacques's belief that the self can transform itself by the magnificence of its own pure natural state. I picture a grown Emile as one of the young people at Rousseau's feet. I'm reminded that all of us late-moderns are Rousseau's students in one way or another. Emile, through Vernon's proxy voice, has tried to follow Jean-Jacques. He has sought his own inner magnificence, believing such an inner state would be substantiated in the heroic acts of recognition. Yet he now discovers that "at once," like a strike of lightning, like a revelation from far outside of him that mystically includes him, he is indeed "*not* magnificent."

This realization proclaims that Jean-Jacques's education has failed. Emile's own performance of the self, the very desire to perform the self, has been met by an impossibility he can never climb over. The pathways of inner genius and heroic action, while seeming so invitingly open, lead nowhere at all. These pathways lead only to the confession that "at once," as if through revelation, he *knew* (knowledge that resonates more with the humanists and early mystics than with Rousseau and the enlightened) that his self, and the ways it has been educated to perform its genius and heroisms, is neither genius nor heroic. The self is only broken and therefore in need of a minister, not a genius or heroic teacher. Vernon and Emile need to be embraced not beyond but right inside the confession of the revelation that they need something outside of them to save them. The amazing mystical revelation is that the self has beauty not in its performance but in its confession. Vernon (or is it Emile?) is more Eckhart's student than Rousseau's.

This third way of mysticism can be seen clearly in the first line of the song, "Someway, baby, it's part of me, apart from me." The line is in quotes, though it's unclear whom he is quoting. But the later refrain "At once I knew I was not magnificent" is connected to this deeply Eckhartian mystical statement in the first line of the song. The confession of the need of the self for something outside the self paradoxically readies the self for a transformation that comes with a word or embrace from far outside the self that nevertheless becomes part of the self. The line could be interpreted as saying that what makes a self—or better, what saves a self—is not what is within the self. Rather, what is outside the self meets and transforms the self into what the self is not. This is not genius or heroism, but the love of ministry. It is an encounter with true otherness. Rousseau's naturalism pushes out otherness. Yet, in recognizing this otherness comes the realization that the self alone is not magnificent. And what's more, this otherness (this inbreaking transcendence) allows you to know, through encounter, that this other that is apart from you has transformed you, becoming part of you. The confession of being "*not* magnificent" becomes the ground for a transformation where something truly other encounters you, becoming fully part of you while always remaining other and therefore apart from you. "Holocene" is articulating a transformation that has its source not in the self but in something wholly and completely other.

Vernon's words of "*not* magnificent," as if they were coming from Emile's mouth, are not defeatist. Not at all! They are beautiful, even singable, because they represent a surrendering to something outside the self that can come into the self and transform the self. To confess that the self is indeed *not* magnificent mysteriously clears a pathway for a deeper kind of transformation. It positions the self to need something from outside the self to break into the self, giving to the needy self the magnificence of something transcendent. This inbreaking miraculously changes the self into something that it has no power to be. Such a pained and beautiful confession leads to a yearning for something far outside the self that might bring the redemption and communion the self lacks but yearns for. The refrain "At once I knew I was not magnificent" is the sure sign, the contemplative and passive confession, that transformation will need to arrive from outside the self to redeem and change the self. "Holocene" and these young people, whether intentionally or not, are seeking the third pathway of transformation beyond the inner genius and heroic action. In this moment of shared voice as night falls on Paris, they point to the path of surrender through confession.

Years before "Holocene" was written and recorded, Justin Vernon had escaped to the northern Wisconsin woods. Broken and in need of confession, like Anthony—the earliest desert father of mysticism—he journeyed into solitude. Realizing that his inner genius and heroic action couldn't save him, he started on a path of surrender through confession, recording each one of his confessions as a song. He never really imagined they were for anyone but himself. Then they became the beloved album *For Emma, Forever Ago*.

I'm now driving into those same woods. Right beyond the cheese factory, the friendly pine trees line the road like beacons, taking my family and me to another Airbnb.

3

Performing Selves Are So Guilty

Why Mysticism and Guilt Are Back

Months before sliding into Paris and the stylish Airbnb next to the Sorbonne, we're driving up to Hayward, Wisconsin. Kara, my wife, has family here. We've been here dozens of times, at least once a summer. This is our first time at this Airbnb. It's usually too expensive, but the price has plummeted for two reasons. First, it's not summer. There's still some snow on the ground, but not much. Where the snow has disappeared, in its place is mud. The gravel road that takes us to the Airbnb feels as soft as the ice-cream cones in town. But it's too cold to be thinking about ice cream. It's spring break and the lakes have just thawed.

This is our second spring break under the tyranny of COVID. The brave—or is it the stupid?—have headed somewhere warm (and saturated with COVID?) like Florida. Or maybe we're the stupid ones driving north instead of south. But it's worth it. Kara's ninety-year-old grandmother, whom Kara hasn't seen in over a year, is now fully vaccinated. We're driving to more wintry lands so that Kara can hug her. Kara and I have had one shot, and our second is scheduled for a few weeks from now. We're thankful that we'll be fully vaxxed before our trip to Europe in the summer. COVID is the second reason the Airbnb is reduced in price. We get the sense that this Airbnb has been empty for a while, a lost year of visitors. But it's perfect for us, hidden in the trees with a direct view of the lake. Our dog tracking in mud is the only complaint.

On day three, to get away from the frustration of the dog's dirty paws, I go into town. It's warm enough to sit outside wrapped in a sweatshirt with a cup of hot coffee. I'm sitting at a distance but close enough to overhear a woman on a video call. I can't help but listen in. As if it's a game, I begin trying to figure out what she does, wondering the context of this meeting.

She's from Milwaukee, it appears. She's been in Hayward for a few months. The cabin that she usually visits each summer has now become home since the shutdowns. My first guess is that she's a pastor. It sounds like a pastoral care call. That's just a guess from inside the purviews of my own life, but it does have that feel.

Finally, it's clear, but not because of my great sleuthing. I hear her say, "This is what a life coach does. They help you listen to your true self, making the badass changes you deserve from the truth of who you are. And you are badass," she says with electricity and a fist pump.

I'm both inspired and exhausted at the same time (though I'm sure Jean-Jacques would have been thrilled to hear those words). It's clear that even with this transition to online meetings, business has been booming for this life coach. She reminds her client that she has fifteen minutes before the next call; she has a full day of calls inside a week of calls. I decide right then that I'm sticking around. What could be better than eavesdropping on at least a few more calls? I know, I feel a little pathetic. Your judgment is justified. But there really isn't much to do in Hayward before the boats are on the lakes.

I begin to hear something interesting. Whenever the life coach isn't reminding her clients that they are "badass" and need to listen to their true self, she is reassuring them. Deeply so. There is *a lot* of reassurance plotted across each meeting. In fact, the calls are mostly reassurance. Reassurance is the most common shape of discourse, more than anything else the life coach says, even more than the "badass" reminders. I think it was the reassurance that made me at first think it was a pastoral care call. Because there is nothing superficial about her reassurance. All the reassurance is saturated with empathy. It's truly compassionate.

Yet, something about it all snags me. In every meeting, the reassurance sounds like this: "I know, things are so hard right now. I know. . . . But, what you need to remember is that *no one, no one*, is doing well right now. . . . Think about it, remember that: *no one* is *doing* well."

I can't hear the response or see the face of the other person. But all signs suggest that these words of "no one is doing well" were just right. They were just the words the person on the other end needed to hear. Why is that? I wonder to myself as I finish my flat white. The Jean-Jacques in my bloodstream almost immunizes me from asking this question. It seems obvious, in an unreflective, unthought way. As I think about that question, I realize I need to go. My eavesdropping has met its limits. As I go, I keep repeating, *no one is doing well*. As I repeat it and think about it, an answer begins to reveal itself.

Grading on a Curve

The life coach from Milwaukee is reminding her clients that "no one is doing well." Now think of Justin Vernon's confession, "At once I knew I was not magnificent." He knows he is not magnificent; he is not a self that can constitute and therefore save his *own* self. When the life coach tells her clients that "no one is doing well," it's far from a confession. Neither the client nor the life coach is surrendering. (You should never surrender in a competition. You need to realize you're still in the game, so get off the mat and keep fighting.) Saying "no one is doing well" is not a confession of being "*not* magnificent" and therefore in need of an inbreaking transcendence.

It's the direct opposite. Saying no one is doing well is a way of reestablishing the self's magnificence even over and against the facts and deep feelings of not measuring up. Sure, it might not *feel like* you're magnificent. To be a good life coach, she has to acknowledge that. But that's *not* because you're not magnificent; it's because you're in a rut. It's because things just aren't going your way. The proof of being a "badass" self may feel absent, but it's because the playing field, in which you're living out your search for your magnificence, is making it hard to play well.

The magnificence of the self is a weighted measure. Your magnificence, your own doing well, is a grade. But luckily, the life coach tells her clients, you're being graded on a curve. You might be feeling like you're doing poorly. But take heart, everyone is doing poorly, everyone is playing on a bumpy, muddy field, thanks to COVID. Hearing this relativizes your feelings of doing poorly. You don't have to feel bad about not actualizing your magnificence as you wish, for at least right now no one is feeling magnificent—which is a weird comfort. But nevertheless, it is a comfort, because ultimately it means you don't need to feel as deficient as you do, anxious that you're failing and falling behind. Failing or falling behind . . . what? That's unclear. But if no one is doing well, you can breathe a little, for what's driving you to keep up can be appeased by the reminder that the whole invisible cohort you're competing against is also *not* doing well. You may not be driving as fast as you would like toward your goals of being a "badass" self. But luckily the speed of the whole competitive race has slowed. It's less of a concern that your own engines are puttering if you get word from your life coach (who is a coach preparing you for this competition) that so too is everyone else you're trying to keep up with!

The Performing Self

The self is assumed to be at its core a *performing self*. We find our way of being inside a constant competition. It can only be good news that *no one is doing well*, only a mantra that can comfort a self, if the self is assumed to be right in the middle of an intense, energy-expending performance. And a performance that is deeply ranked.

Good old Jean-Jacques Rousseau never intended to mold us into performing selves. He'd be more than a little annoyed that the racing of society has so fully captured our imaginations. But when Rousseau's ideas met the rise of a new form of capitalism in the 1980s and 1990s (neoliberalism, which I'll unpack later in this chapter), the drive for the self to perform its own creative magnificence became lodged in our Western cultural imagination.[1] Now everyone in this globalized world of social media, to some degree, is in the middle of a stressful and hurried performance. All of us are chasing magnificence originated by our own energy. This magnificence is won by the performance of a self who expresses an inner genius or broadcasts heroic actions to an audience.

Only inside this never-ending sense that your self is performing (that the only way to be happy with yourself is to be magnificent) could it be a comfort to know that no one else is doing well. Because you're a performing self, it's a great relief to know that you're not the only one struggling to perform. The life coach's mantra would have no efficacy if her words didn't meet a performance anxiety lying heavy on the self. Jean-Jacques opened the door to the self being

---

1. For more on this, see my *The Church after Innovation: Questioning Our Obsession with Work, Creativity, and Entrepreneurship* (Grand Rapids: Baker Academic, 2022), esp. chaps. 2 and 7.

constituted not in its confession of surrender (as Augustine believed) but in its performance of an inner genius or heroic actions. When the inner genius and heroic actions meet a new neoliberal economy that glorifies competition, pushing competition into every corner of our lives, the performance of the self becomes all-encompassing and never-ending.[2]

Not surprisingly, a performing self becomes almost completely fixated on itself. If you don't keep your eye on yourself, you'll lose. Our highest good—the shape even of our moral discourse—pertains to a self inside of a performance. The ultimate telos for late-modern people is to be happy with yourself. And the way to be happy with yourself is to establish the self by the power of your own creativity, as a "badass" who's taking far more Ws than Ls (the competitive language is everywhere). The highest good is to be recognized for the magnificence of your self's performance.

Like hyperalert prey being hunted on the savanna, intensely aware of the smallest change in the environment, we in the late stages of neoliberalism amid the competitive drives of the performing self become hyperaware of our environment. Our hyperawareness makes us extremely sensitive to the playing field. We are astutely aware that this environment is not (and never has been) equal. Those raised on social media are so quickly able to point out the unequal shape of each small part of the environment.

Claims of unequalness become issues of justice. But so often these issues of justice get conflated (particularly on social media) into a sense of fairness in the recognition of the unique performances of the self.[3] It is very hard in late-modern neoliberalism to untangle whether what has been violated is a person's rights or the performative self's longed-for magnificence through expressed identity uniqueness. We see this with language use all the time. Is the use or nonuse of a certain word a matter of justice and a violation of rights or a loss of attention and recognition? The performing self sees no difference between the two. But not seeing the difference between the two further pits people against each other because justice itself is encased in a performative drive for the magnificence of individual selves. Like a swimmer or sprinter who can spot the smallest of advantages taken by a competitor,

---

2. Michael Hardt and Antonio Negri provide a nice definition of neoliberalism: "Neoliberalism . . . [is a social form] of self-management and cooperation, whose value it seeks to extract." Hardt and Negri, *Assembly* (London: Oxford University Press, 2019), 211.

3. This comes together as identity politics, or better and more helpfully, what Charles Taylor has called the politics of recognition. See his discussions in *Multiculturalism*, ed. Amy Gutmann (Princeton: Princeton University Press, 1994).

performing selves also become sharply aware of those with unfair access to recognition and affirmation. Is this injustice or just part of the competitive game of performance? It's assumed to be an issue of justice, because the stakes feel so high and the outrage so intense. But again, is that the heat of the competition of the self or righteous indignation? How are the two differentiated inside the late-capitalist drives of late modernity and our sense of being performing selves?

As we've mentioned, this environmental sensitivity causes performing selves to be extremely sensitive to language use. Performing selves believe they need a society that uses its language to welcome their self's kind of performance. To "welcome" is not just to allow but to affirm the performance the self is undertaking (and the possibility of its magnificence). Welcoming means much more than just the absence of prohibition; it means real embrace of distinct performances of unique identities. What people say (their language) signals whether you'll be affirmed in such a way that it gives your own self real access to victory.

This kind of welcoming is necessary because to be magnificent, the self needs to be recognized as such. To have recognition, you need all society and culture to acknowledge that your way of being a self is indeed magnificent. The words used in the public discourse of society become so important because these words signal to anxious performers whether their performance will be welcomed into the recognition of magnificence. The words foretell whether the environment the self enters is hot or cold to the vulnerable act of performing the inner genius and heroic actions the self uses to secure magnificence. Like pool test strips, language use tells you if the chemicals are safe for swimming. The words used by others, it's assumed, reveal whether a particular performance of the self can achieve (win) the magnificence the self needs to be happy. And when being happy is the highest good, these are very high stakes.

Blasting the Outrage

In our late modernity, a twist on Jean-Jacques has arrived. Society or culture is untrustworthy or corrupt because it obscures your magnificence by not recognizing you as you wish. Society must change what it accepts as a legitimate performance. This outlook is substantiated most concretely in language. Words quickly signal (often without much more substance) whether the environment is safe for your performance. And not just safe from cruelty but ultimately safe from your self being ignored.

The ignoring of your performance has momentous power because it communicates that your self is unwelcome. You are therefore deprived of the affirming recognition you need to be happy as a performing self (being ignored is now a kind of violence). Society needs to be pushed to not ignore your inner genius or not be oblivious to your heroic performing actions. One concrete way to do this is to police language. Using the right words is the clearest sign that the stage is open for your kind of performance. You can even jump-start your performance and assure yourself that you are indeed magnificent by "putting someone on blast," calling out those who ignore or are ignorant to the importance of your unique performance. "Putting someone on blast" is a slang term for embarrassing someone by publicly denouncing or exposing them, especially on social media. Those "put on blast" show they don't have acceptance for your performance because they don't signal it with their words. Your magnificence can be kickstarted by publicly pointing this out.

This "putting someone on blast" is an ideal act for a performing self. It allows you to broadcast your inner genius by the means of a heroic action. You get to claim your unique identity by bravely broadcasting it to the world. And, in turn, the "putting on blast" allows for a kind of moral safety net inside the heated competition of performance. Inside the battle of thousands upon thousands of performing selves clashing over the limited resources of recognition (attention), outrage is an effective tool. Not using the tool of outrage requires a more direct acknowledgment that you're seeking affirmation through recognition. Outside of outrage, real genius and talent must be substantiated. But in a world of competitive performing selves, outrage can cover for a lack of capacity or skill. It can also legitimize your point of view. Your outrage assures you (and others) that you know what you're talking about. If you didn't, why would you be so outraged?

Outrage provides the performing self with a kind of shield. You're now publicly performing your self out of outrage on Twitter.[4] Not (supposedly)

4. Markus Gabriel adds, "Social media are personalization machines. Personalization machines are systems by means of which self-dramatizations are manufactured and marketed. Within this process, what matters is not necessarily that we market ourselves through our Twitter and Instagram accounts but, rather, that others sell our self-images and thereby derive economic profit from them. Each photo we 'share' online says something about our personality. The more photos and other personal information we make available, the easier it becomes to interact with our persona." Gabriel, *The Meaning of Thought* (London: Polity, 2020), 129.

because you're thirsty for affirmation, lost without it, but because you're outraged. Your outrage becomes both the occasion for you to broadcast your inner genius and the supposed fuel that *pushes* forward your heroic actions. Those who read your blunt broadcasts of outrage are supposed to respond with, "You're so brave for saying this!" "You're a real star. I admire you!" "Wow, you're right, people are so stupid not to see this. Thank you!"

The genre of outrage is the safest (and most effective) performance of the self. The outrage affirms the self for its inner genius. The outrage shows that the self feels and sees something others don't, converting some to your outrage and making them fans of your inner genius. In turn, the outrage infuses the performance of the self's broadcast of the inner genius with a sure sense of the heroic (connecting the performing self with an audience who acknowledges the outrage, admiring or being jealous of the attention the outrage has received). Inside a competition of performance, a fight (instead of a flight) will almost always be recognized and celebrated. Inside a saturated environment of competition, a fighter (even a misguided one) will always be applauded and respected. A fight is always more entertaining—a sure measure of magnificence in late modernity—than a flight (welcome to the *Hunger Games*).[5] The performing self of neoliberalism will always cheer on an outraged fighter.

Ironically, outrage is a safe way (at least for the performer, *not* the object of outrage) to test whether the stage is ready for their performance. Outrage is the way to clear the stage from what you perceive to be unwelcoming. Not necessarily unwelcoming to your personhood or humanity but to the anxious performance you need to secure your self's magnificence.

The Always Unrested

Even in finding an open and welcoming stage, through outrage or other means, your self will be far from rested. On a welcoming stage, you'll have to perform more vigorously or point out more fervently that the lack of affirmation you're receiving is due to the unfair predisposition in the social environment. You'll need to point out that there are *still* hidden traps that keep your kind of performance from receiving the recognition your self *really* deserves. These hidden traps (not the construct of the performing self!) are what makes you

5. This wouldn't be true in premodern times. The flight to the desert and the surrender to contemplate only God's goodness is a celebrated act.

unhappy by minimizing your magnificence. The competition never ends; the fight for recognition never stops. It can't stop; the stakes are too high. If you don't get the recognition you need to verify your performance, you'll never be sure that your self is magnificent—and therefore, you can never be happy.

The surest confirmation that a self's performance is magnificent is to receive acclaim for being singularly unique.[6] A self can be magnificent by performing the self like no one else can, a truly unique performance. By the power of your own unique inner genius or heroic actions, you win the magnificence that produces purpose, meaning, and unending happiness. Happiness becomes the confirmation that you have performed well. Happiness verifies that you have secured for yourself a magnificence that you can live with (or, better, live *from*).

Yet, the vicious circle, often hidden in late modernity, is the unfortunate reality that happiness and contentment can only last until the next performance, which, in a neoliberal world, is always coming soon. In such a competitive environment of performing selves, you're only as happy as the recognition you receive for your next performance. The unending happiness that performing selves desire and aim toward is ultimately impossible to attain. A self in performance can never rest; the self must keep performing or risk losing its magnificence, drifting away from happiness (and this drifting produces guilt, to foreshadow the next section). The necessity for constant performance of the self means that the self will never be able to find the happiness and contentment it longs for. The competition coming at us from neoliberalism will not allow it. Rather, endless happiness and pure contentment will remain a mirage amid our constant curating of our self's uniqueness through its many performances.

You desire to know your self as magnificent, and this must be so *at all times*, not just at one moment in time. Only by knowing your self as being constantly magnificent can you be assured of everlasting happiness and contentment. Of course, it is impossible to feel happy "at all times" (because there is always another performance), and this causes you to perform more vigorously, fearing that even the magnificence you've won yesterday has already evaporated. No wonder we're all attracted to outrage. We're actually angry that we're hamsters on a never-ending performance wheel. Unfortunately, that discontentment gets misdirected away from the hamster wheel of performance

6. Andreas Reckwitz has so astutely laid this out in *The Society of Singularities* (London: Polity, 2020).

and toward those who are too dumb, mean, or ignorant to recognize our magnificence. And so the culture wars rage. With the outrage misdirected, the performing can never stop. The anxiety to keep going is always present.[7]

The ultimate problem for a performing self—particularly in a world where everyone else is just as exuberant in their own performance—is that you can never rest. A performing self, trying to substantiate the self as continually and happily magnificent, *must* compete with all other selves *all the time*, giving one performance of the self after another. If you make sure you're always on point, you can ensure that you remain the director, and never the object, of outrage. Your life coach reminds you that while you are resting, your competition is performing. No wonder teenagers sleep with their phones under their pillows, checking Instagram at 3 a.m., watching all the performances on TikTok. If you're not driving to get ahead, you're falling behind. If you're not outraged, you'll become the object of outrage. Your coach can help you keep up. Your therapist, or your pharmacist, can help you cope with the anxiety and depressing exhaustion of it all.

The Strange Effect of Performance

For the performing self, the hurried anxiety that knows no rest seems inevitable. Even the need for a life coach to help manage this unrelenting pace and all the layers of outrage seems justifiable. But there is another element of this grand and all-encompassing competition of the performing self that seems both less apparent and ultimately strange. What's strange is that, by apotheosizing the performing self—making it godlike in its ability to create and sustain its own magnificence—it opens the self to *guilt*, which was not long ago assumed to be disappearing. Jean-Jacques did his part to rid us of guilt. He dug a grave in which to bury Augustine's antiquated *Confessions*. All the outrage, depression, and anxiety verify that we are riddled with cancerous guilt.[8] What a strange reappearance of guilt!

Both the rationalists and the romantics, in their own unique ways, sought to move human concern far beyond guilt. Guilt was something for immature

---

7. Will Storr traces out this reality further in his book *Selfie: How We Became So Self-Obsessed and What It's Doing to Us* (New York: Abrams, 2018).

8. Of course, not all guilt is cancerous. Some is deeply helpful and reforming. However, guilt that produces mystical responses beyond confession and surrender are deeply problematic. I hope to show this in the last sections of this chapter.

minds, something everyone was moving far beyond, from the French rationalists or the German *Bildung* (educated, self-cultivating romantics) to Nietzschean-inspired phenomenologists and Freudian psychoanalysts.[9] It's strange that guilt has returned—and with such force. To go back to our analogy from the previous chapter, it's strange because the hound of rationalism and the terrier of romanticism, while spending most of their days barking at each other, agreed to disregard religion's obsession with guilty souls. For both the hound and the terrier, guilt was clearly part of the past, too tied up with medieval society and its beliefs to have any part in a modern world.

Yet, in late modernity, among its accelerating technology and global capitalist markets, guilt is back.[10] And its teeth are sharp. Early modernity kicked out the teeth of guilt.[11] With guilt removed, there was no reason to assume that confession and surrender had any real importance in human life. Who needs confession when guilt has been tamed? Why surrender when driving toward progress is a salvation we ourselves can create and control? Once guilt had been rendered antiquated, having little part in modernity, confessions of surrender seemed backward and abrasive. Confession and

9. By the way, if the Nietzschean phenomenologists were dogs, they'd probably be standard poodles, all elegant and mean. One of the central forefathers of Nietzscheanism is Arthur Schopenhauer, whom Nietzsche loved and was inspired by. Schopenhauer was a very odd duck. One of his obsessions was standard poodles. He loved his poodles way more than any human being—most particularly more than his mother!

10. Storr adds, "The world is giving us a greater number of opportunities to feel like failures. . . . First, when a public figure makes a mistake there seems to be a much stronger, more intense and quicker backlash. So kids growing up now see what happens to people who make a mistake and they're very fearful of it. This seems to be what happened, for instance, in July 2016, when sixteen-year-old Phoebe Connop took her own life after becoming worried a joke photograph she'd taken of herself would lead to her being denounced as a racist. 'The image had circulated further than she wanted it to,' Detective Katherine Tomkins told her inquest. 'There had been some negative reaction.'" Storr, *Selfie*, 15.

11. Peter Stearns explains how guilt arrived with the Victorians but also was held down by them, only coming to prominence in the later twentieth century. He says, "Guilt, as an experience of self-hate, flourished readily in this context, and again it differed from the reactions that simple scorn from the outside world could generate. Guilt, then, must be added to the other intense emotional attributes encouraged by Victorian culture. The person who could not react . . . was emotionally inadequate. Just as a man of good character had the anger necessary to spur achievement and the courage to face fear, and the capacity to love, so he must, as needs be, have the ability to feel guilt. The woman of good character needed the capacity to love in several forms, and she also needed to be capable of feeling guilty when other emotional norms like serenity of temper escaped her. The harsh bath of guilt did not mean being overwhelmed—for like other intense emotions, guilt must finally be mastered through action, apology, and correction; it should not paralyze. Again we see real consistency in Victorian emotional culture, in which capacity for guilt related readily to other emotional goals." Stearns, *American Cool: Constructing a Twentieth-Century Emotional Style* (New York: New York University Press, 1994), 52.

surrender were assumed to be by-products of all the Catholic and Puritan guilt that the West was outgrowing. With guilt teethless, and with confession and surrender made obsolete, the West divorced itself further from classic forms and concerns of mysticism. True, the German Romantics, inspired by Rousseau, reappropriated a certain kind of mysticism, a certain poetry of expression. Yet, this was mysticism without guilt—or, rather, without guilt baring any teeth.

The German Romantics and idealists loved Meister Eckhart, but more for the German poetry than for his call for guilty souls to let go of their striving and find God in death and nothingness.[12] German romanticism was epitomized in Goethe's novel *The Sorrows of Young Werther*. The novel turned human concern from the mathematics of the rationalists to the passions of the artist in a love affair. Guilt has no place at all in mathematics. Guilt's teeth were knocked out completely by all the battering of theorems and equations. Yet, even with guilt's teeth kicked out, romanticism kept guilt (kind of). Guilt was much more relevant inside the expressions of love and art. Even so, the Goethe-inspired romantics in Weimar and Jena were happy to keep guilt toothless. For instance, a romantic might feel a dull bruise of guilt, but guilt's bite never broke the skin. Like the rationalists, they had moved beyond the experience of standing guilty under a divine righteousness, for instance. That divine guilt was assumed to be only for the uptight, antiquated bishops and their backward theology. If there was a feeling of guilt, even for the romantics, it was a nip without teeth. Guilt could arrive if your passions had failed to be turned into meaningful expressions.

Yet, in late modernity, guilt has shockingly become quite perilous. Guilt has taken on a different form. This new guilt, coming in late modernity, is a kind of cultural evolutionary adaptation fashioned directly for a neoliberal age. With this new guilt, new kinds of mysticism have returned (which, of course, are without confession and surrender). When guilt returns, mysticism becomes an interest for us once again (my point being that mysticism is most often seeking spiritual union through impediment or loss, through an experience of guilt or not measuring up). When guilt is toothless, concern

12. German romanticism, like French rationalism, though in a different way, had little concern for guilt. The new modern "mysticism" of the early nineteenth century was much more concerned with the passions of love affairs and art. Concern for an inbreaking transcendence became less necessary because guilt itself was fading. Goethe's novel *The Sorrows of Young Werther* was a major source of these new romantic concerns.

for the mystical recedes. It could be that attention to mysticism follows the cultural sense of guilt. The experience of guilt causes us to recover new kinds of mystical longings.[13]

In the late twentieth and early twenty-first century, with guilt back, new forms of mysticism proliferated (I'll explain how in the next section). Yet, these new proliferations of mysticism, as a response to guilt's neoteric teeth, were shaped in a way that the framers of modernity (such as David Hume, Denis Diderot, Goethe, Jean-Paul Sartre, or Freud) never would have imagined. All these thinkers in their own way worked to unlink societal structures and human consciousness from guilt. Most imagined that knee-knocking guilt would be evacuated forever. All it took was ending the "superstitions" of the arcane search for mystery through forms of Christian mysticism and its rules. What they could never imagine is that guilt would regain its force *without* any direct link with the divine law, without any real sense of a metaphysic.

And yet it's happened! In late modernity, guilt bares a sinister smile, producing a proliferation of anxiety and depression across every corner of the West. What is shocking is that the source of this guilt is not God or the *Dei verbum. It is the performing self.* We feel guilty to our *selves.* We feel like we've failed to use our time well, to become the magnificent self we should be. We've failed to compare well to all the other magnificent selves we see on Instagram. We've let ourselves down. We are guilty of not curating our self magnificently enough to win us constant happiness. We blew it! Our inner genius and heroic actions are not recognized as they could or should be. All because we didn't perform them well enough.

With the remaining space in this chapter, I'll trace how this new form of guilt came to be and what consequence it delivers. I'll do this by leaning on Michel Foucault's descriptions of the change of power and punishment. Foucault describes a procession that moves from sovereign power to disciplinary power to the power of biopolitics. My contribution will be to drop the shape of guilt and the disappearance and return of mysticism into this procession of power and punishment. This discussion will help us spot why certain kinds of mysticism have returned in late modernity. Inside of modernity, mysticisms without God have given us new cultural pathways of transformation that may need to be adapted or rejected for Christian faith formation.

---

13. It's beyond the scope of this project to explore this claim, but it seems compelling and possible. However, it would need a fulsome genealogy of guilt.

When Guilt Makes a Way for Mysticism

Augustine, and following him Luther, focused directly on guilt. Without the act of God, which comes to the self from far outside the self, sin and guilt were assumed to be inextricable from the human soul. This outlook is something Jean-Jacques could never affirm. And the late modernity that Rousseau's blood runs through agrees with him for the most part. Thus the new arrival of this late-modern guilt is a surprise and therefore must have a different composition. It must be made of a different material.

Zygmunt Bauman, preparing us for our discussion of Foucault, diagnoses the difference of the new guilt succinctly and acutely: "In the past, we were weighed down by an overabundance of prohibitions. Our neuroses were caused by . . . the fear of being accused of breaking the rules. Today, we suffer from an excess of possibility. *We are terrified of being inadequate.* That is the fear that underlies depression."[14] We now feel guilty not in relation to the mark of God's command but in relation to the measure of our own magnificence. The old form of guilt, eradicated by the framers of modernity, was made from the material of the rules of God's oughts (or shoulds). This new guilt is made of a different material altogether. It is made of the possibilities of our coulds, sharpened to make us feel inadequate in performing our selves into their happy magnificence.

Luther felt guilt's teeth penetrate his being in the first form. He lived under the incredible burden of breaking God's law. When Luther first entered the monastery, he was debilitated by being unable to avoid breaking God's and the church's commands. In our time, we've been released from such fear, throwing off divine prohibitions. Or better, we've released ourselves from the burden of breaking God's law or even breaking societal prohibitions (particularly certain social norms). We are released, we assume, from meeting some moral standard outside of us that we must conform to and obey. *Conforming* and *obeying* are bad words in late modernity. The age of authenticity offers a new ethic for a performing self that turns any kind of conforming and obeying into something sinister to the self.[15]

We follow what's true to us, obeying only our own inner voice (the ethic of authenticity). Jean-Jacques convinced us that any outside rules imposed

---

14. Zygmunt Bauman, *Making the Familiar Unfamiliar: A Conversation with Peter Haffner* (London: Polity, 2020), 89 (emphasis added).

15. For much more on this, see my *Faith Formation in a Secular Age* (Grand Rapids: Baker Academic, 2017), part 1.

on us by society or church are not worthy rules to follow. The only rule we should obey is our own inner innocence (Rousseau believed any outer rules of society could be justified only if they reflected the inner life of the people who made up the society). If the self can be free of those exterior societal strictures, it can clearly hear right and wrong coming from its natural, innocent state. There is no reason to experience guilt, to assume the self is guilty. Guilt becomes a construct, an instrument, used nefariously by the powerful.

Sovereign Power

Rousseau, and his frenemy Voltaire, believed that guilt could be used by the powerful because they were coming of age in a world where the rules and prohibitions were set and enforced by sovereignty. The king needed to be obeyed completely. It was the king's calling and burden to order the king's domain as God did the heavens. The sovereign's job was to punish those who violated God's law, as the king and his bishops defined it. Michel Foucault calls this "sovereign power." The sovereign's power to define and rule on what was probate, punishing the bodies of those who broke the rules, created guilt. The king, as God's direct representative on earth, stood over and against the people. It was this standing over and against that imposed guilt and the apparatus of punishment.[16] The king's power, often enacted through dukes, imposed guilt and punishment. Inside this enchanted sovereignty, forms of mysticism thrived. Some of these forms pushed back, in prophetic ways,

---

16. Stuart Elden adds, "Sovereign power is power shot through with asymmetry, founded on some anterior event that it always carries with it, such as divine right, conquest, victory, act of submission, an oath of fidelity, rights of blood, etc. On this model, 'the other side of sovereignty is violence, it is war,' a claim that Foucault makes in *The Punitive Society* and would pursue in detail in the 1975–76 'Society Be Defended' lecture course. Relationships within sovereignty are not isotopic (the same in all places), they are not organized rationally by relations of classification, not a hierarchical table of elements. Disciplinary power, on the other hand, does not work on asymmetry, nor on one-way relations, but is more totalizing and organizing. The example given is military discipline, which for Foucault did not really exist before the Thirty Years' War (1618–48), armies being more agglomerations of disparate forces and mercenaries. Of course, as he would later recognize in *Discipline and Punish* classical Rome provided the model for this later disciplinary model. From the middle of the seventeenth century then, and it is not unrelated that this is the same era as modern states start to emerge, with the allowing of standing armies in the Peace of Westphalia for the territorial princes, a system of discipline emerges in the army, based around career soldiers. These soldiers are not only engaged during war, but also in peace, except for periods of demobilization. Foucault notes that they receive a pension, and thus continue to think of themselves as a retired soldier." Elden, *Foucault: The Birth of Power* (London: Polity, 2017), 117.

against the king's hubris and dukes' decadence. Of course, some forms of mysticism were just empty tools used to perpetuate sovereign power and to punish bodies unjustly. But in whatever form, mysticism thrived inside sovereign power. The abbey and priory were a staple of the medieval period.

In the decades before Jean-Jacques stumbled into Paris from Geneva, sovereign power, sensing threat, was puffing its chest, feeling weak but feigning greatness.[17] Years later, when revolutionaries in Paris, inspired by Jean-Jacques and Voltaire, revolted against sovereign power, they turned the apparatus of punishment on the king himself (a profound, world-turning act!). Louis XVI and Marie Antoinette had a rude introduction to *Madame Guillotine*. When the blade and Louis's head dropped, sovereign power dropped.[18] Now the world was free forever from guilt. Open punishment of the body was finished. No longer did anyone stand over and against the people, holding the rules, demanding obedience, punishing bodies. Or so it was assumed. Inside this incredible societal change of the ending of sovereign power, the mystical receded.

Disciplinary Power

The mystical receded because in the place of the king was now the state (i.e., the people). There was no reason (yet!) to feel guilty to yourself. After all, you were now your own sovereign. But heavy is the head that wears the crown. The sovereign bore the singular burden of discipline for the whole of a society. The king lived under the heavy burden of discipline: he could dispense punishment and guilt on those deserving it in his realm. But now that every citizen was their own sovereign, it was necessary that everyone bear the weight of disciplining themselves. As the order of our societies switched from the will of the king to the will of the people, it was essential that these wills of the people equally, across all of society, discipline themselves.

To ensure this happened, the state offered the "service" of imposing discipline where it was lacking. Supposedly this "service" was provided only, of course (wink, wink), for the sake of the will of the people. After all, if the new social order was to not dissolve into the chaos of opposing wills (allowing the

---

17. In the sixteenth century, many began to question the divine right of kings. For more on this, see Ernst H. Kantorowicz, *The King's Two Bodies: A Study in Medieval Political Theology* (Princeton: Princeton University Press, 1997).

18. Of course, sovereign power kept coming back in France, even after Napoleon Bonaparte. Napoleon enforced a new kind of power , but it didn't stick. The French turned back to a king (with the restoration of the Bourbons) and then away from a king again.

will of the people to set the terms for life), then disciplined order needed to be demanded by all. Each citizen needed to discipline themselves to uphold order. If they couldn't, the state served the people by punishing, Foucault says, *not* the body but the mind of the citizen. The mind was the new place of punishment because the discipline of the will was now fundamental to the social order. The point of the state's punishment, and the reason the will of the people allowed it, was *not* to impose guilt on the body but to twist the mind (to reform the will) to discipline itself.[19]

This new approach had major ramifications for how we interfaced with power and therefore understood guilt. Inside the state, if you could manage your own discipline and were therefore a good citizen, you rarely or never saw the apparatus of the state's machine of punishment. You understood that the state punished, but you never saw it do so. Particularly, you never felt its hovering presence in a way that assured you of its force and power, convincing you that you were always near guilt. The supposedly disciplined citizen was sheltered from this hovering power of imposed guilt. Yet, Foucault's point is that you were sheltered from this felt guilt only if you fit the state's definition of a good citizen. If you didn't—if you were Black or homosexual—the state's apparatus of power and punishment was anything but invisible. Its hovering presence lay heavy on you, reminding you at every turn that you were guilty for not being the ideal citizen. This was a torture of the mind, bound in the way some bodies (such as those who were Black or gay) were demeaned as ontologically or fundamentally undisciplined.

Yet, the idea was that the state was faceless, which of course gave it power. Minds are punished more acutely by the faceless than by those with a face. (The state always has a good alibi: "The oppression is in their mind, those people are paranoid.") The assumption was that, for those who could conform to the disciplined will, no one specifically stood over and against you.[20] No one person, such as a king, stood over you to remind you that you were weak and guilty. In the time of sovereign power, the king's standing over you reminded you that even if you didn't deserve punishment, you were nevertheless small and therefore vulnerable to guilt. The face of the king's enchanted majesty

19. "Problematically Foucault contends that disciplinary power does not need ritual or ceremony to function, but more convincingly notes that it is not discontinuous but continuous." Elden, *Foucault*, 117.

20. To this day, white citizens have a hard time believing citizens of color when they say that the faceless state hovers over them, watching them, imposing guilt on their bodies by torturing their minds. White citizens often say that they just don't see it. They're not supposed to.

assured that message. The state, however, was faceless.[21] For the ideal citizen (white, landowning, heterosexual), as long as you avoided the state's apparatus of punishment, remaining disciplined at work, home, and beyond, there was no force to remind you of guilt. There was no guilt, no person, no laws outside your consenting will that you let down or disobeyed. There were only two categories of people: those disciplined enough to conform to the norms and strictures of the discipline society, and those who had to be bent to do so. Inside the discipline society, groveling, shame, and a sense of hovering guilt—though never completely gone—could be imagined to be forever on their way out.

The only place where guilt still popped up in these high modern times was in the mind. Guilt became an almost completely psychological reality (therefore, confession and surrender as the way to face guilt made no sense). Guilt was neurotic and pathological. Guilt was now a sign, not of sin but of sickness.[22] In a medical age, no one would ever try to deal with sickness using an act of confession. Guilt was a private sickness that lived under the unnecessary tyranny of invisible faces. It was the invisible emotions of your mother and your own repressed sexual feeling for her that was the last remnant of guilt. If a doctor, such as Herr Freud, could sit behind you, hiding his face from you, as you lie on a couch and analyze the way your mind unnecessarily obsessed over these avoidable feelings of guilt, your mind could be healed and guilt could be banished forevermore.

Freud's protégé (and later frenemy) Carl Jung was sure that this face-off with guilt constituted a new kind of mysticism. Surely, he told Freud, psychoanalysis is a mystical operation (again, see how guilt and the mystical are connected). Freud was horrified by the suggestion. He was so disgusted that it ended their budding friendship. Freud was unrelenting in his quest to end any remnant of guilt that would demand any kind of mysticism. In Freud's mind, if Darwin had wounded a religion of guilt, Freud himself would bury it six feet deep. Psychoanalysis is the heroic science to end guilt forever by medically healing the psyche. It was now assumed that the mystical would recede to never return.[23]

---

21. Until a certain point. In fascism, Hitler and Mussolini became the face of the state, and therefore fear and guilt spilled into the society.

22. See Charles Taylor, *A Secular Age* (Cambridge, MA: Harvard University Press, 2007), 610–20.

23. See Peter Gay, *Freud: A Life for Our Time* (New York: Norton, 2006), chap. 2.

The Road That Led to Biopolitics

As the ambitions of Freud show, the disciplinary society gave precedence to reason over expressive romanticism. From our earlier comparison, you could say that the hound of reason always eats first. The terrier was still in the yard, but it was not the state's favorite pet. Therefore, the disciplinary society, overseen by the faceless state, did not concern itself with expressive romanticism like it did with reason. This kept guilt further away from being the central concern. Guilt seemed to appear only in "hysterical" women like those whom Freud studied in a Parisian hospital in 1885 or like Betty Draper in season 1 of *Mad Men*. As we've said, technical reasoning and mathematics have little room for feelings, let alone guilt. Guilt was assumed to be a corrupting force that leads to bad reasoning. It therefore needed to be rationalistically confronted as a pathology and treated with a further dose of reason.

But let's be clear, the state was never completely faceless. It's true that the apparatus of punishment was deeply opaque. The FBI, CIA, KGB, Stasi, and SIS operated completely in the shadows. The king's apparatus of punishment was much different. In sovereign power, punishment was always completely in the open, right in the town square. Bodies were punished—even executed—in full display for all to see. Even small children watched Anne Boleyn's head leave her neck. This openness made guilt an ever-present part of the whole of society and its self-understanding. Guilt was tightly woven into the fabric of social life. On the contrary, in the disciplinary society, punishment is hidden and secret. Guantanamo Bay, a hidden, no-place place, offshore, far from the sight of citizens, is where punishment is mercilessly and secretly imposed by the state. Therefore, guilt was assumed to be gone and over. At least not a direct part of our lives. It was assumed that guilt had no part in the fabric of a disciplinary society run by a faceless state.[24]

Again, though the state's apparatus of punishment was faceless and hidden (a dark op), the state itself was not completely faceless. There were faces like those of Abraham Lincoln, Melbourne, Otto von Bismarck, Winston Churchill, Theodore Roosevelt, Charles de Gaulle, Pierre Trudeau, and John F. Kennedy. When sovereign power ended and the disciplinary society dawned

---

24. Of course, this facelessness was supposed to be for the sake of the fact that it was the people and their will that governed us. But soon this facelessness became a form of power. This happened in both democratic (capitalist) and communist states. Things needed to be hidden from the people for the sake of their own security. The facelessness turned from service to the perpetuation of control.

with the likes of Lincoln and Bismarck, it would be decades before photographs and even television broadcasts of such state leaders as Trudeau and Kennedy were common.

With television, everything changed for the faceless apparatus of punishment and discipline. In the late 1960s, less than two decades after the arrival of television (and with it a new consumerism), the disciplinary society as a whole came under great critique. The state was supposed to enforce discipline, correcting obdurate wills. But the state was caught on film being cruel and therefore undisciplined. In the US, citizens saw with their own eyes that the state was oppressing African Americans in the South and obliterating Vietnamese peasants a world away. The citizens saw that the state itself was guilty of atrocities. Even so, the state and its leaders could ignorantly or implacably deny it. Maybe they could deny it because, to the great frustration of many, the state knew no language of guilt. Therefore the state continued to justify its actions with theorems and other technocratic sleight of hand. The hound of reason barking out the numbers. Robert McNamara (Kennedy and Johnson's secretary of defense) famously used spreadsheets to quantify the progress of the Vietnam War, measuring success by body counts and never even considering that those were bodies of human beings; he was rationally counting.

Over and against the state's wishes, guilt was back. It had returned on the back of the state itself. The state was the object of guilt. With guilt directed at the state and the state confused by such talk, guilt's source was not yet directed toward the self. Rather, guilt's return came through the realization that the state's apparatus of punishment was itself guilty (of course, this is still an open debate with deep tensions between those who chant "Black Lives Matter" and those who chant "Blue Lives Matter" in return).[25] This made the state, as a whole, corrupt—at least in the minds of the young and the radical. The idea of the disciplined society was wounded and staggered across the West by the youth revolts of 1968. The youth revolts sought to rebuke the hound of reason by cuddling up with the terrier of romantic expressivism. The young opposed the disciplinary society by taking on the marks of an expressive

25. When people chant "Black Lives Matter," they are not chanting that other lives matter less. They are prophetically asserting that inside the still-existent disciplinary society's apparatus of punishment, Black lives have mattered less. Black bodies have felt the unjust force of punishment for being "bad" citizens. What has made Black citizens "bad" is that they are Black. To chant "Black Lives Matter" is to assert that the faceless apparatus of punishment has been a machine that chases down and punishes Black bodies indiscriminately and far outside the disciplinary society's values and laws.

lack of discipline. They were loud (with chants and guitars), dressed outrageously (with tie-dye), and grew their hair long. They turned their backs on the disciplinary society and dropped out. To be countercultural was to follow the lead of the terrier and oppose all things bound by disciplined rationality.

This return of guilt, attached directly to the state's apparatus of punishment, brought forth a new age of spirituality (new-age spirituality). Inside this new-age spirituality, the mystical, in broad strokes, appeared with cultural force in modernity for the first time. The Beatles ditched their suits and matching haircuts, releasing albums like *Magical Mystery Tour* and *Sgt. Pepper's Lonely Hearts Club Band*. The impetus for this new mystical spirituality was *not yet* the guilt of the self (that would come next). The push was the revelation of the guilt of the disciplinary society itself. Inside this opposition to and outrage over the state's guilt, a generation sought the spiritual as a way of opposing the rational. A move into the mystical was a way to push back against the technocratic state. This occurrence is what Charles Taylor has called the arrival of the "nova effect." Inside this moment of the state's guilt, all sorts of third-option spiritualities are birthed. They are third-way options because these new spiritualities are equally rejecting classic (state-friendly) forms of organized religion as well as opposing rationalistic unbelief.

This nova effect of third-way options brought forth spiritualities made by and for pure expressivism. This expressivism of the new generation was learned from the radical descendants of Jean-Jacques Rousseau. The stoned beat poets in New York, promiscuous bohemian painters in Paris, and traumatized intellectual exiles of Nazi Germany taught a new generation new fringe spiritualities, bringing them from the fringe to the center of our cultural imagination. Particularly, these intellectual exiles, who took teaching positions at growing US universities, had concrete proof of the rotten center of the disciplinary society. They pointed this out to their young students. These exiled intellectuals were not shy in drawing stark parallels between the FBI and the Gestapo. After all, both were central to the apparatus of punishment in a disciplinary society. Both were caught red-handed, guilty, with the blood of the innocent painted from wrist to fingertip.

This shift set the conditions for the arrival of the performing self, and with it the ability for guilt to turn toward the self. Shockingly, for the performing self and its new teeth of guilt to arrive, those who originally opposed the new spiritualities of the counterculture needed to turn the counterculture's expressivist momentum against itself. A new conservative collective that had no stomach for the counterculture and its desires made sure that if disciplinary power was being replaced, this new collective would set the terms for what would take its place. It took another decade, post-1968, for the disciplined society to be replaced for good. In the dying days of the 1970s and the dawn of the 1980s, the disciplined society, ironically, was buried by the very conservatives who had despised the revolts of 1968. The youth revolts wounded the disciplined society, but it was the economists of the new right who killed it and buried it in a shallow grave.

The Power of Biopolitics or Guilt in the Shadow of Neoliberalism

The counterculture, to its credit, overthrew disciplinary power. But to its derision, its overthrow created a vacuum of power it had no ability to fill. Rushing in to fill that role was this new conservative collective of economists and libertarians. They imposed a new form of power, bringing forth a post-disciplinary world, by claiming that the problem with disciplinary power wasn't its guilt, necessarily, but its size. Big government and its regulations were the source of evil. In their mind, America was guilty of strangling capitalism with its big government regulations. If the disciplinary society was bad, this new collective asserted, it was because disciplinary power demands big government.

The disciplinary society was cold but sturdy. Companies and workers, as long as they stayed disciplined, were given protections, securing their future. Yet, feeling the economic lag of the mid-1970s, the economists of the new right believed protections like pensions and employment security stagnated growth, weaking the economy overall. Margaret Thatcher and Ronald Reagan birthed a neoliberalism that promised fewer regulations for companies and even fewer protections for workers.

But why would workers accept this? By following the expressive individualism of the counterculture, neoliberals could paint the disciplinary society as guilty for its big government intrusion on *your* freedom. Fewer regulations and protections were *good* for your own individual freedom to be your own magnificent self. The individual sense of *your* freedom was key. In the logic of the counterculture, freedom was defined expressively. And it was defined this way for economic gain. To allow businesses the freedom from the regulations of big government, the disciplinary society had to grow through all-out competition. To thrive—even to just survive—we needed to let competition, and therefore achievement (but *not* discipline), reign in all corners of our lives. Soon competition and achievement were the ethos of nearly every part of our lives. Workers needed to be convinced that it was *good* and in their best interest to welcome competition over protections, better to have flexibility than pensions, better to be rewarded for your individual achievements than slowed by the collectivism of a union.

To make this all work as a form of power, an apparatus of social control was necessary. True, a form of the apparatus of punishment in the disciplinary society continues (Guantanamo is still open, and the police still profile African American men). But ultimately it was much cheaper and better (more conducive to small government) to make every individual, every bios or body, responsible for their own life. The body (bios) politic turned from a group or community to the sole individual. We are now all asked to be our own body politic. The body politic takes the shape of the individual, so much so that we are now responsible for our own punishment.[26] The force of responsibility is now your own self. The stick that makes sure you take on this responsibility of your own self is the unrelenting competition that spills into every corner of every part of our lives.

This new power is what Foucault calls the power of "biopolitics."[27] The new apparatus of punishment is the self against the self. The new economists asserted that if a new economy, with few regulations, had its way, there would be little reason for the disciplinary society's apparatus of punishment. Because now what matters is not being a good citizen but being a winner, being all you can be.[28] Being magnificent!

26. Michael J. Thompson makes a similar argument in *Twilight of the Self: The Decline of the Individual in Late Capitalism* (Stanford, CA: Stanford University Press, 2022).

27. What Foucault means by "biopolitics" is complicated and has a deeper genealogy than I can offer here. It has much to do with our shifts in medicine. Yet, Foucault links the arrival (or, better, perfection) of biopolitics with the rise of neoliberalism. See his *The Birth of Biopolitics* (New York: Palgrave, 2008). This is the part of biopolitics I'm trying to highlight.

28. Byung-Chul Han adds, "Within the neoliberal regime, even power appears in a positive form. It becomes smart. In contrast to repressive disciplinary power, smart power does not cause pain. Power becomes altogether decoupled from pain. It can do without repression. Subjugation takes place through self-optimization and self-realization. Smart power operates in seductive and permissive ways. Because it parades itself as freedom, it is less obvious than repressive disciplinary power. Surveillance also takes on a smart form. We are constantly asked to communicate our needs, wishes and preferences—to tell our life stories. Total communication, total surveillance, pornographic exposure and panoptic surveillance coincide. Freedom and surveillance become indistinguishable." Han, *The Palliative Society*, trans. Daniel Steuer (London: Polity, 2021), 10.

If being magnificent is the goal, if everyone becomes their own individual, expressive competing business or brand, fighting for their own interest (with little concern, even hatred, for altruism, à la Ayn Rand), then the apparatus of punishment can migrate from outside the self in society to be locked right inside the self. We do the punishment ourselves now. The structures of disciplinary power remain. Prisons are still open and punishing; we continue to live with a sense of disciplinary power. But this disciplinary power rarely creates a direct experience of guilt. Thanks to the competition of neoliberalism and its biopolitics, we now acutely feel guilt. Guilt is again everywhere—but now in a new, self-directed way. We are guilty to ourselves. We punish ourselves for not winning, for not being magnificent. "I'm my own worst critic," people say. The self-talk of upwardly mobile people is often harsh; after an embarrassment, it wouldn't be uncommon for someone to look in the mirror and shout, "You're so stupid! Get it together!"

In the wake of neoliberalism, the disciplinary society is replaced by the *achievement society*. What matters now isn't discipline—following the rules—but instead pursuing and gaining recognition for your achievements. You need to concern yourself with winning. And you can only win by showing what your own self is able to achieve, doing magnificent things, being amazing in all general ways. In biopolitics, a society is run by the ambitions of its workers and the creativity of our own selves. Inside the power of biopolitics, the self runs surveillance on itself, punishing itself, driving itself to reach for what can never be had: pure magnificence. If everyone is on their own, and everyone is competing against everyone else, then everyone will obey, working on their self at every turn so that they don't lose, so that they don't fall behind and feel guilty for doing so. If it's sink or swim for everyone, with tests of merit everywhere, then the apparatus of punishment becomes native to the system itself and guilt mobilizes constant performance. Punishment, and therefore deep feelings of guilt, is what we do to ourselves by constantly judging our performance.

Now your very self is assumed to be an achievement. The only way to mitigate risk in this kind of achievement society of biopolitics is to try the impossible and win pure and lasting magnificence for your own self. Neoliberalism clears out as many regulations and protections as it can so that competition can be as intense as possible. Winners achieve, not only at work but in every part of their life. The self in an achievement society is always, without end, right in the middle of a competitive performance. The self is fully and always a performing self.

Concluding and Moving Forward

From inside this environment of achievement through performance, and the acute guilt it produces in us (experienced as low-grade and high-grade anxiety and depression), a new late-modern mysticism comes to be. This new mysticism is equal parts expressive romanticism of the counterculture and all-out competition of neoliberalism. It's a mysticism born to assist selves in becoming unique and authentic, while in turn always winning, performing, and achieving. Inside this environment of guilt (which grows on both the expressivism and the competition), we become interested in knowing who is spiritually coping or even thriving. We wonder (even search for) who is turning the guilt and exhaustion into authenticity and victory. We need something spiritual, both as a balm (relief) to the rash of constant competition and as a way to position ourselves for further victory inside this competition. The guilt resulting from knowing that we're not thriving in this competition of selves against selves causes us to reach for (or be open to) new forms of mysticism. It leads us to admire the mystic. But the mystic and mysticism itself need to be molded specifically for the constant expressive competition and those sharp teeth of new guilt. These new spiritualities with their own mystical exemplars (call them heroes, celebrities, influencers, gurus, personalities) include, to name a few, exercise, time management and organization, healthy eating, travel, socially conscious activism, mindfulness, self-growth, being a great parent who gets your kid into Yale, and all sorts of megachurches that promise to assist you in your individual competitions of the self. There is always the danger that even talk of God becomes captured by this logic, making God the one who demands our performance.

Driving for the magnificence of the self that neoliberalism demands, inside a hypercompetitive environment, makes guilt ever-present. This guilt clears the ground for these new mystical pathways. These new mystical pathways come to us in many different media. But maybe one of the most direct, powerful, and reflective pathways is the contemporary memoir. The memoir demands spiritual reflection on a life. The memoirist, reflecting on their life, can often name, beyond the failings and guilt of the self, the mystical route to victory.

Memoirists might just be our new late-modern mystics, coming out of the shadows of the new guilt we bear.

As we move forward in this project, we need to ask, What kind of mysticism do these new mystics advocate for the achievement society? Bound in the power of biopolitics that punishes the self, can this mysticism really confront the guilt and exhausting drive for the magnificence of the self? Does this new mysticism, birthed from the performing self, have any room for confession and surrender? Does it still have space for Justin Vernon's discovery in "Holocene" that "Someway, baby, it's part of me, apart from me" and "At once I knew I was not magnificent"? Does Vernon's call back to more classical forms of mysticism still have a place in late modernity?

We are closer to exploring a dozen memoirs to see if the cultural pathways of these new forms of neoliberal mysticism can be mapped to help us get a better handle on the issues of faith formation and the practice of ministry in late modernity. But before we can do that, we still have work to do. We need to explore how this return to mysticism remains modern and grounds itself in the everyday, and then we will draw our map and plot these secular mysticisms on that map.

4

•————————•

When the Everyday Houses
a Mysticism without God

To stretch my book budget, I'm happy to buy used books. If the book is at least $8 cheaper used, I go used. There are two gambles with used books. First, the speed of shipping. Sometimes a used book comes in two or three days. Other times it can take two or three weeks. No matter what the seller says, it's impossible to know.

My second concern is markings. I'm not too concerned about dust jacket or old library markings. But I don't want a heavily underlined book, especially if done haphazardly. I hate paging through a used book and seeing the thick, askew orange lines of an out-of-control highlighter (who are those maniacs by the way?). I particularly hate when the highlighting is met with blue or black ink from another reader. And I go a little crazy if there is a third underliner using pencil. The blaring cacophony of readers and their mismatched utensils is just too much.

However, I don't mind reading along with someone. I even like it. I just prefer a reasonable solo underliner with a clear point of view. I particularly enjoy those who make small, detailed summary comments in the margins. I know this reader was preparing for a seminar or precept discussion. The reader's anxiety of needing to understand and communicate something important about the book is like a time capsule. Although the imagined discussion that this reader is preparing for is *long* over by the time I receive the book, I can nevertheless still feel the grinding anxiety to grasp the point of the text. We're doing that together. This blurs time and space in a weird way. The pages and their comments become a unified point where the chasm between past and present is merged into our single reading. It's also fun to try and imagine who this other underliner might be, speaking to me across time and space but now contemporaneous. I do my deciphering by the variables of marking style (some people just underline words, others whole paragraphs), choice of utensil, and handwriting.

Since my reading of Tara Westover's *Educated* in the sand, I've been buying more memoirs. I particularly like to read them when I travel. I purchase Julie Yip-Williams's *The Unwinding of the Miracle*. It arrives just hours before my flight to Europe. This is the same trip that will end in Paris. Yet, before we get to Paris, in the shadow of the Sorbonne, we visit an almost empty Prague.

We arrive in Prague by train from Berlin. Our Airbnb is a short walk from the station, right across the street. That should've set my expectations. I should have been prepared for a useful but worn apartment. As we enter the large doors, we meet David, the Airbnb host. I notice right away that the apartment is spacious but needs a coat of paint. There is no smell of Febreze covering any secrets. It's comfortable enough. David warns us, however, to never leave with the windows open and to always make sure we lock the door. "It's not a dangerous area, but not *not* dangerous; things can get stolen," he tells us in his broken English. He then gives me a detailed twenty-minute overview of the espresso machine. I work hard to feign interest. David finally ends by showing us his favorite pub on a giant map of the city. We take his advice by filling our travel-weary stomachs with burgers and Czech beer (the beer is delicious and cheaper than the water, just as he said).

Back in the apartment as the June sun disappears in a splash of orange brighter than any highlighter, and with the murmurs of the European Football Championships heard across the city, I pull out Yip-Williams's memoir. Before I know it, I'm four chapters in. Yip-Williams tells the heartbreaking story of being a healthy, happy mother of two small children when she experiences excruciating pain while visiting family in Los Angeles. Rushed to the emergency room, tested and retested, she learns that she has late-stage colon cancer. In the fight of her life, she battles arduously yet beautifully and honestly, as she searches for some meaning to her illness. Ultimately, in the end, she dies. The sorrow of leaving her children and husband, the bravery of facing her mortality, is haunting and stunning.

Like the mystics, she walks a path into liminality. Her cancer forces her into a new space where she must face the deepest questions of existence. Yet, she does this not in a monastery but in the everyday life of children's birthday parties and the heavy realization that she will not see her daughters graduate from high school, not even middle school.

Per usual, I have my yellow highlighter in hand. I'm looking for the mystical pathway, interested in the experiences and ideas of grief, loss, and confrontations with mortality. I bracket paragraphs that point to this, boxing them in yellow. On other pages, I carefully underline sentences that point to this wrestling.

But as I begin reading, I realize I'm not alone. There is another reading along with me. This unknown other has a red pen. She doesn't bracket anything. Her marks are careful, precise. Her red pen cautiously underlines certain words and phrases. Her marks appear only once every ten pages or so, and just a phrase or half sentence is marked. As we move together from chapter to chapter, it's clear we're reading in a much different way. There is little to no parallel in our underlining. We're basically reading two different books. I begin to notice, even more closely than usual, that her red pen is emphasizing the names of treatments, hospitals visited, studies done, medications taken, diets tried, and the process of arranging for hospices.

By chapter 3, I begin to form an understanding of who this person might be. I start calling her red-pen reader. I know why red-pen reader is reading. Her partner, the one she loves and can't live without, also has colon cancer. She's reading as a lifeline. She reads with an awareness that her life is on the precipice of a grief she can't face—that right now she won't face. Red-pen reader is not ready. The book must have been recommended by a friend to get her prepared for the inevitable end. But she's not ready to face it. She reads looking for answers. Red-pen reader's underlining is a hunt for some way out. She still believes there is some kind of exit from this enclosed room of doom. Even as she watches the room fill with water up to her neck, she reads for a solution. Her red pen underlines the breadcrumbs in an evil forest, and she believes those crumbs can lead her out, setting her beloved free from the cancer-monster that has captured them both.

I finish Yip-Williams's memoir on our last day in Prague, right before we do one last walk over and back on St. Charles Bridge. With the book closed and finished, the spell that unites past and present inside our joint reading is broken. I wonder what's happened with her. I ponder how red-pen reader is doing. I wonder how she's gone on without her love. I wonder if any of the treatments worked. I even begin to consider that maybe red-pen reader was the one with cancer. Maybe I was reading along with her as she, like Yip-Williams, was beginning to face her own mortality. Maybe this book I'm holding was sold after a family member in grief cleared out her room, giving away the last possessions she didn't let go of herself. I could imagine her lying on the couch, wrapped in a blanket on a summer day—the chemo in her body always making her cold—paging through this very book I now hold. With the cancer in her body, red-pen reader was at first interested in researching how she could beat the beast. But by the end of the book, she was aware that her own end was coming fast. Whether red-pen reader was a relative of a cancer patient or herself overtaken by the cancer, I wonder if she ever found herself on the mystical pathway that Yip-Williams did. I contemplate whether Yip-Williams, from the grave, like a saint, had guided red-pen reader into a mystical journey.

What's Come Before

In the last two chapters I've sought to show both how and why certain kinds of mysticism have returned in late modernity and our secular age. We have yet to unpack the specifics of what constitutes these certain kinds of mysticism. We've named these paths (inner genius and heroic action), yet we've not traced these new late-modern pathways of the mystical. That will be the task of the next chapter. In this chapter here, we will prepare for this tracing. So far I have articulated how mysticism has indeed returned in late modernity. This new form of mysticism, manifest particularly in contemporary memoirs, is often a mysticism without God—*something once thought impossible or at least oxymoronic.*

A mysticism without God has its origins in the German Romantics who were inspired by Jean-Jacques Rousseau and his new confessions. Jean-Jacques's confessions asserted that the inner self was naturally magnificent, not bound in sin. Along with many other perspectives, this flip of the Western Augustinian sense of the self and its inner life opened the possibilities for the creation of a performing self. Inside neoliberalism, the performing self needs to race to compete against everyone, everywhere, all the time (with *all* your time!). The self's magnificence is won through a competitive performance of recognition. The self's won magnificence is the only sure way to be happy.

Yet, this pursuit of magnificence—this need to curate and always work on the self—creates the conditions for a new kind of dire and acute guilt to evolve. We get a mysticism without God because we shockingly create a guilt without God. When guilt is present, new forms of spirituality and mysticism race like antibodies to our cultural forefront to meet the guilt. Even in late modernity, with its many critiques and avoidance of religion, guilt reappears (first as the guilt of the state and then as the guilt of the self's inability, against the backdrop of constant competition and comparison, to use its time to secure its own magnificence). This reappearance of guilt opens us to—even creates a yearning for—mystical spirituality.

Charles Taylor has told us that a secular age like ours is not void of belief and spiritual longings but creates surpluses of what we assume are many equal and yet divergent ways to believe. Taylor calls this buffet of spirituali-ties a "nova effect." My contention is that guilt is what primarily fuels this explosion of mystical spiritualities. This self-attacking guilt makes for a buf-fet of beliefs, but it also imposes a fleetingness on all those beliefs. Feeling the acute guilt and intuitively recognizing that the specific spirituality you're using to meet the guilt is only one among hundreds—and unsure whether the option you've chosen is really assisting you in reaching magnificence—fragilizes the belief and practices you hold loosely. You're always wondering whether you should go back to the buffet for another spirituality, a different mystical exemplar on another mystical path that might help you better cope with your guilt.[1] Might a different spirituality help you win and be happy as opposed to exhausted and anxious, feeling like you're falling behind and losing? You wonder if another spirituality might better clear the way for the true performance of your self's true magnificence.

What fragilizes belief (fragilized belief being the core dynamic of living in a secular age) is (1) the sharp teeth of guilt and (2) the surplus of spiritual options used to help the self navigate this guilt and move toward a magnifi-cent performance. These two dynamics move us to always be looking for and trying on spiritualities and yet never fully settle on one. ("I was vegan for a while." "I used to be hard core into CrossFit." "I was in a mindfulness club." "For about year I went to an Alpha group." "I got pretty deep into this UFO channel on YouTube.") Our beliefs are fragile because we need something to

---

1. For a rich discussion of modern forms of mysticism, see Harold Netland, *Religious Experience and the Knowledge of God: The Evidential Force of Divine Encounters* (Grand Rapids: Baker Academic, 2022), chap. 6.

protect us from guilt's teeth, and yet we are hyperaware that the spiritualities and mystical gurus we use as guards against guilt are anything but static and sure. We're aware that there are so many other people seemingly performing the self better than us who are using different spiritualities and belief systems. These are the pressures that fragilize our beliefs.

Yet, there is one more element. This other element gives these new secular spiritualities and these new pathways of mysticism their particularly modern shape. This element, as we'll see, is the ability of these secular mystical spiritualities to attend to the *everyday*. Attending to the everyday has not always been something that mysticism could embrace. Yet, these new late-modern paths of the mystical have done so. Below I'll show that the location of the judge who imposes guilt directly shapes the arrangement of the mystical. Where the judge resides (for instance, in the self or in heaven) directly shapes the topography of the mystical pathway.

Mysticism and the Punisher

To excavate the shape of mystical pathways, think about it like this: Guilt is the awareness of a failure. But guilt has no teeth if failure is met with a weak form of punishment. Every parent of grown children has experienced something like this. Around middle school, your adolescent suddenly doesn't care that you've declared him guilty for a household violation. He scoffs because now, as a seventh grader, he finds your elementary punishments trivial—he even finds you, in some ways, trivial. The perception of the power of the one who judges you as guilty is essential (that power could have many forms: the power of a parent or the power of a soldier with a gun). The power of the judge who renders punishment and therefore creates guilt will determine if the guilt has teeth, and the sharpness of those teeth. If the judge has no real power, then even if you have been declared as having failed and therefore guilty, the guilt you carry is light, even laughable.

This concept has important practical theological ramifications. One of the abiding temptations inside late modernity, particularly for mainline churches, has been to gut God's judging power for the sake of an emphasis on God's acceptance. Judgment and acceptance have been set up as an either/or. Either God is a punishing judge or God is accepting and loving. It can't be both. This false dichotomy (true love itself is a judgment) has too many ramifications to unpack here. But one ramification that relates to our task at hand is that when God's judgment is cut out, so too is the perception of God's power and otherness. When the judgment and the otherness of God are downgraded, it limits the imagination for a living, moving God who makes claims and callings. It is little wonder that inside many mainline churches, divine action is flat and mystical longings for an inbreaking transcendence become suspect. Yet guilt still lies heavy because within the vacuum of God's lost judgment, the self becomes its own domineering judge. Ironically and surprisingly, in late modernity our own self judges us more directly (and harshly) than God does.

How does this happen? Remember, for guilt to have bite, the judge who imposes guilt must be powerful, and that gives us an important insight into the late-modern construction of the self. For the performing self to feel guilt acutely, the self needs to be a dynamic construction that furiously (and mercilessly) judges itself. This can happen only if magnificence (as opposed to weakness, sin, and death) is assumed to be both natural to the self and yet an achievement of the self. The power of the self to judge the self is to hold the self to a magnificence that is supposed to be native to the self that for some reason the self just cannot reach through its hurried performance.

The magnificence of the self casts a staggering light on our guilt. It is not a holy and other God who reigns in heaven who imposes guilt through God's own magnificence. It is our own self who is the new object of magnificence. We are guilty, whether before God or ourselves, because our own being is exposed as being in opposition or contradiction to magnificence (or glory). It's particularly harsh to come to realize that this magnificence you can't reach isn't outside you but within you. It's your own fault that you're not magnificent. Again and again, you keep failing to reach it. Inside this realization, you come to see yourself as a real failure for being unable to possess what is right before you.

Attention to magnificence has migrated, in small and large ways, from God to our own self. Our own self is now our harsh judge, locking us in a heavy guilt. In needing to make the self into something that can magnificently win and be happy through victory, the self possesses deep power to damn the self for its failure to perform well. The enclosed but potent location of the late-modern self as both judge and guilty defendant makes it possible for a mysticism without God to arise. This location of the judge also gives this new mysticism without God its particular shape or arrangement, placing it directly in the everyday.

To understand how this occurs, and give it more breadth, we need to step back. We need to return to when mysticism was arranged much differently from how it is today, when it was located somewhere other than the everyday— and never without God. This was a time when the location of the judge who imposed guilt through punishment was as far outside the self as could be imagined. This location was the eternal magnificence of heaven. Stepping back will help us spot how the arrangement of mysticism is bound to the location of the judge who renders guilt and how a secular mysticism for the everyday could possibly arise.

How Mysticism Was Once Arranged

The mystics of the thirteenth and fourteenth centuries contended that God was a powerful judge (Psalm 7 makes this more than clear). They, and with them all of humanity, lived under God's transcendent and complete power of otherness. God brought judgment (the king's hands were God's own). This made all those who were judged feel the heavy burden of guilt. This sense that God was powerful and other (transcendently bound in heaven) gave both guilt its bite and mysticism its disposition or arrangement. The guilt brought mysticism to the surface; the location of the judgment and punishment that produced the guilt molded the shape that mysticism would take.

For instance, because the location of the judge was in a heavenly, eternal realm—far beyond us—mystical activity happened in set-apart places like the monastery or the desert. The power and otherness of a transcendent judge who produced the guilt demanded a departure from the everyday. It demanded this departure because the power of judgment and the location of guilt were located in eternal otherness. Therefore, at least some people, for the sake of other guilty souls, needed to depart from and abandon the everyday. Since mysticism's earliest Christian days, it was a departure from particularly the everydayness of the city. The founder of Christian mysticism, Anthony the Great, in the late third century left Alexandria for the desert, seeking the mystical by abandoning the everyday for the sake of his own and his society's guilt.

The desert and soon the monastery became the direct locale of the mystical. The mystical pathway led away from the everyday. These were set-apart places, outside the everyday, intended for direct communion with the divine and for encounters of forgiveness that bring a union of spirit. With their reading of

Scripture and Plato, the early church fathers of the East were sure that God was completely other, judging from outside the everyday. Heaven or eternity was the place where God delivered judgment. Therefore, following the path away from the everyday was the way into the mystical life.

However, while this was true, it would be an unfortunate caricature (and one perpetuated by early Protestants and Enlightenment rationalists for different reasons) to claim that the monastic life of the cloister or desert was a repulsive turning from the world.[2] It was *not*. Basil, for instance, a founder and advocate of the monastery in the fourth century, saw the monastery as a necessary institution to care for the poor and hungry. There was no theological legitimacy in abandoning the world. But there was importance in departing from the everydayness of the world to attend to the mystical pathway of renunciation and prayer.[3]

Departing from the everydayness of the world was justified because the source of judgment was a powerful God who was other, and therefore guilt itself was bound in the power of an eternal otherness that was starkly different from the everyday. This sense that the source of judgment that declared guilt was bound in an eternal otherness gave medieval mysticism its shape. Mysticism was a response to the guilt coming from the punishment of a completely other God. Guilt's heavy presence made mysticism necessary. The fact that the source of this guilt was an eternal God of heaven arranged or shaped mysticism as a turning from the everyday, but *not from* the world. The cloister became the concrete locale or home of the mystical.

Inside these cultural realities and social imaginaries, it could never have been assumed that mysticism could be disconnected from God. How could that possibly be? Mysticism was a response to the guilt imposed by the judgment of God. A mysticism without God would be like marrying yourself. The thought that there could be a mysticism without God was unimaginable, because it was unimaginable that the self could be judged guilty by the self—that

---

2. Martin Luther, for instance, was harsh in his refusal of the monastery.

3. Rowan Williams explains, "Certainly the desert fathers and mothers were in flight from the social systems of their day, from the conformity and religious mediocrity of what they found elsewhere. But they were clearly not running away from responsibility or from relationships; everything we have so far been considering underlines that they were entering into a more serious level of responsibility for themselves and others and that their relationships were essential to the understanding of their vocation. Flight, as this saying of Macarius's suggests, is about denying yourself the luxury of solving your problems by running away literally or physically from them (sit in your cell) and about taking responsibility for your sins (weep)." Williams, *Where God Happens: Discovering Christ in One Another* (Boston: New Seeds, 2007), 70.

the self could be both guilt-ridden and a raging judge.[4] The fact that this has come to be is an utterly singular late-modern construction. This relocation of the judge who imposes guilt has moved mysticism into the everyday. This move into the everyday has happened because the self judging against the self resides within the performances of the self in the everyday. It is a viciously self-referential circle.

To connect some dots, we need to explore a much different relationship to the everyday born out of a rejection of the cloister. We need to see how the everyday became a place for God's presence, a phenomenon that allowed the everyday to eventually house a mysticism without God.[5]

Recovering the Everyday

This significantly different (and therefore new) relationship with the everyday, even the ordinary, started in the mid-fifteenth century.[6] Clerics who were turning from the everyday, living in the monastery, became malformed by the corruption of the cloister itself. The clerical class that turned from the everyday and the ordinary began to imagine themselves as controlling (even owning) the apparatus of punishment. They believed they had direct controls of all guilt. Inside this hubris, they began to revel in the power of dispensing punishment, even asking people to pay for forgiveness. This slowly but surely led to the blurring of their calling to bear, in prayer and petition, the punishment of those bound to the tasks of the everyday. It steered those in the cloister to stand over and against (even to disdain) the everyday.[7]

---

4. One wonders whether those who judge the harshest on social media are those who feel most overwhelmed with the guilt of not measuring up.

5. "As Francis envisioned his new order, he and his followers were to own nothing at all, not even a place in which to live, and they were to subsist solely by begging. The vow of poverty was as ancient as monasticism itself but the emphasis on mingling with the world and preaching to the laity was not. Up until that time, monasticism had been all about leaving the world behind and praying for it, not ministering to it directly." Carlos M. N. Eire, *Reformations: The Early Modern World, 1450–1650* (New Haven: Yale University Press, 2016), 49.

6. Carlos Eire, in his large and stunning book *Reformations*, tells this story, starting in 1450.

7. "Beginning with Martin Luther, who had come to loathe 'monkery' and everything associated with it as the ultimate corruption of Gospel principles and genuine Christianity, Protestants attacked the institution and its members with great virulence, sometimes even with physical violence. Luther filled his writings and sermons with antimonastic invective and even dedicated a long treatise to debunking the 'error' of monastic vows! Ulrich Zwingli called monks 'fattened pigs in disguise' whose vows were 'grounded solely in hypocrisy and idolatry,' adding that there were no people on earth 'richer than monks and none more avaricious.' In

This led to constant tensions. By the early sixteenth century, it exploded. The many movements for reform over a hundred years finally burst into a Protestant Reformation. At its center, Protestantism found this departure from the everyday and the ordinary to be a vile disobedience. It was a sure sign of theological corruption. Flipping things on their head, the Reformers believed that departure from the everyday and the ordinary was itself a guilty act. What rendered it guilty was the judgment of the Word of God. The Sacred Scriptures unveiled an incarnate Christ born not in a cloister but in a manger. The everyday and ordinary became the place of God's presence, and thus also the locale where people lived under guilt, in need of forgiveness. By disdaining the everyday, the clerics left the people in the guilt of their everyday lives.[8]

Martin Luther saw that forgiveness itself was not dependent on the apparatus of punishment owned and controlled by Rome. Rather, forgiveness and the release from guilt and divine punishment was offered freely to all inside their everyday lives. In the everyday flow of reading the sacred text that turned hearts to God, and in the everyday obedience of doing ordinary work faithfully, one could be given the gift and promise of forgiveness. This forgiveness came about through the profound but ordinary act of faith. In the everyday we could now find our guilt met by the mercy of God who judged but who also died in the everyday so that we could live. As opposed to the apparatus of virtue built on top of the apparatus of punishment, faith was for everyday people. The everyday, not the cloister, was now the place to encounter forgiveness and to live out a forgiven life.

By consequence, monks such as Martin Luther and Philip Melanchthon married nuns. They turned the monastery in Wittenberg into a house filled with children and students, a house spilling with the everyday. This Protestant attention on the everyday could be held together only because both Luther and

---

Protestant pamphlet literature, monks figure prominently as exemplars of every vice, and as social parasites living comfortably while others toil for them." Eire, *Reformations*, 417.

8. Carlos Eire gives us some context: "As if this were not bewildering enough, the clergy were divided into two very distinct groups: *secular* and *regular*. The secular clergy, whose name seems to be an oxymoron or a contradiction, were those who lived in 'the world,' among the laity to whom they ministered. The secular clergy were directly under episcopal jurisdiction, in the parish churches, as the historical descendants of the ancient presbyters. The regular clergy were the monastics, the descendants of the ancient Christians who had fled into the desert and established isolated communities. The original monks had little to do with 'the world.' In fact, the very first monks had been hermits, and the origin of the term *monk* is the Greek word for one who is alone, *monos*. But by the fourth century, monks began to gather into communities, and that way of life became normative. These men came to be known as 'regular' clergy because they followed a written rule (Latin: *regula*)." Eire, *Reformations*, 25.

Calvin never failed to speak of guilt. They reminded parishioners that God was indeed full of love. But this love was never without judgment (as we have now come to contrast the two). Forgiveness was central because guilt never lost its teeth. And, therefore, God was never anything but God. For both Luther and Calvin, the God of the Bible was a God who killed (judged) before God made alive (brought salvation). This was a God of judgment and grace, guilt and forgiveness, even punishment. Yet, it just so happened—marvel of all marvels—that this very God turned the apparatus of punishment onto God's self, making us all free to live in and celebrate the ordinary and everyday. This was the *evangel*, the good news, for those bound in the everyday who lived against the backdrop of cosmic guilt. It was the centrality of this good news in and for those in the everyday that made the Reformers, and Protestantism as a whole, evangelical.

When the Everyday Opposes the Mystical

Yet, this new and needed veneration of the everyday led to a different problem. Attention to the everyday seemed to slowly but surely strip the mystical out of Protestantism. Late in his life, Luther worried about the enthusiasts (called Schwärmer by Luther), who inside the everyday made mysticism an emotionalism. There were outliers, like those from the radical reformation (early Anabaptists) and the likes of Jakob Böhme (a Lutheran mystic), who sought to reach for the mystical in the everyday. Slowly but surely, in broad ways, the mystical couldn't hold inside the dawn of modernity in the Protestant nations.

Even the Lutheran and Reformed Pietisms of the seventeenth to nineteenth centuries found it hard to not allow their everyday spirituality to be turned into either rigid fundamentalism or hyperemotionalism. The temptation for Protestantism as it moved into a modern world was to gut the mystical from the inside out. Fundamentalists did this by turning the Bible, and certain everyday Christian practices, into scientism, demanding rational affirmation of principles. The everyday was flattened and made immanent by these principles and propositions. For conservative Protestants, the passion of the mystical was ejected from the everyday by the fundamentals of belief (the Azusa Street Revival tried to bring back a modern kind of Protestant mysticism in the early twentieth century, with both successes and shortcomings). For the fundamentalist, mysticism was stripped from the everyday because guilt ironically bore no mark of the otherness of God. Guilt, though heavy and spoken of often, was also cold and stiffly bound to the consent to principles. What rendered you guilty was not the otherness of God but your own inability to meet the standard of rational belief in the principles. The shape of fundamentalist power, punishment, and guilt made no space for the mystical inside its fetishizing of the rational.

The modernists or liberal Protestants also extracted the mystical from the everyday. The modernists or liberals represented the *mainline* of Protestantism. They were the representatives of true Protestantism inside the historically Protestant cultures and societies of the West.[9] They were the bastions affirming (even valorizing) the everyday and the ordinary. As the everyday became more modern, discourses (even psychologies) of guilt, as we've shown in the previous chapter, were less necessary. For someone like Harry Emerson Fosdick, guilt was a sickness that psychologically informed pastoral care could heal. Any other residue of guilt was bound in larger systems like the child labor of industrial factories. The objective was not to bear the guilt of punishment but to make the shape of the everyday more humane. With guilt bound in either abstract systems or ailments addressed by psychology, mysticism seemed backward and therefore anti-modern. Throughout the nineteenth and twentieth centuries the shape (and affirmation) of the everyday, and the exclusion of discourses of guilt and punishment, made mysticism antiquated, and therefore caused its practices to become absent. Modernist (liberal) Protestantism never much liked mysticism because it appeared to be a departure from the task of tending to the ethics of the everyday. Mysticism was assumed to be a form of superstition that yearned for something beyond the ordinary.

The dominant forms of Protestantism and the shape of modernity itself agreed (because both were linked) that mysticism had no real place in the everyday (this is what makes the appearance of Pentecostalism, and charismatic movements inside classic Protestant denominations in 1970s and 1980s, so interesting and important; their arrival was seeking a return to mysticism without losing the focus on the everyday). Mysticism was assumed to be antithetical to the everyday. Mysticism was for the cloister only. This mutual rejection of mysticism by the warring siblings of Protestantism was possible because both the fundamentalists and the modernists turned from the direct commands of a living God who is other. Fundamentalists put people under

9. This flipped in the late twentieth and early twenty-first century. Now evangelicalism (as the children of fundamentalists) is considered the *main* deposit of Protestantism—at least in America.

the weight of principles of belief, modernists/liberals under the "oughts" of cultural responsibility.[10] In different ways, they equally rejected the importance of any mystical pathway. The mystical pathway being walked by Catholics, even in the West, was all too anti-everyday for Protestants.

When the Mystical Enters the Everyday

Surprisingly, by the second half of the twentieth century, mysticism was rising again. Charismatic movements were popping up in fundamentalist and mainline Protestant denominations, and mysticism was even coming to exist outside Protestantism. Even more shockingly, mysticism was appearing outside of organized religion completely. Mysticism without an operating theism was on the rise. It arose from within two much different forces with much different concerns. One was a cultural feeling or sense of being guilty in your everyday competitions, the other the breakthrough of new ideas in phenomenology. What connects these two divergent late-modern concerns is their mutual location of mysticism squarely in the everyday. The mystical had been assumed to be antithetical to the everyday. It was thought that mysticism could not grow in the rocky soil of the everyday. Mysticism could exist in modernity but only if it turned its back on modernity by returning in direct or symbolic ways to something like the cloister (pre-1940s Pentecostals did something like this, turning from the institutions of the modern world). Yet, these two very different forces (a cultural reflex and new intellectual reflection) made it possible for the mystical to find a foothold in the everyday itself, and so much so that a mysticism without God came to be.

1. The Tyranny of the Everyday Self

In the last decades of the twentieth century a new mysticism arose without any need or concern for God (the previous chapter tells how). This mysticism without God could arrive because guilt returned. This guilt did not come from a divine command, with eternal consequence or practices of forgiveness. Instead, this guilt came about because of the demand to make the self into something magnificent (hence the escalation of self-help, self-development, and self-esteem movements and markets in the 1980s and beyond). You now feel guilty that you can't win inside the never-ending competition of the self's

10. This divide continues today in America especially.

performance. Mysticism returns without God because guilt returns with such overwhelming force in late modernity.

Again, the location of this guilt is not in the eternal but in the competition of the self. Guilt feels heavy because the force of punishment is so fierce. What delivers this punishment is no longer a God of grace, judgment, and mercy, but your own self. We need life coaches, blog gurus, thought leaders, social media pastors, and pop psychologists to tell us to love and forgive the self because it just so happens that the self is a tyrannical judge. The most harsh judgments of the self are aimed at the self. The self is so cruel that there is often no route to restoration and forgiveness. It becomes hard—an overwhelming life task—for late-modern people to learn strategies to forgive themselves (always by themselves). We are desperate for doctors, coaches, and celebrities to help us do so.

It is so difficult to forgive yourself because forgiving yourself is an empty restoration that keeps you locked within yourself. After all, the self is what put you under this heavy guilt. Forgiving yourself is to assume the tyrant of punishment can also be the balm of peace and forgiveness (the abuser is the lover). It was once assumed that only a divine reality could hold those two together, taking you out of yourself to give you the life of the divine being. But now you need to forgive yourself for not being magnificent using solely the magnificent power of yourself, which you don't have and are feeling guilty for failing to accrue. You become locked further within yourself as you feel the bite of guilt imposed by the self that must then forgive the self by the magnificence the self doesn't have—which bites you further with more guilt. To keep this circle from crushing you, you adopt mystical spiritualities that can help you (at least for a while) cope with the piercing burden of guilt's vicious cycle.

This mystical spirituality without God is directly and unequivocally located in the everyday. This new secular mysticism is a mysticism because it directly engages guilt, responding to punishment, for the sake of the self reaching union (union with your own self). Because the one imposing this guilt is not the divine eternal being, there is no reason to depart to the cloister (to even enter any form of organized religion). Rather, the judge who imposes guilt and whom you seek union with is in the everyday—it is your own self. It is the self that is seeking to win inside a hurried performance in the everyday, achieving recognition in the everyday. Therefore, the shape or arrangement of this late-modern mysticism—the topography of these secular mystical pathways—will be bound in the everyday. You are looking for the spiritual to help you not to escape the everyday but to deal with it.

Yet, there is a second force that allowed the everyday to take on new weight, bending toward the mystical. This second force preceded and, in many ways, cleared the ground for this cultural feeling or sense we've just discussed. The new attention to the everyday of this second force allowed the first force to sense the weight of the everyday, seeking spiritualities bound in the everyday.

2a. The Phenomenologist

It may have been certain concerns in Protestantism that rejected mysticism for the sake of the everyday. But it was a particular Jewish thinker and one predominant Catholic, both residing in Luther's Germany in the early twentieth century, who spotted that the everyday itself bore an inimitable depth. It was non-Protestants in the Protestant West who saw the multitudinous reach of the everyday. These thinkers saw that there was a copious profundity to everydayness. The everyday was a potent field. Yet, even when examining this profuse depth of the everyday, these thinkers discovered that the everyday never escaped being the everyday.

Edmund Husserl (1859–1938), the eminent Jewish thinker, stumbled into the profuseness of the everyday. Like many before him, Husserl was trying to grasp how we know things inside the everyday (often called "epistemology"). Husserl recognized that any structure of consciousness is bound inside a first-person perspective. Whatever you know, you know from within your own perceptions. No one can escape perceiving something through their own mind, seeing with their own eyes, for example. You can never stand outside your mind and perception. It's from the point of view of the knower, from inside their own experience, that the knower knows anything at all.

This wasn't really a breakthrough. Long before Husserl, René Descartes and Immanuel Kant already understood this. They knew that the experience of the knower mattered. Kant stated that there was no way of knowing a thing in itself (*Ding an sich*). We always know a thing from within our perceptions of it. It was the other side of the experience of knowing that Husserl emphasized. Husserl argued that when trying to come to grips with what we know, we always focus on the subjective experience of knowing and not on the objects we experience. Our minds might know colors, for instance, and it's interesting that minds can know such abstract things. But Husserl's point is that this kind of attention keeps us from recognizing as directly as we should that any experience we have of colors is never of purely the color. Rather, our experience of colors is an experience with a concrete object (a thing in the world) that possesses that color. We know things not solely in our head but in how we experience the objects and things in our everyday world. What we subjectively experience is not color but objects that possess a color. To really understand the mind and how it knows, we must give attention to our direct experience with everyday objects and things.[11]

Attention to everyday objects is the other side of the enigma of knowledge. Our experiences of everyday objects and things, when examined, are bound in a great depth of knowing. This attention to objects and things in the everyday birthed a new philosophical school called phenomenology. Phenomenology teaches us that our experience of ordinary objects in the everyday bears heavy (at least for Husserl, epistemological) weight. We know things inside a world of objects; the phenomena of interacting with these objects fundamentally shape our lives. These objects in our everyday lives deserve more attention because our ways of knowing are tied up with our experience of our everyday surroundings.

Modernity followed Protestantism and turned its back on mysticism by focusing on the everyday. But unlike Protestantism, modernity released the everyday, slowly but surely, from any direct divine engagement. This made the everyday safe from divine wrath and punishment (endangering guilt until it would return in late modernity, this time without God). Ultimately, the everyday became immanently flat. The immanent flattening risked making the everyday

---

11. Peter Salmon discusses these core epistemological commitments in Husserl: "For Husserl, the first of these, intentionality, became the 'indispensable fundamental concept of phenomenology,' and the key to any attempt to unite the incredibly strange realms. Descartes had argued *cogito, ergo sum*, 'I think therefore I am.' But what is it to think? Consciousness does not simply 'think,' it 'thinks about'—about trees, or what to have for lunch, or the problem of the concept of number. An ego alone in the universe, thinking, with no objects of consciousness, bears no relation to our own. In order to describe consciousness—and therefore do philosophy—one has to acknowledge and incorporate an 'intentionality,' a directedness to our thinking. By interrogating consciousness in this form—by describing how it is for consciousness to be in the world—we can attempt to establish and understand this concord between consciousness and the outer world. Husserl's revolutionary insight is that this analysis does not require an investigation of one of the major questions that had dogged philosophy, overtly and covertly, since its inception: the question of the actual existence of the world. What is important is not, for instance, whether or not the tree I am experiencing actually exists, the important thing is my experience of it, as a first-person phenomenon. I am to describe this phenomenon and analyse it. This task of description and analysis is the task of phenomenology." Salmon, *An Event, Perhaps: A Biography of Jacques Derrida* (London: Verso, 2020), 47.

vapid. Human concern and practice became dull and meaningless in such a world. This flat plane of existence with its utterly boring and tepid ways of life became the target of attack for Friedrich Nietzsche. In the late nineteenth century, the everyday, Nietzsche believed, was so flat and dull, bound in meaninglessness, that heroic action was called for. There was no way back to divine consequence (God was dead!), but the bold, the true heroes, could take actions to mold the everyday, to impose their wills upon it, filling the everyday again with consequence—at least for those who took heroic control. Nietzsche made a case for the depth of the everyday. He did not claim the significance of the everyday. Rather, he made a case for the everyday by seeing it as a stage on which the bold hero thrusts his or her will, reshaping the everyday by such passions.

Husserl affirmed this heroic return to the everyday, but in a very different way. Husserl's concerns were far more epistemological. He agreed that the everyday could escape the vapid. Yet, for Husserl this escape happened by examining the seemingly dull objects and decorum in the everyday, revealing a gravity to our experience. Husserl's phenomenology, in its own heroic way of reflection, returned a depth of meaning to the everyday. It may have had less flair than Nietzsche's, but it had more precision. Husserl's phenomenology was a bold, heroic move beyond stiff rationality.

Husserl and Nietzsche opened a door to the everyday, escaping its deadening flatness. They both gave the everyday direct attention. Husserl particularly opened dimensions not seen before. Therefore, after Husserl, the texture and gravity of the everyday returned through phenomenology (the French thinkers of the mid-twentieth century put Nietzsche and phenomenology together more tightly in calls for the heroic acts of deconstruction). The structure of knowledge and the heroic actions to perceive and name it (not the divine command, as it was for Luther) showed the depth of the everyday. The everyday became reanimated by the phenomenological.

Yet, it would take one of Husserl's students to move his phenomenological reanimation of the everyday toward the mystical. This genius step toward the mystical, taken by a Catholic-educated boy, would be intentionally done without God.

2b. The Phenomenologist's Student

Husserl is known not only as the founder of the school of phenomenology but also as the teacher of the twentieth century's greatest and most contentious philosopher, the Catholic Martin Heidegger (1889–1976).[12] Heidegger's writings are unequivocally groundbreaking, and the shape of his everyday life is just as undeniably perplexing and worthy of derision.[13] Though having learned so much from Husserl and once being so close to him, Heidegger, in the 1930s, cut him off. Heidegger joined the Nazi Party. Hannah Arendt, herself a great philosopher of the twentieth century and Heidegger's mistress in Marburg, couldn't forgive him for this. Arendt, herself Jewish, saw Heidegger's treatment of Husserl as particularly cruel. It was an ancient betrayal of a son to his intellectual father. And for no other reason than the latter's Jewishness.

Arendt knew better than anyone that Heidegger's original and groundbreaking work built directly off Husserl. Husserl taught Heidegger to focus on the everyday. Heidegger took this from Husserl, doubling down on it.[14] Husserl remained concerned with epistemological questions. He turned to the objects in the everyday, to our experience of these objects (phenomenologically), for the sake of cracking the code of how we know. Heidegger on the other hand believed that all this concern for knowing had distorted a larger truth. That we *are*. That we *have being*. The everyday was not just a significant component in the equation of knowing but the very location of *being* itself. It is being, particularly being alive in the everyday, that is the central concern. It's not that we know or don't know things, but that we exist, Heidegger believed. Where we exist is in the world of everydayness—it's in our everyday practices, languages, and interactions with objects, people, and perspectives that we become directly in touch with our being. The everyday is rich, because the everyday is the *there* of our *being*.[15] It is the place of *Dasein* (being there) that is so central to all Heidegger's thought.

12. Heidegger's father was a "sexton" or "sacristan" of a Catholic church. Peter Trawny, *Heidegger: A Critical Introduction* (London: Polity, 2019), 19.

13. Peter Gay offers some texture: "When the Nazis came to power, Heidegger displayed what many have since thought unfitting servility to his new masters—did he not omit from printings of *Sein und Zeit* appearing in the Nazi era his dedication to the philosopher Husserl, to whom he owed so much but who was, inconveniently enough, a Jew?" Gay, *Weimar Culture: The Outsider as Insider* (New York: Norton, 2001), 83.

14. "The concept of 'world' or 'life-world'—already used by Husserl earlier on—corresponds especially to this concept of 'life.' It provides possibilities of a differentiation necessary to the full-development of the conception of 'life.' Thus 'world' is always 'environing-world,' 'with-world' and 'self-world.' We live in 'worlds' that merge concentrically and that may eventually form a unified 'world.' I live with my friends, loved ones, and enemies, etc.; I live each time in a 'personal rhythm.' On the basis of such a differentiated understanding of 'world,' Heidegger carries out his phenomenological analysis." Trawny, *Heidegger*, 12.

15. "This 'taking care' of everyday matters occupies Dasein in a specific way. At this point in the phenomenological-hermeneutical survey of everydayness, Heidegger introduces a concept

So, indeed, this is a world of things, but in this world of things what impacts us is not that these things are objects of knowledge but that they shape the environment in which we *are*. The everyday is not just a field of epistemological objects; the objects are the essential furniture of our everyday existence.[16] These objects or things are essential to our everyday experience with being. The everyday matters because being matters, because the everyday is where being is located and unveiled. We are only in touch with our being (*Sein*) inside there (*Da*), inside the everyday activities and languages. Heidegger, who was trained by a Jew and whose closest early colleagues were Protestants, made no plea for returning to the monastery. He affirmed with vigor the everyday. But unlike his teacher and many of his early colleagues, Heidegger paid such dogged attention to being, and therefore the affirmation of the everyday, that he developed a unique emphasis on the mystical.

Heidegger was maybe the first modern mystic of the everyday without God (or maybe, as Arendt believed, he was the last of the dying and departing romantics).[17] His impact has been immense. Heidegger made it possible for a mysticism in the everyday without God to become a staple of late modernity. This emphasis on mysticism was both an affirmation of his Catholicism and an escape from it. Heidegger himself announced, as a way of turning from his Catholicism, that he denied mysticism. As John Caputo has explained in his exquisite book *The Mystical Elements in Heidegger's Thought*, Heidegger claimed to deny mysticism for the sake of the linguistic. It was not silence in the cloister that unveiled being but language inside the everyday that did so. Language directly revealed that the everyday possessed a

---

or, better put, a terminological distinction that still invites criticism today. First, let us recall that Heidegger indeed asked 'who' Dasein is in the everyday. He now answers this question. Dasein's everyday 'taking care' always happens in accordance with a particular 'way of being.' When I ride the bus or go to work, when I take out a loan or buy myself a pair of pants, I do all this as 'they' do. In the everyday, that is, in the everyday public sphere, Dasein 'takes care' of matters as 'they' 'take care' of matters. In the everyday, Dasein appears in the 'way of being' of the 'they.' Heidegger distinguishes this 'way of being' from the possibility of 'authentic' existence. Dasein 'takes care' of everything it is 'authentically' concerned with—like love or friendship, death or birth—in a different manner than when it 'takes care of' everyday affairs. The 'they' is the 'neuter' of the everyday public sphere; by contrast, 'authentic being-a-self' grants Dasein the possibility to live beyond everydayness." Trawny, *Heidegger*, 41.

16. Richard Cohen adds helpfully, "What Heidegger proposes, instead, is a phenomenological-hermeneutical account of everydayness as lived. In practice, then, everydayness means that each self defines itself in terms of attributes." Cohen, *Elevations: The Height of the Good in Rosenzweig and Levinas* (Chicago: University of Chicago Press, 1994), 47.

17. This was particularly how Arendt saw Heidegger's late work.

depth of being.[18] Heidegger's late work—starting around the time he rejected Husserl—embraced the thought of the fourteenth-century Rhineland mystic Meister Eckhart. But where Eckhart emphasized God, Heidegger replaced God with *Dasein*. Where Eckhart sought an unveiled communion with the divine being, Heidegger's pursuit was to lead his readers into an unveiling encounter with *Dasein* in the everyday (*Dasein* as the everyday). Heidegger rejects mysticism because he rejects both the cloister and God (more than rejecting God, he affirms *Dasein*). And yet Heidegger was mystical in his contention that *authentic* language and practice in the everyday took us into the profound depth of being itself. Authentically living and speaking is to be taken into the depth of *Dasein*.

Authenticity in the everyday can deliver a depth of meaning by connecting us to being: this concept makes Heidegger the first mystic of a late modernity without God. Authenticity became the direct experience of *Dasein*, replacing God.[19] On the back of Heidegger, the memoirists of the early twenty-first century forge new mystical pathways for the everyday without God. They can follow the trail of *Dasein*. Unknowingly connected to Heidegger, they almost all affirm the deeply held sense that the self's authenticity can free itself from guilt. By intuitively and unknowingly following Heidegger, these new mystical pathways without God take the shape they do. Some even, again unknowingly, draw from Nietzsche and Husserl by affirming the heroic.

Heidegger teaches us all that authenticity in the everyday delivers the depth of being. Authenticity is what releases and protects you from guilt. Authenticity is the substance of this spiritual state that loves the self for the sake of the self. Late-modern people imagine that if we can find an authentic way to *be* in the everyday, we'll touch something profound, something ontological

18. "Language is much more than a simple 'medium' or 'instrument' at the disposal of human beings who can then control things and themselves as they become 'informed.' Even though language can appear as 'information,' it also harbors possibilities that go far beyond that. This beyond is what is at stake. Heidegger's philosophy grasps language as a 'dwelling' in which the human being 'dwells.' In an emphatic sense, this 'dwelling' can exist only if 'being comes to language.' From this point of view, we see how different the conception of language as 'information' is from the view of language as 'house of being'; this difference is decisive for 'dwelling.' For Heidegger, a world dominated by the cybernetic conception of language has eliminated the possibility of 'dwelling.'" Trawny, *Heidegger*, 109.

19. Peter Eli Gordon adds, "It is important to note here that Heidegger uses the term *authenticity* in order to designate that special mode wherein Dasein understands its 'ownmost potentiality for Being.'" Gordon, *Rosenzweig and Heidegger: Between Judaism and German Philosophy* (Berkeley: University California Press, 2003), 224, quoting Heidegger, *Being and Time* (New York: Harper and Row, 1962), 307.

in our self. We'll be baptized in the river of *Dasein*, washed with its meaning and purpose, the everyday touching something mystical through our inner authentic genius and heroic actions. We will be magnificent selves because we will be authentically encountering being. *This will allow the mystical to land squarely in the everyday.* The everyday needs authentic language to unveil the mysteries of Dasein. No wonder the memoirist is the new mystic of the everyday in late modernity. They unabashedly dive into authenticity through language and reflection in the ordinary, opening up a mystical space in the everyday. These memoirs give testimony of a transformation by the force of *Dasein* (not necessarily the God of Israel). The fact that it's a transformation of being means it can't be ignored—it has a true depth. And yet it becomes a confusing challenge for ministers and churches because it takes no account of God's own being to make sense of it.

This drive for authenticity in the everyday, these mysticisms without God, leads some to wonder if Christianity itself can *really* deal with the everyday at all. It's a cold irony that Protestant Christianity honors the everyday so much that it has become perceived as losing a sense that it can deal with the everyday. It may be true that Protestantism is responsible for validating the everyday. But Protestantism—and Christianity as a whole, some contend— remains too concerned with sin and the divine Word to allow for those in the everyday to reach for authentic ways of being in the everyday. It is now assumed that without the authentic, the mystical dimensions of the everyday cannot be experienced. The magnificence of the self's performance in the everyday is assumed to be unachievable. Therefore, for some, organized religion is as- sumed to be a vapid kind of spirituality.

Jews with a Different Emphasis

Next to guilt's new teeth and the recovery of the depth of the everyday (now without God), we can spot at least two new mystical pathways. Both path- ways, for the most part, are constructed without God. We've already been calling these pathways "inner genius" and "heroic action." We can now see how their very topography is shaped by, and bound in, the everyday.

Husserl and Heidegger cleared the ground within the everyday for these two pathways to exist. To do so, both pathways had to assert that the self can seek magnificence for itself—either through its heroic will or through embraced authenticity. The mystical became locked solely and completely within the self when met by other cultural realities such as the post-1968 counterculture and neoliberal capitalism. It lost Justin Vernon's assertion in his Bon Iver song "Holocene" that "someway, baby, it's part of me, apart from me." The new pathways of the mystical in the everyday have lost sight of that which spiritually connects me, becoming part of me but always (irreducibly) apart from me. They ignore or deny that even, or particularly, in the everyday, transcendent otherness can be encountered inside the deepest of unions.

At the same time that Husserl and Heidegger were pointing to the everyday's depth, two other Jewish thinkers were doing their own work in claiming the profundity of the everyday. Unlike Husserl and Heidegger, they attended to the everyday with God's otherness squarely at the center. These two Jews were seeking a mysticism in the everyday directly with God. The mystical path they sought, while also holding an utter commitment to the everyday, contended that what becomes part of me is always beautifully and irreducibly apart from me.

When a Mother Leaves

In 1928, Husserl was giving a lecture in Heidelberg. He was at the height of his fame; his thought was making a stir across Germany. Living in Heidelberg and interested in what Husserl was saying, Martin Buber walked into the lecture hall unannounced. He thought he could slip into a corner and listen. But Buber was spotted and asked to sit on the panel at the head table. When Husserl arrived, he greeted the panel, shaking hands with each person. Husserl was stunned when this short, stocky man with a long beard like a prophet said, "My name is Buber." After a long pause, Husserl asked, "The real Buber?" Buber just shrugged his shoulders sheepishly. Husserl responded, "But there is no such person! Buber—why he's a legend!"[20]

Martin Buber is the greatest Jewish intellectual of the twentieth century. Much like Husserl, Buber was seeking the depth of the everyday. Yet unlike Husserl, and in a much different way from Husserl's student Heidegger, Buber embraced a form of mysticism with God. Both the everyday and the mystical, from the beginning, were essential parts of Buber's life. They were linked in a sad way.

Buber's mother left the family when he was only three years old. Buber's first memory was of her departure. He ran to the large French windows of

---

20. Maurice Friedman, *Martin Buber's Life and Work*, vol. 2, *The Middle Years, 1923–1945* (Detroit: Wayne State University Press, 1988), 121.

their Vienna home, pounding on them and shouting, "Momma, momma!" But she didn't even look back. She left him for good. Her departure—and worse, her seeming ambivalence—was a piercing experience of loss that never left Buber. He carried the wounds of her departure his whole life.

It was through this rupture that Buber held together the everyday and the mystical. The everyday itself has mystical weight through the deep relations of a mother to a child. Buber, as we'll see, centered his thought on the profundity of human relationships. He centered it on the I and Thou, on the *Ich und du*. Thou (or You) might seem formal in English, but the *du* in German is the second-person form of address used, particularly in Buber's time, only in intimate settings by those in intimate relations. It's the kind of form that's used particularly in the discourse of mothers with their small children.

This everyday discourse, Buber believed, has a mystical depth bound not in a metaphysics but through a spirit of relationships. There is no doubt, particularly in the late nineteenth century in Vienna, that the mother was a representative, even embodiment, of the everyday. In a Jewish German-speaking and Yiddish-speaking household, her person firmly shaped the everyday. Her family experienced the everyday through her. Yet Buber understood that this shaping and filling of the everyday was not (and never could be) simply functional or instrumental. The mother's importance is not in her tasks but in her relations. She shapes the everyday not through her duties but through the mystical relations she has with her children. The everyday bears the marks of the mystical, not by her gender role or operations but by the spirit of her relations, by her love for *du*. Buber knew this because he lived inside the crater of its absence.

The everyday and its warm spirit had become completely void for little Martin. His everyday home was uninhabitable. The everyday was a frigid nightmare. A cold home with a lonely father in despair was no place for a small boy. So little Martin was sent to his grandparents' home. Martin's grandfather, Solomon Buber, became the most influential person in Martin's life. Solomon, an intellectual force in his own right, "liked to pray among the Hasidim and used a prayer book full of mystical directions. He liked to take his grandson Martin to a small Hasidic Klaus or synagogue to pray."[21] Buber grew up feeding on Hasidic tales and fables. His everyday life was

21. Maurice Friedman, *Martin Buber's Life and Work*, vol. 1, *The Early Years, 1878–1923* (Detroit: Wayne State University Press, 1988), 95.

filled with the mystical pursuits of the Jewish community, balm to his lost relations.

Seeking to articulate how the mystical could be inside the everyday, Buber turned to Meister Eckhart, like Heidegger after him. He went to Berlin to write his dissertation on Eckhart. But soon the world changed. After World War I, Buber's focus on the mystical was met by a more direct attention to the everyday. The longings and losses of his childhood took more direct form. The I and You was born out of the horrible ways that the Great War turned the everyday into the deepest of animosity. The everyday spirit of nations mobilized for murder. The Great War imposed the loss of the *Ich und du* for so many. It was the ending of so many relations of discourse. So many mothers were left without sons.

After the war, discourse (conversation) became Buber's focus. Discourse between persons in relationship is the way the everyday bears the mystical. The mystical is shaped by relations of persons bound and yet differentiated in their I and You relations. Like Heidegger, Buber saw that the everyday bears the mystical through communication, through speech. The human *being* is never without, and always shaped by, some form of speaking. Buber shared Heidegger's attention to being and its connections to the linguistic. In the 1950s Buber invited Heidegger (after his ugly Nazi Party affiliation and rudeness to Husserl) to visit him in Jerusalem. They shared a commitment to the everyday, a longing for the mystical, and the importance of speech. Though so close, their emphases were nevertheless too different. Heidegger focused on language as the very house of being. It was the authenticity of language that unveiled *Dasein*, bringing the mystical into the everyday. Language opened us up to the mystical and to an encounter not with God but with *Dasein*. (Arendt may have been right that Heidegger appeared to be the last romantic, as he leaned on the poet Friedrich Hölderlin to make these points.)

Buber, too, affirmed speech. But for him the everyday bore the mystical not through the linguistic but through discourse, through the spirit of relations. It wasn't that *Dasein* was unveiled in authentic language use but that speech was a discourse of persons sharing in spirit. Both a linguistic focus like Heidegger's and a discourse focus like Buber's raised the importance of speech. But for Buber the importance of speech was in the discourse of persons in relationship. The everyday bore the mystical by the beauty and pain of persons sharing in the spirit of one another through the I and You discourse. This I and You discourse brought forth a concrete relation to the ultimate

You—the God of Israel. The linguistic could perhaps be done without God, but the discourse of persons in relationship is always done before God, Buber believed. Any I and You discourse witnesses to a God that Heidegger replaced with *Dasein* (ironically the Jewish Buber was closer to the core of Eckhart's teaching than the Catholic Heidegger).

Buber saw this important nuance because of his own experience of suffering, because Buber had lost the *du* in the everyday. Buber moved in the direction of discourse as relations because he watched so many I and You relations, so many *Ich und du* discourses, end in the horror of the trenches of the Great War. Ironically, suffering, surrender, and confession were more central to the Jewish Buber than to the Catholic Heidegger. Like Justin Vernon in his Bon Iver song "Holocene," Buber recognized that the mystical spilled into the everyday through discourse of confession. In confession, the self was *not* magnificent but nevertheless bound in spirit to another *du* who loves you inside your lack of magnificence such that the mystical envelops the everyday. The beauty of the discourse of this confession was the direct mystical encounter. *Ich und du* is the joining point of the everyday with the mystical.

Like Eckhart, Buber knew this joining point of the everyday and the mystical through the *via negativa* (negative way).[22] Buber knew that relations of discourse bring the mystical into the everyday because he felt its aching absence. Loss and departure in the everyday—negative realities[23]—assured Buber that discourse relations have mystical depth. Following the sorrow led to a ground of depth inside relations of person in communions of discourse.

---

22. Friedman shows how Buber is a kind of theologian of the cross: "In 1914, the year after the publication of *Daniel*, Buber wrote two separate essays which cast a curiously contrasting light on his relationship to mysticism. In 'The Altar' Buber described the famous Issenheim altar, a triptych by the painter Matthias Grünewald, whom Buber called a brother to Meister Eckhart, who preached two centuries before in the same Alsatian cloisters. The traditional Christian figures in the painting emerge in Buber's treatment as the characters in a drama of color pointing to a new sort of mysticism—found within the world of sense rather than apart from it. The glory above color is the spirit of heaven which does not disclose itself to earth. 'Our world, the world of colors, is the world.' Yet we are not condemned to a fragmentary existence. The person who realizes the teaching in a central life becomes one through the strength with which he embraces the world. He rejects none of its colors, yet he receives none of them before it is pure and intensified. Through this the real world, the world of colors, is revealed. This is not the original unity. It is the unified glory achieved out of becoming and out of deed. 'He loves the world, but he fights for its unconditionality against all that is conditioned.' And we can do the same: 'We cannot penetrate behind the manifold to find living unity, but we can create living unity out of the manifold.'" Friedman, *Martin Buber's Life and Work*, 1:90.

23. Byung-Chul Han, the Korean-German philosopher whom we will explore in chapter 7, will have much more to say about the negative.

This was a kind of mystical depth Buber sensed when praying in the Hasidic Klaus with his grandfather.[24]

Yet ultimately, it would be from the wells of the beauty of a deep friendship, and a friend's journey in sickness, that Buber would find assurance that the mystical was in the everyday, that even in a modern world after a Great War, God was still a You to address and to be addressed by.

Where Sick Friends Reveal Another Way

Unlike Martin Buber, Franz Rosenzweig was raised in an assimilated Jewish home. There were no walks to the Hasidic Klaus for mystical prayers. As a matter of fact, most of Rosenzweig's cousins converted to Christianity. Why not, they figured; they were essentially already Christian, living in Luther's Germany. Rosenzweig decided that he would follow them. But unlike them, he wanted to intentionally convert to Christianity as a Jew—just like Paul before him. Therefore, in July 1913, Rosenzweig went to Yom Kippur (the Day of Atonement) services. He thought of it as his last act as a Jew. It ended up being his first true step.

We're not exactly sure what happened in the service, only that after it he saw no reason to convert. Something in the practice of confession and surrender changed him. Rosenzweig wrote his cousin that there was no reason for him to convert now. He had turned and then turned again, coming full circle. His path took him out and back again. Rosenzweig was the *ba'al teshuvah*, the "master of the turning." He had "turned away from Judaism but [was] now turning back."[25] Rosenzweig's turning and turning again is an example of the "believing again" that Charles Taylor contends is the faithful way to live for God in the late-modern secular age.

Rosenzweig's turning and turning, as a way of learning to confess and surrender, met a suffering for which his bourgeois background had not readied him. As the Great War broke out, Rosenzweig joined the Kaiser's army. Living among the piling bodies—their stacks were a sadistic monument to how the everyday could be turned into hell—Rosenzweig wrote. On postcards he

---

24. "Hasidic piety has its true life in 'holy insecurity'—the deep knowledge of the impotence of all 'information' and possessed truth. Although Hasidism took over Kabbalistic theurgy, its true life as revealed in the legends is not *kavanot*, special magical and mystical intentions, but *konana*: everything wants to be hallowed, to be brought in its worldliness into the *kavana* of redemption, to become a sacrament." Friedman, *Martin Buber's Life and Work*, 2:233.

25. Friedman, *Martin Buber's Life and Work*, 1:282.

sketched out a new philosophy for living in the everyday—not beyond but before God. He sent the postcards to his loving mother (the kind of mother Buber never had and yet longed for), who kept the postcards in a shoebox. After the Great War, those postcards became one of the most important philosophical and theological books of the twentieth century, *The Star of Redemption*.

We'll have occasion in the final chapter to go deeply into Rosenzweig's thought. Yet, what is important to say now is that the experience of both his conversion and the war led Rosenzweig to affirm the everyday. The everyday is so important because it is unequivocally and beautifully the place of revealing. It reveals a strangeness that produces an encounter that opens the everyday up to the mystical—to a direct encounter with God. For Rosenzweig, the everyday is the place where God reveals God's strange being in action. The everyday is the place of revelation. The mystical is set free from a medieval metaphysic to be encountered concretely in the everyday through God's own unveiling in the world.

This revelation (that the everyday becomes the place of revealing) is concurrent with the revealing of the strange beauty of my neighbor. This latter revelation calls me, it turns me, toward participation in redemption.[26] The mystical is the participation in redemption inside the everyday. My embracing of my neighbor in their true strangeness is a mystical encounter with revelation through the event of redemption. Redemption—a turning toward true life—happens nowhere other than in the everyday. Care for my neighbor, discourses of confession and surrender with and for them, occur next to, and never in opposition to, their concrete *du*. This fills the ordinary with a transcendent quality—with the mystical. The ordinary becomes infused with the mystical by encounter with something that's part of me apart from me. It is a union with true otherness—the otherness of God and my neighbor.

Ministry to my neighbor, then, floods the everyday with the mystical.[27] But I can only see my neighbor as strange and I can only be called into a relationship of redemption if I'm able to enter a discourse wherein I surrender my own magnificence for the possibility of an event of confession—an event where

26. Eric Santer explains, "Rosenzweig's understanding of the notion of love central to the biblical traditions—love of neighbor—will thus have to be framed as an encounter with one's neighbor in his or her death-driven singularity, as an encounter, that is, with my 'neighbor-Thing.'" Santer, *On the Psychotheology of Everyday Life: Reflections on Freud and Rosenzweig* (Chicago: University of Chicago Press, 2001), 80.

27. I am giving Rosenzweig my own language of ministry.

my neighbor and I confess inside a mutual discourse our shared humanity and find a union of care and love, most often through our shared sorrow.

This was just the kind of friendship that Rosenzweig and Buber shared. Buber, always so self-protective outside his family, only called Rosenzweig *du* toward the tragic end of Rosenzweig's life. Rosenzweig and Buber's friendship was one of deep discourse, never without suffering. When Buber read Rosenzweig's *Star of Redemption*, they became close, entering into long nights of conversation. The friendship was bound in the everyday, in the ordinary, and yet so tangibly tasted of the mystical. They eventually decided, as an act of friendship, to translate the Hebrew Bible into German. Yet, only weeks into the project, Rosenzweig started having weird sensations. Parts of his body stopped working. As a young father with a small boy he loved, Rosenzweig was diagnosed with ALS. Full paralysis and death was on its way.

Like Yip-Williams, Rosenzweig was now directly on a journey where loss and surrender were central. Buber joined the journey as a friend, keeping the discourse going. Even when the paralysis was nearly complete Rosenzweig continued to remain in discourse, to taste the mystical inside the everydayness of sickness and surrender. The surrender infused with a spirit of mystical union through the discourse of friendship. Rosenzweig's brother-in-law created a machine from Franz's typewriter that allowed him to dictate letters, even doing translations with Buber. When the paralysis was so bad that Rosenzweig could only blink, he continued to speak to his friend. His wife counted his blinks to decipher letters, taking hours upon hours to dictate his correspondence. In that discourse of confession, in walking the pathway of surrender, Rosenzweig, like Yip-Williams, found a fullness of spirit, a union as deep and as transcendent as it was sad and heartbreaking.

This is a different mystical pathway from the ones blazed in the everyday by Husserl, Nietzsche, and Heidegger. But though distinct, this different mystical pathway nevertheless is unequivocally bound in the everyday. We've called this third mystical pathway "confession and surrender." This chapter has articulated how a return of the mystical is ordered inside the everyday. This gives us three particular pathways of the mystical from within the everyday of late modernity: (1) inner genius, (2) heroic action, and (3) confession and surrender.

The first two, as we'll see in memoirs below, are dynamic mystical spiritualities but often without God. The third pathway has seen usage, but it is much less traveled in late modernity (and often not initially by religious people). Yet when it is traveled, God is often acknowledged in a way that is not true of the other two pathways. As Yip-Williams's memoir so beautifully articulates, the self cannot be constituted as magnificent but only as a relation of love and loss. Yip-Williams calls this a miracle. Confession and surrender is a core dynamic of an everyday mysticism before God. Confession and surrender are central to the shape of transformation.

I wonder if red-pen reader found this. Did she ever taste the mystical sweetness in her bitter loss?

5

The [Bleeping] Triangles Are Everywhere

How Triangulated Dilemmas and Conflicts Map the Mysticism of a Secular Age

I confess it was a performance of the self. A way of broadcasting my cleverness. A way of showing my reach. I wanted an audience to recognize my magnificence, to see that I was a person who visited magnificent places, saw magnificent things. I wanted this audience to comment on my magnificent wit. Honestly, there was no other reason to post it to Twitter.

We have just arrived in Madrid on a late August night. By luck of circumstance, this is our second trip to Europe this summer due to the cancellations and postponements from the 2020 shutdowns. During our first trip, in late June 2021, it felt like the last days of COVID. The pandemic anxiety was evaporating like the virus itself in the warm soothing sun of early summer. Paris was unlocked and celebrating.

Yet, by August and late summer, the ease and glee of early summer has dissipated. The world now realizes that late June was only the last days of the Alpha variant. Delta is now on the loose. Cases are spiking like the heat in Madrid. Our anxiety is rising with it. Our particular anxiety comes in two parts: first is the Delta variant; second is a canceled Airbnb. Twelve hours before our flight, our Madrid Airbnb host messages us to inform us that there is a leak in the apartment. The water needs to be shut off as well as the electricity. This means no air-conditioning as the temperature touches 108 degrees. It is necessary to change apartments, and quickly.

We arrive late. The cab slowly winds its way through dark, busy Spanish streets. We lug our bags up six flights of stairs. We don't trust the rickety elevator in the dark hallway. There are three locks on the door, all with strange distinctive mechanisms. All three locks look like they could be on Hogwarts doors. We struggle for twenty minutes to unlock them all in the right order. The large doors finally swing open and welcome us into a spacious apartment with beautiful views of the streets below. Overall, however, the apartment is run-down. The floor is broken, and paint is flaking and falling in a corner of the living room. But there are four bedrooms, all air-conditioned, giving us far more space than we need. And best of all, Madrid's two most renowned museums are just a short walk away. After some sleep, the Prado Museum will be our target.

The Prado is stunning. Every floor is worth the time. But I can't find what I've come for. I do eventually find some Picassos, but not many. Most are in Paris. The few on the wall, on loan from Paris, are from the surrealist and cubist period. The triangles pop with bizarre depictions of people. Each is mystical in its surrealist portrait. The triangles are everywhere. Everywhere a triangle, giving depth and form, making the mind spin.

But I'm here to see a particular masterpiece. I want to see the huge *Guernica*, the massive, 11×25 foot, black-and-white painting Picasso created in 1937. It is a cubist, surrealist piece. But unlike the other pieces on the wall of the Prado, *Guernica* isn't a portrait. It's a depiction of horror. It's a landscape of the murder of war. In April 1937, Franco, the violent dictator of Spain, gave the Nazis permission to bring hellfire from the sky on a Spanish town, to test out the power of their weapons. They obliterated the city of Guernica with a downpour of bombs. Picasso's massive painting is his depiction of the atrocity.

It takes me too long to realize it, but I discover I'm at the wrong museum. *Guernica* isn't at the Prado but the Museo Nacional Centro. Lucky for me, it's also a short walk from our Airbnb. After a day in the Prado and fifteen thousand steps, I have no other interest in the Museo Nacional Centro than to see *Guernica*. We wait until 5 p.m., when the last hour of the day is free. We line up and, luckily, get in. We walk directly to the room of *Guernica*. It's where everyone else is headed as well.

We finally enter the room. The painting is massive, taking up one whole wall of the large, open space. I'm not sure if it's the size or aesthetic of the painting, but it has a tangible presence. There's an aura to it. Like the feel of the room, I'm agitated. Everyone is buzzing like bees, moving quickly around the room, chatting away. The museum attendants are responding. They're either scolding people for taking selfies with *Guernica* or shushing the room as the noise climbs in volume, nearing the level of a party or even preconcert.

The attendants are doing their best to remind the patrons that this picture is *not* the Statue of Liberty, *not* the Eiffel Tower. It's not even the *Mona Lisa*. This is not a cool selfie spot. This is a picture of war, of hell come to earth. This is a painting to contemplate in silent reverence.

Picasso's celebrity and surrealism give it too much distance. *No one* can stay silent, let alone contemplate. There is no stillness. I can't be still. I sneak to the back of the room and act like I'm checking my email, grabbing a selfie for Twitter later. I'll say to my few followers, Look at me! Look at my performance! I'm in Spain. I'm seeing *Guernica*. Aren't I interesting? Don't you wish you were performing your self like I'm performing mine? Tell me I'm great! Tell me you're jealous!

The addictive buzz of the room now paints everything in a vapid dreaminess. I was so excited to see *Guernica*. I worked hard to see it, standing in line, in 100-degree heat, for an hour. Now I am here. But I can't get myself steady enough to be here. All of us strangers in the room, like a hive, are too busy buzzing to be able to escape Picasso's celebrity and allow the painting to speak to us. We are too frazzled to be reminded of death, evil, destruction, and grief. The shushes of the attendants plead with us to show reverence. But we all choose selfies instead. Without silence, the beckoning of the violent painting is lost on us. It is rendered mute.

My eyes are wide like an eight-year-old on too much sugar; my is mind racing for what's next. I say to Kara, after fifteen short minutes, "Let's go." She gives me the side-eye and hands me her phone—not for a selfie but to listen to

Rick Steves. I put on the headphones and the room goes silent (enough). My attention is drawn into the painting. I'm seeing it for the first time. Each part is discussed. I keep seeing the triangles. The whole painting is mapped by triangles, the numinous pull of the painting all hanging on the triangles. I pause. I'm inside it now. It's speaking. The triangles are taking me in, allowing me to see.

I step back and let the painting reach for me. After a while, after a moment of connection, I take off the headphones. Just then I overhear a young man with an Irish accent say to his friends next to me, "Triangles. It's always damn triangles with this bloke. More [bleeping] triangles."

Triangle Fights

It is indeed always triangles. But like viewers of *Guernica*, we often miss them inside the fog of war, inside the dizzy buzz of our accelerated lives. The dizzy fog leads us to see parallel lines, thereby missing the triangle. Inside a culture war we often imagine—because we're so often told—that there are two sides in a face-off. Our issue is polarization, we're informed. Polarization gives us a picture of two sides in opposition, a chasm between them. Conservatives versus liberals. Right versus left. Pro-life versus pro-choice. Democrats versus Republicans. Pro-vaxxers versus anti-vaxxers. Believers versus unbelievers. We imagine two sides in battle. This assumption leads us to map Western modernity as such a polarization. We think it's always a conflict between two sides.

Yet, we see in part 5 of *A Secular Age* that Charles Taylor believes this isn't quite right. Rather than two sides, faced off in fury—nose to nose—Taylor believes the conflicts and contentions (he calls them "dilemmas") at the heart of modernity are shaped more like triangles. There are not two sides in conflict but three. We keep contending there are two sides to make it simpler, because the fog of war confuses the landscape. But the real complication of our conflicts and contentions/dilemmas is that there are always three sides to the disputes in Western modernity. These three sides shift, and shift again, the alliances, animosities, agreements, and angsts. The three sides can make for strange bedfellows. Each side is against not one but two sides at a time, teaming up with one over against the other, only to shift and join the other side in a new dilemma. In other words, *the conflicts are always triangulated!*

Taylor explains that we can see this triangulation most clearly around the conflicts and critiques of religion in late modernity. There are two sides in the triangulation that oppose religion's commitment to there being something *beyond*. Christianity holds that within everyday life, while the everyday always remains the everyday, we should seek something beyond the everyday, something within the everyday that nevertheless is beyond. This *beyond* is religion's claim that there is (1) something *beyond* death and (2) something *beyond* human flourishing. Neither of these beyonds is a pure metaphysics; rather, both are locked in the everyday. Dying and longing are squarely everyday realities, and yet religion seeks to go through them, to find something beyond them that gives them meaning and purpose. Let me explain this by first succinctly unpacking these two "beyonds."

What "something beyond death" means is self-evident. To the annoyed eye roll of one side of the triangulation of modernity, religion contends that there is something beyond this life, something that this life is preparing us for (Martin Hägglund's *This Life* is an example of a disdain of religion's beyond).[1] "Something beyond human flourishing" is less obvious. To the disgust of the other side in the triangulation, religion contends that life is about more than just securing happiness, affirmation, and even rights in a functional social order. It's not that most religious people are opposed to happiness, affirmation, and rights. They, too, think these are important; a functional social order is necessary. But religion has most often contended that there is something beyond all this, something beyond these human drives. Even something more important than human flourishing itself. There is a deeper, even an inbreaking, transcendent command than to just make the world a better place. There is something beyond the maintenance of the social order to which the human being is called. This leads certain people (Martha Nussbaum is an example[2]) to assert that religion guts our true humanity by pushing us to seek something beyond these social forms of flourishing.

Ultimately, what these dimensions of resistance to religion's beyond reveal is that there is not a singular, unified critique to religion. The more we dig into these oppositions to the beyond, the more we see that these are not simply two parts of a critique held by one group standing in polarized disapproval of those who hold to religion's belief in the beyond. Rather, there are actually two different groups who critique religion's beyond. And, interestingly, linking us with our discussion in the previous chapter, these two sides share a strong

---

1. Martin Hägglund, *This Life: Secular Faith and Spiritual Freedom* (New York: Pantheon, 2019).

2. See particularly Martha Nussbaum, *Cultivating Humanity: A Classical Defense of Reform in Liberal Education* (Cambridge, MA: Harvard University Press, 1997).

critique that religion cannot deal appropriately with the everyday. These beyonds (whether beyond this life or beyond human flourishing) are assumed to be corrupting forces to the everyday. The everyday is undercut—dangerously or vapidly so—by this attention to the beyond. This beyond violates the everyday.

Yet, importantly, the very fact that it is believed that religion/Christianity cannot deal with the everyday exposes that these are triangulated sides that oppose religion. The closer we look at how these two sides conceive of the everyday, the more we can see that they are as much in conflict with each other as they are with religion. What, then, are these two sides that make up a triangle with the religious or, rather, with those who hold to dimensions of the beyond (which I'll call the "Beyonders")? It's now time for us to name these other two sides.

Getting Straight on the Sides

Now we can begin to name the sides. Though we use the term "side" here, it's really the corner of the triangle that is the ideal of that group. We'll talk more about this soon as we plot certain thinkers on the triangle.

We can name the first side the Exclusive Humanists (E.Hums). This side has a deep commitment to humanism, believing all human flourishing comes from within humanity itself. It sees no value, only problems, in openness to the beyond. For this group, humanism is underlined and bold, humanism in an exclusive form.[3] It contends that flourishing can be wrought only by human attention. It is exclusive because flourishing is only for the sake of more flourishing (ultimately, flourishing becomes equated with happiness). There is nothing outside (or beyond) flourishing that flourishing witnesses to or longs for. Flourishing has no greater purpose, no larger vision, no deeper narrative than humans flourishing by the efforts of humans. It is a flourishing exclusively bound in human drives, and it therefore denies anything beyond. For example, inside this kind of exclusive humanism, flourishing has no eschatological visions, no *imago Dei* to define what is human, no MLK-like dream that shapes and sets the terms for flourishing. This makes it difficult to even define flourishing or to rule out actions and attitudes that would violently oppose those who refuse this exclusive humanism, demonizing such opponents.

---

3. There are other forms of humanism that are not exclusive. One example is Jens Zimmerman's development of incarnational humanism in *Incarnational Humanism: A Philosophy of Culture for the Church in the World* (Downers Grove, IL: IVP Academic, 2012).

Ultimately, those on this side, the E.Hums, believe that when we look beyond, we risk imposing false forms of flourishing that deny freedom. The beyond of religion, they contend, mutilates the everyday by telling us to repress our most base-level humanness (we can hear an echo of Rousseau here). Religions of the beyond ask us to deny our natural drives and passions. They ask us to make something beyond, something other, more essential than our felt identities and our efforts toward an accepting social order. Religions of the beyond, the Beyonders themselves, attack the authenticity of our everyday lives by asking us to see something else as more essential than the flourishing of human freedom and desire. When a beyond narrative is placed on top of human flourishing as the freedom of desire, that narrative must be exposed and deconstructed so that we can get back to the base of our humanity.[4] As we'll see, the E.Hums share this with the other side of the triangle, which I will

4. Sarah Coakley offers an important discussion on our contemporary understanding of desire. The whole introduction, and this large quote as a representation of it, is worth reading. Here Coakley articulates an E.Hum sense of desire and its place within the modern moral order ethic. Coakley says, "Before I go any further in this account I must say something important about the very category of 'desire' in this book, and its relation to words more commonly utilized in contemporary debates about religion and sexual ethics: 'sex,' 'sexuality,' 'gender,' and 'orientation.' When people talk about 'sex' and 'sexuality' today, they often presume that the first and obvious point of reference is sexual intercourse or other genital acts. (This is especially true in North America, I have found, where the word 'sexuality' has more of these overtones of actual physical enactment than in Britain.) The presumption, then, is that *physiological* desires and urges are basic and fundamental in the sexual realm; and to this is often added a second presumption: that unsatisfied (physical) sexual desire is a necessarily harmful and 'unnatural' state. From such a perspective, priestly or monastic celibacy is indeed monstrous—a veritable charade, necessarily masking subterfuge and illicit sexual activity. A popularized form of Freudianism is often invoked in support of this latter view about the 'impossibility' of celibacy. But this is odd; because Freud himself—who changed his mind more than once about these matters in the course of his career—never taught that social harm comes from what he called 'sublimation.' On the contrary, he argued that sublimation is entirely necessary for civilization to endure. Chaos would ensue otherwise." Coakley, *God, Sexuality, and the Self: An Essay 'On the Trinity'* (London: Cambridge University Press, 2013), 7.
    Coakley continues, giving us a Beyonder sense of desire: "It follows that, if desire is divinely and ontologically basic, not only is human 'sex' to be cast as created in its light, but 'gender'— which nowadays tends to connote the way embodied relations are carved up and culturally adjudicated—is most certainly also to be set in right subjection to that desire. In short, the immense cultural anxiety that, in a secular society, is now accorded to 'sex' and 'gender' (and to their contested relations) can here be negotiated in a different, theological light. Not that 'sex' and 'gender' do not matter, on the contrary, the profound difference that incarnation makes to Christian Platonism will prove that they do indeed so 'matter,' and deeply so. But it is not in the way that contemporary secular gender theory would (almost obsessively) have it. Such an obsession, I dare to suggest, resides in the lack of God as a final point of reference. As for 'orientation,' too (another modern verbal invention): what orientation could be more important than the orientation to God, to divine desire? That is why this particular book will not divert to a detailed discussion of the so-called 'problem' of 'homosexuality.' For it is concerned with

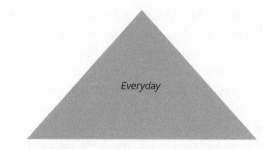

Exclusive Humanists

call the Counter-Enlightenment. These two sides are at times friends and at other times deep foes. Though both sides want to critique and expose religion, what differentiates the E.Hums (Exclusive Humanists) from the Counter-Enlightenment is that the E.Hums are committed to "modern moral order."

What mobilizes the E.Hums is a commitment to the idea that our social order must be organized around mutual benefit. Taylor calls this the "modern moral order." The modern moral order contends that freedom cannot be imagined outside, but only within human flourishing. To affirm and advance the modern moral order, we must affirm politeness, manners, and certain ways of talking so that all can flourish. We must uphold a social order that affirms our individual freedoms to be our unique selves.[5] Our norms *should not* be preparing people for something bigger and beyond the everyday. And the purpose of our norms is not to obey something outside the everyday that reorders our everyday. Rather, our norms should create a society wherein every person is free to *be* authentically *themselves*. To find their inner passion and genius. To express themselves. What is considered bad or wrong (unethical) is measured by what prevents others from the benefit that they mutually deserve to freely be themselves by finding their authentic passions.

---

a deeper, and more primary question: that of putting desire for God above all other desires, and with judging human desires only in that light" (11).

5. David Goodhart has an insightful critique of the modern moral order: "Nor is this kind of particularism morally inferior to the more universalist views of some Anywheres. If everyone is my brother, then nobody is—my emotional and financial resources are spread too thin to make a difference. The novelist Jonathan Franzen puts it like this: 'Trying to love all of humanity may be a worthy endeavor, but, in a funny way, it keeps the focus on the self, on the self's own moral or spiritual well-being. Whereas, to love a specific person, and to identify with his or her struggles and joys as if they were your own, you have to surrender some of your self.'" Goodhart, *The Road to Somewhere: The Populist Revolt and the Future of Politics* (London: Hurst, 2017), 110, quoting Jonathan Franzen, "Liking Is for Cowards. Go for What Hurts," *New York Times*, May 28, 2011, https://www.nytimes.com/2011/05/29/opinion/29franzen.html.

There is a deep call to action here (producing a critical edge). Inside a commitment to the modern moral order, Exclusive Humanists believe we should fight (and hard!) for the growth and expanse of this modern moral order. We should call out those who restrict the freedom of individual identities, who oppose anyone's equal regard to flourishing as a free expressive self. Of late, such "calling out" has taken on very sharp edges as it fuels itself by outrage (as discussed in chap. 3). This is a call to fight to make the world safe for all selves to have mutual equal regard and therefore flourish inside a polite (or politically correct) social order. As we'll see, these sharp edges haven't happened in a vacuum but are the result of the triangulation.

That is one side of the triangle. Taylor's point is that this side tends to be skeptical of, even disgusted by, religion's contention that there is something beyond human flourishing. There is now quite a phenomenon of those who were raised as some form of a Beyonder who have immigrated to the Exclusive Humanist side. These former Beyonders believe the E.Hum position holds far more veracity. The E.Hums' fiery, uncompromising commitment to the modern moral order becomes an updated *evangel* that these ex-evangelicals find far more ethical. Yet, the E.Hums' passionate dedication to the modern moral order creates inner tensions, particularly around religion. For instance, when a Muslim woman wears a burqa on a bus in Detroit, the E.Hum is divided. At one level, the modern moral order asserts that this woman has every right to live out her identity as she wishes, and diversity is to be celebrated. And yet, the Muslim woman herself would say that wearing a burqa is *not* about the freedom of her identity but comes from a command from beyond her. This makes the E.Hums very uncomfortable, wondering whether the woman's flourishing is being lost (whether her freedom is being smothered in the repressive command). After all, the command of the beyond seems to violate mutual equal regard (it seems neither mutual nor equal). And mutual equal regard—the modern moral order—is what makes up the core of the Exclusive Humanist ethic.

On the other side of the base of the triangle is what Taylor calls the Counter-Enlightenment (CE) or Neo-Nietzscheans.[6] Those in this camp are galvanized and mobilized by defiant rejection (it's no surprise that defiant

---

6. By Counter-Enlightenment, Taylor is borrowing from his teacher Isaiah Berlin, though Taylor is using Counter-Enlightenment a little differently than Berlin. When Berlin says Counter-Enlightenment he means the Romantic response to the French Enlightenment starting with the Magus of the North, Johann Hamann. Taylor often means Nietzsche, a more biting opposition to the modern moral order, when he says Counter-Enlightenment.

rejection media—talk radio, Fox News, and red pill websites—have become the new salons of the Counter-Enlightenment). The CEs are the group of rejection! They simultaneously reject two things. First, at their core, they reject religion's contention that there is something beyond death. They find this naive at best and an opioid at worst. To believe in a delusional hope in the beyond keeps people from fighting in the everyday (Marx). It neuters their will to power (Nietzsche). Concern for the beyond tranquilizes the will for the heroic. Belief in something beyond death is essentially an opioid crisis.

The E.Hums can agree with this rejection of the beyond. They are happy to jump on board this attack, teaming up with CEs against the Beyonders. Yet, though the E.Hums join the opposition to the Beyonders, the CEs violently reject the E.Hums for another reason. The second rejection reveals that the conflicts of modernity are not binary but triangulated. The CEs directly reject the modern moral order. They hate it! They find the modern moral order a shameful castration. The modern moral order and its assertion that we need a polite, affirming, properly speaking, open society where people manage their language and actions so that all have mutual equal regard is bogus and even poisonous. Talk of mutual equal regard and the "freedom of identities" to "be safe" to "find and express desire" is only a ploy for control. It's the move of the weak elite, to keep the strong and powerful from exercising their will. It's a way of scraping out the truly heroic from the human spirit.

The gun in American society, for instance, symbolizes much more than the gun itself. It symbolizes much more than the basic freedom and protection of the Second Amendment. The gun and the battle to keep it are the concrete symbol of the heroic. The person with guns (the more, the better) stands in opposition to the weak people who support the modern moral order. The gun is a symbol of the refusal to allow E.Hums to eliminate the great heroic action in exchange for their slippery, weak ways of control. The

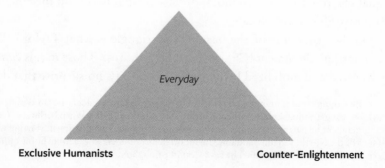

Everyday

Exclusive Humanists   **Counter-Enlightenment**

gun therefore comes with all the other accoutrements of the bold hero—the flag, the truck, the fatigues, the "screw you" attitude of a WWE wrestler or Beth from *Yellowstone*. It's assumed that those who support the modern moral order produce an antiheroic (repulsive) way of speaking about freedom that truly hates freedom. The snowflake E.Hums want hugs, not merit, not force, not boldness. What makes America great is the heroic boldness, *not* the modern moral order (this is what divides the American consciousness and, in turn, American Protestant Christianity).

It's no wonder that militias and congresswomen with guns and chants of "Let's Go Brandon!" (even in some church services!) have escalated. They are the Counter-Enlightenment rejections of the modern moral order and of the soft, overeducated E.Hums that run the country.[7] Donald Trump is assumed to be the president of the working class, not because he's *from* the working class and understands any working-class person's struggles, but because he brazenly and heroically opposes the modern moral order.

Yet we should be careful as we move on. The examples I've just given may wrongly give the impression that the Counter-Enlightenment side is always right wing. It's not, nor has it always been. Taylor believes these positions are much more deeply embedded in Western modernity than any political moment or fleeting conditions of a certain Zeitgeist. For example, in the mid-twentieth century, even up to the late 1990s, the CEs were more left than right (just think of the heavy metal movement). Radical intellectuals deep in conversation with the hermeneutics of suspicion (Marx, Nietzsche, and Freud) opposed the modern moral order—particularly in its neoliberal form. These intellectuals provided substance for many left-wing politicians, particularly in Europe. Even today a radical leftist thinker such as Slavoj Žižek would need to be placed squarely on the Counter-Enlightenment side of the triangle.[8]

I've already alluded to who sits at the top of the triangle, even giving them a name: the Beyonders. But I need to reiterate that the beyond of the Beyonders is not metaphysical. The beyond does not refer to a pure longed-for

---

7. For a story of the rise of new Counter-Enlightenment leaders and their success in a Trump era, see Andrew Marantz, *Antisocial: Online Extremists, Techno-Utopians, and the Hijacking of the American Conversation* (New York: Viking, 2019).

8. See Žižek, *A Left That Dares to Speak Its Name* (London: Polity, 2020), a book of essays in which Žižek deplores Trump and all American Republicans, but he is hopeful that Trump's presidency will bring the end of the modern moral order and neoliberalism. He's hopeful, and he even celebrates Trump's victory, because it's much better than four or eight years with Hillary Clinton, an elite of the modern moral order.

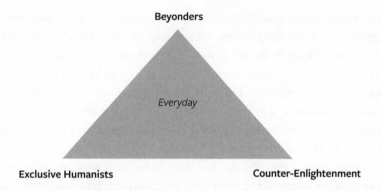

metaphysic. Rather, beyond means "beyond exclusive human flourishing," beyond the assumption inside the everyday that there is nothing beyond death. The Beyonders are not transcendental monks returning in late modernity. As we'll see, there is a transcendent attention within the Beyonders (but so too within the other groups). What gives the Beyonders their name is the commitment that there is both something beyond exclusive human flourishing and something beyond death. This something that lies beyond significantly shapes our everyday lives. (The whole of my project, and this work as well, is to make a case for the possibility of being a Beyonder, to call Protestantism back to the beyond.)

I have asserted, following Taylor, that these religious commitments to the beyond, and the distinct critiques of them, reveal that our modern conflicts are not binary but triangulated. Up to this point I've only named the sides. Before we see the triangulation in motion, though, I need to say more about the Beyonders and the late-modern conundrum we Beyonders find ourselves in. Doing so will help us understand why contemporary expressions of Protestant Christianity (particularly in America) have had difficulty not sliding toward one corner or the other of the triangle. It seems ever difficult for Protestantism to stay at or near its point of the triangle. The cultural gravity of our secular age pulls Protestantism down one side of the triangle or the other. American Protestantism has often sought cover from these critiques and dilemmas thrust upon Beyonders by joining hands, in one form or another, with Exclusive Humanists or the Counter-Enlightenment.

Taylor asserts that E.Hums critique the Beyonders for holding to something beyond human flourishing, and the CEs critique the Beyonders for deeming that there is something beyond death. Taylor explains that the two critiques coming from these two distinct sides of the triangle create a major dilemma for the Beyonders (for religion and the religious). The two critiques create two horns. If one horn doesn't wound the Beyonders in the mind of the larger society, the other will. "It seems hard to avoid one of these criticisms without impaling oneself on the other."[9]

Let's examine this. The core critique of the E.Hums against the Beyonders is that they are repressive. They force people to bury and deny their true humanity. The assumption is that when the Beyonders hold that there is something beyond human flourishing, they attack human desires. Supposedly, Beyonders paint human desires as evil and wrong, asking people to mutilate such desires by repressing who they really are. For our free desires make up who we really *are*. The Beyonders respond to this critique by saying, "No, this isn't a repression or mutilation; rather, this is a way into a true acceptance, a divine hope of humanity, a freedom to be who you were created to be. It's not about the repression of desire but encountering love, joy, and peace. God is accepting and so, too, should be God's church! Religion, or better, the church, is a training ground to embrace your truest desire—to love and to be loved by God. To come to know that you're accepted completely." When Protestantism feels this critique, it's quick to make acceptance everything, dividing churches and pastors between those who are accepting and those who are not. Accepting becomes the very beginning and end of justice. Nuance becomes nearly impossible.

Yet, this acceptance-centric rebuttal from the Beyonders exposes them to the loathing criticism of the CEs. The CEs respond, "Yuck, how soft and sweet. The denial is stomach-turning. What a dumb drug! You Beyonders think the world is a Disneyland ride filled with cotton-candy acceptance. Your dreams of an accepting God who hugs you is like talking bears and princesses, all your dreams come true. Religion is a fairy tale and a weak one at that. It can never deal with reality as it is."

Taylor's point is that the response to E.Hums *may* address the critique of repression, but it immediately opens the Beyonders up to the CE critique that religion bowdlerizes reality. Religion, and Beyonders, are scared of the dark, they say. The Beyonders' story of reality edits out all the horrible parts of nature, history, and human capacity. It's not a way of life in the everyday for the honest and grown up.

9. See Charles Taylor, *A Secular Age* (Cambridge, MA: Harvard University Press, 2007), 624, quoted in James K. A. Smith, *How (Not) to Be Secular* (Grand Rapids: Eerdmans, 2014), 109.

"No," the Beyonders rush back, asserting, "we believe that nature, history, and the human being is lost and trapped in death without God's intervention. We believe that human beings and all we put our hands to are stained with sin. Evil is real and it must be resisted, and Jesus is strong and powerful to do so. The church is God's gym. We believe that God judges and hates sin, coming to destroy evil and all injustice. God is mighty!"

The Beyonders, now like a sous chef with too many orders, are hit again by the E.Hums, who, hearing all this talk of sin, death, and a mighty God, respond, "See! All your talk of acceptance, joy, and peace is actually none of that, because you believe that human desires and constructions are fundamentally sinful! You and your God fetishize power instead of accepting freedom. You believe there is real darkness in us and in our work that we can't solve ourselves. That's a dangerous way of embracing a repulsive repression. You make all desire bad." And back and forth it goes from one horn to the next. James K. A. Smith says it well: "If you try to avoid pie-in-the-sky hopefulness . . . you're going to sound awfully dour—in which case you're going to be newly subject to the repression critique."[10] The dilemma for the Beyonders is that if we're not disemboweled by one horn of critique, we'll be eviscerated by the other.[11] Welcome to Protestant America!

Like Picasso's bull in the upper left corner of *Guernica*, this is a sharp, double-horned dilemma. Recognizing these two sharp horns leads us to spot two things. First, we can see why Protestantism has been so divided in late modernity. The one-two punch of repression and bowdlerizing, bowdlerizing and repression, has led Protestants to seek shelter in the house (more like garage) of either the E.Hums or the CEs. Feeling the pull of immanence next to the sharp stabs of critique, different Protestant groups have slid down the slope of one side of the triangle or the other, linking up in some degree with either E.Hums or CEs. Inside an immanent frame, as Taylor calls it, it's become very hard for laypeople and (even more so) pastors to balance themselves and stay near their point of the triangle. It's increasingly difficult to hold squarely to being a Beyonder in the everyday.

10. Smith, *How (Not) to Be Secular*, 109.
11. It's been my objective in my work to try to balance this critique, which I know well. I've done so with two interconnected perspectives: the theology of the cross and the personalist structure of humanity (the hypostatic). I remain deeply committed to these two perspectives, bringing all my work in and out of them, because I think they have the potential (though no trump card) to deal with the heart of the critique of the beyond. My work desperately tries to make a case for the beyond. But I need to always keep the dialectic living of *theologia crucis* and *hypostasis*.

Unable to keep balance, for example, some Protestants became modernists in the 1920s, sliding down and linking up with E.Hums. Their core tenets were as bound in exclusive humanism as they were bound in the sacred tradition. In the 2020s, some Protestants have slid down the other side of the triangle, linking arms with right-wing CEs. The core of their faith is as much a heroic nationalism as anything else. Over the last hundred years, mainline and evangelical Protestantism have been increasingly divided as they've shielded themselves from the horns of critique by sliding down opposing sides of the triangle. The more that they have linked up with the views, practices, and ethics of either the E.Hums or the CEs, the more distance has emerged between them. With this distance, they have come to name the other Protestant side as the real enemy![12]

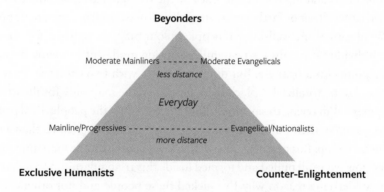

These two sharp horns also reveal how this triangulation works. For instance, as much as E.Hums and CEs are opposed to each other, they're happy to team up against Beyonders. Beyonders, at least in late modernity, have had a hard time finding their own identities, purposes, ethical practices, and discourses of significance without linking up, in small or large degree, with E.Hums or CEs. But in turn, the Beyonders, in small and large ways, have been happy to team up with either E.Hums or CEs. What gives distinction to the kind of Protestant you are is *whom you team up with* (gone are creeds and confessions as the mark of distinction).

All this means that a person or group is typically never solidly located at one point or the other of the triangle but almost always directed along one side in a partnership, depending on the issue or conflict. (This makes for strange

12. Our ecumenical issue is not so much doctrine but how different Christian collectives respond to the conflicts and dilemmas of modernity, how they cope with critiques of the beyond.

bedfellows, such as fundamentalist Christians and antireligious libertarians joining forces for funding for private education in Maine.) To understand the conflicts and positions of those in late modernity we need to locate certain parties within an interactive map of triangulation. Let's do that now.

An Interactive Triangle Map

You'll notice in the diagram of the triangle that the absolute corner is the ideal of that group, whether it be the Beyonders (top corner), the Exclusive Humanists (bottom-left corner), or the Counter-Enlightenment (bottom-right corner). Nobody really fits into the ideal, though. Any one person or thinker will be plotted along one of the sides of the triangle based on how they are pulled either closer or farther away from the corners, similar to magnetic poles.

By placing some well-known people on our map, we will see how groups and individuals are always triangulated inside modernity, moving between three points on a triangle. But doing so comes with two cautions. First, no person can be totalized. I place these people on the map only for illustrative purposes—I'm trying to say more about the map than the people. Real people (as opposed to their public personae) are much more complicated than a tidy point on a map. But placing some well-known people on the map might help show how we're all pulled and formed inside this triangulation. Second, there is no underlying reason why I've picked these people and not others. They just came to mind. There is no other larger point. The only reason to name these people is to show how this triangulated reality shapes us all. Naming these people gives some texture to our map.

We can start with a few people already named above. We can locate the philosopher Martha Nussbaum just right of the E.Hums. She could be considered *the* contemporary philosopher of Exclusive Humanism. Because she has little interest in (or concern with) religion or any talk of the beyond, she's best plotted on the line between E.Hums and CEs. But Nussbaum also has no stomach for CEs, though she is more directly in dialogue with them than she is with the Beyonders. Martin Hägglund can also be plotted on the plane between E.Hums and CEs—though closer toward the CEs. Hägglund's interest in Beyonders is only to critique them. He reserves his opposition only for those who think there is anything beyond death.

We've also mentioned two other thinkers, Charles Taylor and Slavoj Žižek. Plotting them on our map shows how they are two very different kinds of thinkers. Žižek is a CE leftist. He's as committed to the Counter-Enlightenment as Nussbaum is to Exclusive Humanism. Therefore, we can plot him right near the point of CEs, with a slight tilt toward E.Hums. Charles Taylor, on the other hand, needs to be plotted in the middle of the plane between the E.Hums and the Beyonders. Taylor is deeply committed to forms of humanism, even some of its exclusive element. But this is always tempered and shaped by his openness to the practices and visions of both present and ancient Beyonders.

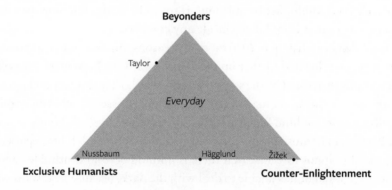

Mapping thinkers is both difficult and easy. It's difficult because these philosophers' positions are well reasoned and well thought-out—they've given them deep thought, taking account of the other positions and perspectives. In turn, it's easy because their positions are well reasoned and such thinkers specifically look to locate themselves. But my claim is that this triangulation is the shape of everyone's everyday world in late modernity. Therefore, let's move beyond philosophers to public figures. We've already mentioned one, Donald Trump. We could plot Trump near the CEs—he was the first Counter-Enlightenment president (or maybe it was Andrew Jackson). Trump brags continually about his will to power. Depending on your own place on the map, you'll find this either disgusting or exciting. There is no need to connect Trump at all to the E.Hum plane, who are his enemies. Trump is in alliance with and willing to support those with some interest in the beyond (as long as they align with his Counter-Enlightenment wishes). Trump cannot be located too closely to the Beyonders, though. Only enough to plot him a click or two toward that plane.

Speaking of Trump's enemies, we can plot Hillary Clinton on the complete other side of the triangle map (no wonder they hate each other so much). Hillary is very close to E.Hums—which is why evangelicals, even those somewhat close to the Beyonders on our triangle, have hated her and refused to vote for her. They hate her because she is located completely on the other side of the map. These evangelicals have some distance from Trump as well. But at least Trump touches, even if superficially, one line on the map that they live within. Therefore, these evangelicals may not like Trump's will to power or rude attack on the modern moral order, but he's better than Hillary (and so Trump won in 2016).[13] However, in plotting Hillary, we need to tilt her slightly toward the Beyonders (but still far away from the evangelicals who hate her). Hillary's own Methodist faith is important to her—though more personal and private than it is mobilized inside any conflicts.

Joe Biden beat Trump in 2020 for many reasons. But one important reason is that Biden is located further up the plane toward the Beyonders. He is still not completely trusted by the same evangelicals who hate Hillary and refused to vote for her. But as our map shows, the distance is lessened, allowing enough of them to vote for him. Biden is further up the plane of the E.Hums, toward the Beyonders because of his Catholicism and (importantly!) his experience of loss. He cannot foreclose that there is nothing beyond death. He cannot contend that religion is unable to deal with the dark, because he lost his wife and two children. He has known grief and religion's ability to comfort the human spirit (not smash its desire). For some evangelical voters in 2020, the distinction between them and Biden on the map was shorter than it was with Hillary (allowing enough of them to vote for Biden). Voting for Biden still felt like a violation, but Biden was close enough on the map for them to do so. Trump was farther away. Trump shared their mobilizing political plane, the CE plane that these evangelicals mix with their beyondness, to varying degrees.[14]

---

13. Alain Badiou says provocatively, "I think the success of Trump was possible only because the real contradiction in today's world, the true opposition between two antagonistic visions, could in no way be symbolized by the choice between Hillary Clinton and Donald Trump. Because, to tell you the truth, Hillary Clinton and Donald Trump, however different their styles may be, both belong to the small worldwide oligarchy that is capitalizing its profits on a worldwide scale." Badiou, *Trump* (London: Polity, 2019), 2. He continues, "Here we have a lesson in dialectics, a lesson in the different forms of contradiction. The contradiction between Hillary Clinton and Donald Trump, however intense, was nonetheless a relative rather than an absolute contradiction, a contradiction within the same parameters. The contradiction between Trump and Sanders was at least the possible beginning of a vision of the world that might go beyond the one that is imposed on us" (22).

14. You can also notice on the map how close Biden is plotted to Charles Taylor. In a podcast with Center for Faith and Culture at Yale Divinity School, Taylor has said that Biden is his kind of Catholic, holding similar views to Taylor himself. Charles Taylor, interview with Miroslav Volf and Ryan McAnnally, "Charles Taylor & Miroslav Volf: What's Wrong with Our Democracies?," *For the Life of the World* (podcast), October 2, 2021, episode 87, 40:37, https://for-the-life-of-the-world

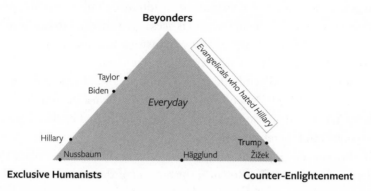

We can also add to our map some popular figures who nevertheless shape people's social imaginaries in the everyday. For instance, Jordan B. Peterson, the YouTube professor, can be plotted near the CEs with a few clicks toward the Beyonders. Peterson actually doesn't have much interest in the Beyonders. But his Jungian symbolism gives him some openness. He knows Beyonders who lean toward CEs listen faithfully to him. Yet ultimately what sets apart Peterson, and what has made him popular, is his attacks on the E.Hums and their drive to make the modern moral order pure. Peterson finds this kind of fight for freedom and desire oppressive. He wants individuals to stop listening to these defeatist E.Hums and heroically take back their lives (starting with making their beds).

Peterson's opposite across the map would be Glennon Doyle and her plat-form. Some progressive Christians have come to admire Doyle. She blends E.Hum commitments with a language that Beyonders, seeking acceptance and freedom for their desire in the everyday, can identify with. Her call to love and accept yourself fits perfectly on the low plane between E.Hums and Beyonders.

In locations similar to those of Peterson and Doyle, respectively, we can plot Mark Driscoll and Shane Claiborne. Driscoll is the epic pastor in the key of a heroic Counter-Enlightenment brawler. He purposefully crosses every line of the modern moral order, feeling his God-given call to stick his finger in the eye of E.Hums and any Christians who find themselves associated with E.Hums and their idolatrous modern moral order. Driscoll's biblicism means he has some (odd) connection to the Beyonders, but only the Beyonders who

-yale-center-for-faith-culture.simplecast.com/episodes/charles-taylor-miroslav-volf-whats-wrong
-with-our-democracies-fear-of-replacement-post-truth-and-entrenched-tribal-factions-part-1.

are fighters adopting the CE attitude he so admires. Claiborne is his opposite. Claiborne is an activist believer who is seeking, as his call to the beyond, to make the moral modern order more expansive and therefore more just and accepting. His main opposition are those like Driscoll and their churches who worship real and symbolic guns. Claiborne literally pounds guns into gardening tools.[15] Both Driscoll and Claiborne see themselves standing against idolatry. Yet their definitions of idolatry are conditioned by their location in the triangle (and therefore completely opposite).

To throw a few pop culture figures onto our map, we could place the comedian and podcaster Joe Rogan at the bottom of the triangle. Rogan has no interest in any beyond (he thinks religion is the result of paleolithic humans taking psychedelics). But Rogan's podcast, while not completely opposed to some themes of the E.Hums, is mostly a CE project. It points out the stupid inconsistencies of the media and other elites who fetishize the modern moral order. Bill Maher, the HBO talk show host and comedian, can be located near Rogan. Maher finds Beyonders to be the most ignorant of fools.

Important historical figures such as Martin Luther King Jr. and Malcom X can also be located across the triangle. King called the US to honor its constitutional and moral commitments. King knew better than most how the modern moral order was shaped for the everyday. He called Protestant America to honor the mutual benefit and equal regard of the modern moral order and see that America is violating the flourishing of African Americans. King's vision of flourishing is humanist but not exclusively so. King had a deep operative sense as a preacher that there is a beyond, that justice itself needs a longing for and living toward something beyond the modern moral order and mutual benefit. King was one of America's true prophets, heralding that late modernity needed some kind of beyond in its modern moral order or else great division and major crisis would come home to roost in America (and, oh, how this has happened).

Malcom X, unlike King, is not sure the ideals of the American project (of liberal democracy at all) are worth saving. He's not sure the E.Hums' modern moral order can produce the freedom and esteem the Black community deserves. Malcom X's Muslim commitments give him some openness to the beyond, but unlike King, he needs to be plotted on the CE line and further away from the Beyonders.

15. Shane Claiborne and Michael Martin, *Beating Guns: Hope for People Who Are Weary of Violence* (Grand Rapids: Brazos, 2019).

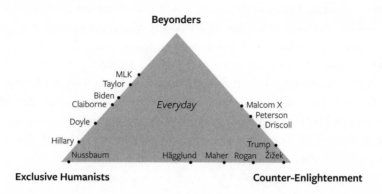

Now, who could be plotted closest to the Beyonders? (And remember that in modernity you can never be exactly on the point: everything is triangulated.) Thomas Merton first came to mind. But Merton, though admirable, doesn't qualify. This is a map of the triangulations of conflicts in the everydayness of late modernity. Merton, though he wrote political critique, spent most of his time in isolation from the everydayness of society—and not just in a monastery but in his own remote hermitage on the property of a monastery. Also remember that this is a map of modernity, so someone like Francis of Assisi or Teresa of Ávila wouldn't qualify. Five examples come to mind of those who can be plotted close to the very point of the Beyonders.

First, Dietrich Bonhoeffer. Bonhoeffer, while so deeply engaged in the everyday—his thoughts never turning from the everyday—nevertheless believed even ethics was not ever about asking what is right or wrong but asking what is the will of God. Such a view goes beyond human flourishing. And his (supposed) last words to a follow prisoner were, "Tell my friend Bell, for me this is the end, no not the end, the beginning."[16] This is a confession of something beyond death. To plot Bonhoeffer, however, we'd have to locate him near the Beyonders' point but just a click or two on the CE side. Bonhoeffer's Prussian conservativism and his lifelong love for Nietzsche gives him this slight CE flavor.

Across from Bonhoeffer we could place Desmond Tutu. Tutu is a Beyonder, with a click or two on the E.Hums plane. Tutu showed his full commitment to the beyond in his construction of the Truth and Reconciliation Commission

16. Eberhard Bethge, *Dietrich Bonhoeffer: A Biography* (1970; repr., Minneapolis: Fortress, 2000), 927.

in South Africa. The commission was built around practices of the beyond, confession and forgiveness, and the necessity of mutual surrender to see the other (whether violator and violated) as a human being. This humanness is not bound in individual desire but in a spiritual interconnection that includes but is beyond individual desire. It is a freedom for being with, for forgiveness.

We could add a few more people, with less room to articulate why: Henri Nouwen and Simone Weil both sought something beyond. We could also add one of the earliest Beyonders in modernity (maybe the father of all modern Beyonders): Danish recluse Søren Kierkegaard.

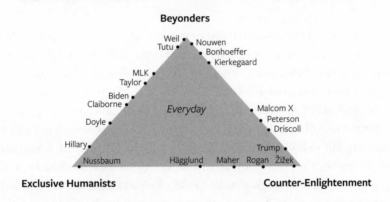

Back to the Mystical

I've gone to great lengths to tease out this triangulation, making it into a map, so that we can return to our discussion of the surprising appearance of mysticism in late modernity. The triangle map will help us locate the different mystical pathways we've already named in the chapters above. We'll soon see how the pathways of inner genius, heroic action, and surrender/confession are bound within this same map. The memoirs we'll explore in the next chapter can be plotted similar to how we've located the figures above. These mystical memoirs are also triangulated (they're never just one thing). For instance, a certain memoir may be committed mostly to the mystical experience of the inner genius of Exclusive Humanism. But that same memoir might also click toward the heroic action of the Counter-Enlightenment. The mystical paths of late modernity, not surprisingly, are also a triangulated movement across these three options, never strictly one but often mostly one with a little of another.

This triangulation reveals the assumed operative shape of transformation, conversion, and spiritual renewal that moves across our larger cultural realities and in turn finds its way directly into pastoral ministry and the life of the church. These different pathways to transformation have their origins inside the three triangulated ways of being in Western late modernity.

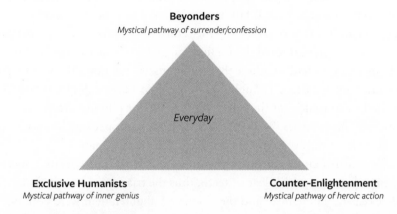

Beyonders
Mystical pathway of surrender/confession

Everyday

Exclusive Humanists
Mystical pathway of inner genius

Counter-Enlightenment
Mystical pathway of heroic action

We have yet to answer one big question: How does this triangle map of conflicts and commitments also describe the landscape of late-modern mysticism? In other words, How could it be that Exclusive Humanism and the Counter-Enlightenment could come to house certain forms of mysticism, particularly distinct mysticisms without God? It seems more logical for mysticism, even in modernity, to appear for Beyonders, and only Beyonders. Nevertheless, a mysticism for each side of the triangle has arrived. As we'll see, it is a native mysticism formulated by and for each of these points of the triangle. Each point has its own distinct mysticism that offers a particular shape of transformation. The arrival of these native mysticisms within Exclusive Humanism and the Counter-Enlightenment has in turn had the effect of confusing and unbalancing the Beyonders. It has led the Beyonders, as they've slid down the sides of the triangle, to lose touch with or confidence in their own shape of the mystical and transformation. Pastors have let go of Beyonder forms of transformation in exchange for these E.Hum and CE means of transformation.

How did all this happen? How did E.Hums and CEs, who critique (even disdain) religion for its beyondness, nevertheless produce a native mysticism?[17]

17. Though it has to be stated that it is not that native. Both the E.Hums and CEs, while often imagining themselves to be unique, are always drawing from religion to make their

And why did E.Hums and CEs come to embrace a mystical spirituality within their own commitments to either the modern moral order or the will to power?

It happened because both E.Hums and CEs re-embraced transcendence. Which seems inconceivable because E.Hums and CEs share a critique of religion's beyondness. Yet, as I'll show, many on the bottom side have made a space for transcendence (a revamped kind of transcendence that matches their inner commitments). Both E.Hums and CEs had to make this space; it was not optional. It was necessitated by the return of a monster on the horizon: guilt. This monster attacked the E.Hums and CEs as much as any Beyonder. E.Hums and CEs had to admit that the monster was not a figment of the Beyonders' imagination. Though they don't often admit it, E.Hums and CEs have had to concede that they were responsible for flipping the switch and animating this monster. To everyone's surprise, guilt became like a film of algae on top of the everyday for all three parties on the map.

This return of guilt is surprising because the E.Hums and CEs were able to appear only because guilt lost its teeth, thus the triangulation becoming the map. Exclusive Humanism and the Counter-Enlightenment were both born in times when guilt had become toothless. Both E.Hums and CEs scoffed at Beyonders, and religion as a whole, for thinking guilt was anything but an imaginary monster, a childish illusion that stupidly keeps people believing in something beyond human flourishing and death. With this hubris, both E.Hums and CEs asserted that guilt was an imaginary object used either to repress desire and therefore identity or to keep people from the heroic exercise of the will to power.

Yet, what allowed guilt to return with new fearsome teeth—fear that leaves a film on every part of the everyday—was the E.Hums' and CEs' shared view of the self. Both the E.Hums and the CEs took their core DNA for the self from Rousseau, who was a unique kind of thinker who equally inspired both the E.Hums and CEs. Both E.Hums and CEs call Rousseau to one degree or another a forefather. Both embraced conceptions of the self that allowed the self in late modernity to become conceived as performative. Both the E.Hums and CEs hold that the self is always and necessarily in a battle of performance.

For the late-modern E.Hums, the self is an individual whose free desires need to expressively broadcast the self's inner genius. The competition for

---

claims. The modern moral order itself can only come to be because of many Protestant breakthroughs and then readaptations.

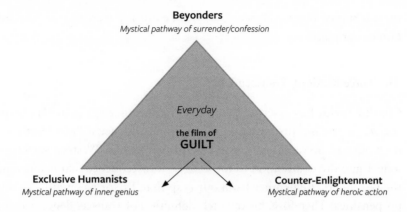

Beyonders
Mystical pathway of surrender/confession

Everyday

the film of
GUILT

Exclusive Humanists
Mystical pathway of inner genius

Counter-Enlightenment
Mystical pathway of heroic action

recognition of unique identities proliferates inside the modern moral order, which is the stage or playing field of competitive performance. For the late-modern CEs, too, the self is an individual who is competitively and heroically acting in the world. The self performs heroic actions that win esteem and therefore power. The self's power is in rejecting what all the dumb, scared lemmings follow. Both sides take as dogma from Rousseau the belief that the self is magnificent—magnificently unique or heroic. This magnificence is substantiated and verified inside the constant and never-ending performative battle (thanks to neoliberalism). The triangulation of conflicts and dilemmas demonstrates further the essential competitive nature of all existence.

Because both E.Hums and CEs hold to a performing self that is seeking constant confirmation of its own magnificence (as a deep existential need), both become open to a piercing and penetrating kind of guilt.[18] Needing to cope with the guilt, both E.Hums and CEs ironically but intently embrace a kind of transcendence. Transcendence—an embrace of spirituality—is the core way to deal with the guilt and exhaustion of constant and unrelenting performance. This embrace of transcendence creates distinct and native mystical pathways and views of transformation. As mentioned in the previous two chapters, the reappearance of guilt makes new mystical pathways necessary and potent.

These are distinct forms or kinds of transcendence. To get a handle on these mystical pathways and views of transformation, we need to tease out

18. My core source for this cultural guilt is Alain Ehrenberg, *The Weariness of the Self: Diagnosing the History of Depression in the Contemporary Age* (Montreal: McGill-Queen's University Press, 2016), and Byung-Chul Han (whom we'll explore in-depth in chap. 7).

these forms of transcendence. This will be our last step and the final addition to our map.

The Three Kinds of Transcendence

Charles Taylor has asserted that to live in a secular age is to experience a society in which transcendence is lost. Transcendence is "lost" in that it is no longer an overarching, organizing principle. Our Western societies no longer give direct attention to the kind of transcendence that is inherent to the Beyonders. Remember from our map that Taylor has major Beyonder propensities. Therefore, his own felt definition of transcendence is colored by the form of transcendence he holds to, a Beyonder form (more on what makes it a Beyonder form in a bit). Yet, Taylor's point applies to the whole of our age. Transcendence, or the supernatural, is no longer assumed to be the base reality of our everyday lives. Our societies run on the rails of the natural. But the train cars that move on these rails of immanence and naturalism are anything but antispiritual. Above the rails there is a nova effect of spiritualities, a myriad of ways to be spiritual (and to cope with guilt) along the three sides of the triangle.

To say we live in a secular age of the loss of transcendence doesn't mean that transcendence itself is completely absent. In a neoliberal epoch of the performing self, only a very small part of even the E.Hums and CEs are absolute materialists. The creative drives for recognition and the fight for victory upend absolute materialism. Spirituality is a way both to cope and to get an edge inside the all-out competition. It's no wonder, then, that in these hypercompetitive environments of performance, high-achieving victors speak often of transcendence—the ecstasy of victory, the transcendental state of being in the zone. Professional athletes and celebrities thank God and are happy to expressively broadcast their many spiritualities. Even Kanye West leads worship services.

This myriad of spiritualities, while exponential, can nevertheless be located inside three distinct forms of transcendence. These three forms of transcendence are concomitant with the three points on our triangle map. There is a concomitant form of transcendence each for E.Hums, CEs, and Beyonders. These different forms make all the spirituality claims across our conflicting triangulation confusing. William Desmond, in his book *God and the Between*, articulates these three forms of transcendence. My contribution is fitting these three forms of transcendence on our map of conflicts and dilemmas, connecting Desmond and Taylor.

Desmond calls these three forms of transcendence T1, T2, and T3. Proactively firing all three into motion, Desmond says, "We turn from God (T3), turn towards ourselves as immanent transcendence (T2), and lay hold of our own power to master the flux of equivocal transience (T1)."[19] This is an intricate statement, and Desmond uses 350 pages of dense, fine print to unpack it much further. But what is most helpful for us is to spot how each of these three forms of transcendence (these three Ts) is bound inside the three sides of our triangle map.

T1 and its "laying hold of our own power to master" is a kind of transcendence that produces a mysticism bound in a self who is mastering the self by heroic actions. It is a form of transcendence embraced by the CEs. The CEs' mystical pathway is bound to a transcendence in which, through heroic action, the person lays hold of their power and masters something, often through the energy of rejecting what the E.Hums value. This form of transcendence ("laying hold of our own power to master") creates a mysticism without God for CEs (this was Nietzsche's point after all!). This is a common pathway many memoirists walk in their stories of transformation. This is a form of transcendence that is located *externally*. It's a transcendence found inside gallant external action. Action is swept up into the intrepid spirit and therefore testifies to transcendence. Though it must be reiterated that T1 transcendence has its source completely in the performing self (not in something beyond the self). This transcendence is external because it is a lurching or grabbing for something outside the self but is nevertheless fully contingent on the power of the performing self. To embrace your power to reject what the lemmings are doing and lay hold of your own destiny leads to transcendent euphoria. This transcendent euphoria sends the self out again and again in battle inside a neoliberalism of conflicting performances.

This takes us to Desmond's T2. If T1 is found in external action, then T2 is found in an *internal* awareness of the self. Transcendence 2 is bound in the longing for freedom "as the promise of self-determination."[20] Determining the self, finding the self's true identity, is a freedom that becomes fully transcendent. The location of this transcendence is not external (as it was with

---

19. William Desmond, *God and the Between* (Malden, MA: Blackwell, 2008), 59.
20. Desmond, *God and the Between*, 22.

T1 for the CEs) but inside. The center of gravity in both T1 and T2 is bound in the self; the self is the one who produces this transcendence. The self is the most fundamental cog, even the engine, of transcendence in T1 and T2. In T2, the self finds transcendence when the self finds its inner genius, its true identity. When the self is free to determine itself, it steps into a transcendent and deeply spiritual place. This is a form of transcendence completely concomitant with the E.Hums. T2, as concomitant with the E.Hums, creates a mystical pathway, again without God, that finds its effervescence in the expressions of the self's inner genius to produce its own freedom. The lauded sages of this E.Hum transcendence are those who have found, and boldly live out, who they are. Receiving recognition for their marvelous boldness to be their magnificent self, they live inside out, with their inner identity of genius in successful performance.

As we'll see, there are many memoirists who present their own transformation in just such a way. Their transformation, the mystical acceptance of who they truly are, is the awakening to their own inner genius to determine their own freedom. They often have a conversion into seeing the truth of the modern moral order itself. This kind of mystical pathway is concomitant with the E.Hums because in order to flourish it needs the modern moral order and the commitment to equal mutual regard. T2 is a mysticism that believes that the fullness of flourishing is internal acceptance of your desires as your identity. It is a flourishing that moves into an internally bound transcendence. T2, then, is a form of transcendence that can cohabitate with (and even propagate) exclusive humanism. Such transcendence is inseparable from the exclusivist view of flourishing.

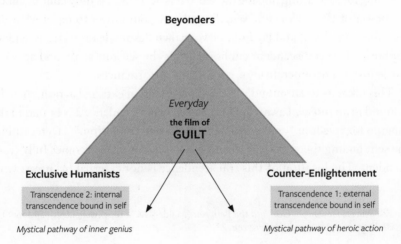

The E.Hums and the CEs happily team up in conflicts with Beyonders. Both agree that the Beyonders' beliefs and their form of transcendence are dangerous. They both equally assert that their own beliefs are much less dangerous because their own beliefs in the modern moral order or the will to power are more entwined with the everyday. Their own distinct views of transcendence are therefore less delusional. But in the twenty-first century this has not been shown to be true. Rather, inside both camps, the E.Hums and CEs, conspiracy theories and delusions of grandeur have proliferated. These have been very dangerous to our everyday lives, particularly to democracy and the shared public good. Transcendence 1's external drive to lay hold of the self's own power to reject has produced dizzying forms of conspiracy theories that have come from the likes of QAnon and Alex Jones. All of these conspiracy theories are enacted by a raging rejection of the modern moral order. They assert that the modern moral order is not just misguided but a conscious ploy of control run by a small cabal of E.Hum elites. The true believers in the CE camp are dangerously open to being pulled into conspiracy fits of rage. These outbursts are a blood-pulsing kind of transcendence in T1.

The E.Hums have a similar issue. Inside the drives to provide access and tools toward the expanse of the modern moral order through the free broadcasting of the inner genius of identities, Silicon Valley elites have been swept into delusions of grandeur. With great hubris these young tech giants believe their optimization can change the world—even solving the problem of death (Google is working on it now). They believe somehow that (functional/technical) connections alone are a transcendent magic that can make the world from corner to corner safe for the modern moral order—Andrew Yang and his blockchain is a case in point.[21] Inside these digital tech breakthroughs of social media, the experience of transcendence in T2 (the internal drive for freedom) is so electric, so potent, it blinds itself to the damage and limits of technology.[22]

---

21. For discussion of this spirituality of grandeur, see Siva Vaidhyanathan, *Anti-Social Media: How Facebook Disconnects Us and Undermines Democracy* (New York: Oxford University Press, 2018).

22. No wonder conspiracy spouters and big tech have turned on each other as enemies. These two distinct forms of transcendence are facing off in conflict. They are both overinflated and both are now in some ways the dominant form of E.Hums and CEs in their conflict. Yet oddly they need each other. Conspiracy needs the tools of tech and tech needs the traffic of conspiracy, and E.Hums have to balance this against their belief in the modern moral order and mission to expand mutual equal regard of identity broadcasting.

Both of these are fundamentalist forms of E.Hum (T2) and CE (T1). And yet the E.Hums and CEs keep scoffing at Beyonders, saying Beyonders can't be trusted because of their complicity in the Crusades. Beyonders' real complicity, though, is their sliding down too close toward either the E.Hums or CEs. This, of course, has happened in evangelicalism, as QAnon and other CE forms of T1 overtake conversative Protestant congregations like a virus.

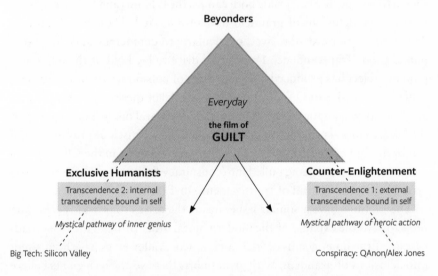

Putting the extremes aside (none of the memoirs we will explore went to these levels), it is nevertheless the evolution of these forms of transcendence that allows for new mysticism without God to arrive. These are mysticisms without God (even if some like Kanye speak of God), because these forms of transcendence take no account of the beyond. Moreover, because they are concomitant and native to the modern moral order of E.Hums and the will to power of CEs, they consider a transcendence that is beyond to be dangerous.

What both sides find dangerous is that at its core the transcendence of the Beyonders makes a much different claim about the self. The Beyonders' form of transcendence leads the Beyonders to claim that, in the shadow of transcendence (T3), the self is revealed—to quote Bon Iver again—to be "not magnificent." This confession of un-magnificence deeply upsets (even angers) E.Hums and CEs alike. The un-magnificence risks not only the substance of their distinct beliefs (striking at parts of the modern moral order and the will to power) but in turn counters the very constitution of their forms of transcendence. If the self is not magnificent, then both external-bound and internal-bound forms of transcendence are thrown into question.

The Beyonders hold to what Desmond calls T3. If T1 is external and T2 internal, then T3 is "superior," Desmond says. What Desmond means by superior is not evaluative. He is not necessarily saying that it is a better form of transcendence. Rather, he's saying that T3 is a form of transcendence (the original form) that is bound to an encounter with something beyond. It's a transcendence coming from outside the self. "Superior" is equal to "beyond" for Desmond. Transcendence is *not* externally or internally situated. It has no animating location in the self at all. Rather, it's a form a transcendence that is beyond, outside, superior to the self. Therefore, its form of transcendence relativizes the self, leading to confessions of un-magnificence. Because the source of transcendence is not in the self at all but far outside it, the self is not a producer of transcendence from within the self's own performance. The self is only and finally a recipient. Transcendence 3 is bound in the encounter with otherness.

It may be best to call this kind of transcendence *inbreaking*. It is an eventful inbreaking that comes from outside the self, unveiling that the self cannot, and will never be able to, control this transcendence. This transcendence is so bound in the everyday that it is simultaneously completely other and outside the everyday. When this transcendence breaks upon the self, the self can only receive it as a gift, a promise, a judgment, and an invitation. This inbreaking transcendence (T3) can only be encountered in surrender and confession. It is met with an openness to something beyond that cannot be controlled. Only in the disposition of release and expressed need is the self stopped in its performance to receive what is beyond it that can save it.

T3 is the mystical pathway of the Beyonder, bound to a form of in-breaking transcendence. The mystical path is to surrender and stop all performances by confessing the need for the inbreaking encounter with true otherness. This makes for a very different shape of transformation than that imagined by either the E.Hums or CEs. This Beyonder mystical path is still walked but not with the traffic of the other two, because it is the path that cannot be walked without an encounter with the living God of becoming. This form of mysticism cannot be done without God, for it must surrender to the fact that the performing self cannot save itself. Therefore, it needs an encounter with the living God—with true otherness—who breaks in and makes new. This mystical pathway must remain in the everyday, but it seeks a redemption that it knows must come from an encounter with an inbreaking otherness.

Confession and surrender are the dispositions that the museum attendants think are appropriate to being in the presence of *Guernica*. They ask us to surrender to the silence. To confess the horror of war. To experience the painting as a cipher of otherness. With those dispositions, the painting may participate in moving us viewers into transformation. But we can't surrender. We have no interest in confession. We choose more immediate (and, honestly, flattering) forms of transcendence. I take a selfie to broadcast my identity through my genius wit (T2). The Irish lad next to me rejects the whole thing, sick of all the triangles. His friends laugh. He feels the warm glow of imposing his will and power in his rejection (T1). There are more triangles at play in the room than just those on Picasso's huge canvas. The Irish lad is right, the [bleeping] triangles are everywhere!

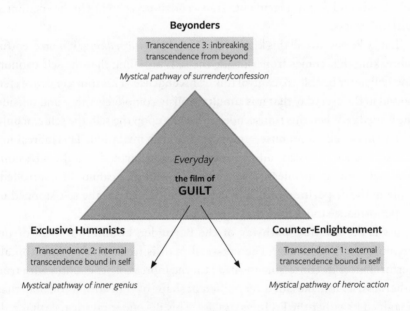

6

Mystical Memoirists

Mapping the Spiritual Pathways of a Secular Age

When you fly west, even in the land of the rising sun, you rise long before the sun.

It's mid-November 2019 and we're in Tokyo. In a few days I'll be teaching a class in Hong Kong. Hong Kong is in a state of unease. Riots have been raging, right near the seminary where I'll be teaching. We're not sure, even while in Tokyo, if it's safe to go to Hong Kong. I keep checking my email. It's hard for me to imagine that a trip I've been looking forward to, that I'm even right in the middle of, could be canceled. Little do I know that not far away, in Wuhan, China, a virus has appeared that will cancel nearly all my 2020 plans. On our return flight through Shanghai, there is a small army of airport personnel laser shooting foreheads for temperature checks. We have no idea why. It seems so odd in November, not so much in December.

In Tokyo, we have an Airbnb near Shinjuku, not far from the Metro stop. But it always feels longer when you're lugging bags and looking for the spot. We find it off the main road. The Airbnb directions tell us to go to a lockbox on the ground floor, use a code, and get the key to the flat. But we can't get the lockbox open. Our westernized minds are not able to work the high-tech Tokyo gadgets. Jet lag is not helping either. After thirty minutes and messages back and forth to the Airbnb host, we finally get in. The room is small but meticulously clean, inviting in its spareness. Everything is basic. Except for the toilet. The toilet looks like a spacecraft, possessing more buttons than the flight deck of the Millennium Falcon. Overall, the Airbnb is perfect.

I go straight to sleep. It's a heavy, but not long, sleep. It's 2:58 a.m. and I'm staring at the ceiling in the grip of jet lag. We already know where we're going for breakfast, Robot Donut. The donuts are to die for. But this amazing place doesn't open until 5 a.m. The only option to cope is to browse my iPad.

Before I know it, not only does the jet lag have me but so does the YouTube algorithm. I'm right in its wake. I click on one David Foster Wallace video and now I'm deep. I watch his famous Kenyon College commencement address, then a few interviews with Charlie Rose. Then a few more snippets of other interviews. At one point, on the top of the list of suggested videos is a clip about the rumors of a coming *Friends* reunion. I start thinking about Chandler. I wonder what Wallace thought of him. Chandler the *always* sarcastic, ironic, and much-loved character. I watch a *Friends* clip from 1998. I once loved Chandler. I now find him very off-putting. And I don't think it's the jet lag but rather the death of irony.

In one of the earlier interviews the algorithm queued for me, Wallace explains that novelists, particularly countercultural ones, started using irony in the mid-twentieth century. Irony and cynicism became a way to push back against and disrupt the dominant narratives. Irony's power was its ability to be the burr in the saddle of a straight earnest society. Yet, Wallace's point is that by the mid-1980s, and coming to fruition in the 1990s, irony shifted. It went mainstream. The arrival of neoliberalism and the hyperdrives for performance opened the gate to irony, allowing it to run throughout all of society. Irony became the mass-produced medicine of a new neoliberalism. Irony, like Tums, was a quick way to cope with the stomachache of an all-out drive for performance and achievement. Irony was a defense that could turn into an offense against guilt and the new need to be all you could be. Wallace doesn't go here directly, but his writing by the mid-1990s points to these themes. The reflections are present in *Infinite Jest* and in his nonfiction piece on cruise ships called "A Supposedly Fun Thing I'll Never Do Again."

Wallace's overall point is that consumer capitalism in its last decades used the forms of the avant garde novelists of the midcentury to sell cereal and light bulbs. Television, the medium Wallace loved and hated like a mistress, became the new epicenter of irony. Chandler Bing was the prom king and Grand Poohbah of over-the-top sarcasm. Unrelenting irony came like a machine gun from every line Chandler uttered. With *Friends*, network television hit its peak of cultural relevance. *Friends* perfected neoliberal irony to sell consumer goods. After *Friends*, a decline set in and TV took a turn (a happy one in my mind) from the ironic to the sincere. HBO dramas and AMC series led us into the golden era of realist and sincere television (television shockingly became more serious than cinema—television went serious, cinema went superhero).

Wallace never lived to see this golden era of realist/sincere television. But he did his part in bringing it forth. His novel *Infinite Jest* in particular was an ur-source for the sincere journey of the soul who desperately searches the vapid everyday for meaning and purpose. Wallace explained, in those mid-1990s interviews, that the novelist needed to depart from irony and turn to a new gritty sincerity.[1]

Now twenty-five to thirty years later, the sincerity is so heavy, molded so tightly around the performing self and late capitalism, that humor itself is nearly dead. Stand-up comedians are canceled; ironic jokes (particularly about

1. Chuck Klosterman too calls this the "New Sincerity" and analyzes it very similar to how I do here. Klosterman says about its rise in the 1990s, "There have been many versions of the New Sincerity, always unified by the same motive: the belief that people should be honest about what they feel, and that consumers of art should not reward artists who use emotional estrangement as an intellectual crutch. In the late eighties, there was a New Sincerity music scene in East Texas, although the musicians were all too sincere to succeed nationally. In September of 1991, *Esquire* ran a long story on the New Sincerity that mostly mocked the idea, claiming that habits like cocaine were part of the old Sincerity ('it made you improvise, lie, and cheat for amusement') while ecstasy was a drug for the New Sincerity ('it kills irony'). *Esquire* used two different covers for the issue: one with David Letterman smiling and one with David Letterman scowling. The theory was that people who supported the New Sincerity would want the copy where Letterman looked nice. New Sincerity logic was (very briefly) applied to movies, and particularly movies made by Kevin Costner. But the zenith of its influence occurred in the late nineties, when it temporarily became the dominant way to think about literature. The movement was driven (as was so often the case) by a David Foster Wallace essay, but the term was most incessantly applied to writers like Dave Eggers and Zadie Smith, eventually leading to pro-earnestness polemics like *For Common Things: Irony, Trust, and Commitment in America Today*, a 1999 nonfiction book from a twenty-five-year-old home-schooled Harvard graduate named Jedediah Purdy." Klosterman, *The Nineties: A Book* (New York: Penguin, 2022), 21.

He continues, "The New Sincerity offered no gray area—either you cared about it too much or you didn't care at all. To those who saw ironic distance as a creeping cultural affliction, there was no creative crisis more damaging; to almost everyone else, it seemed liked an imaginary problem that could not matter any less than it appeared. But what the New Sincerity was, and what it always is, was anxiety over the comfort of emotional uninvestment, magnified by the luxury of introspection" (211). Klosterman concludes, "This was the crux of the psychosomatic problem: I think I should feel guilty for enjoying something I don't actually care about. The solution was to be less cynical, and one way to be less cynical was to elevate the expression of sincerity. But trying to be sincere on purpose is like trying to be spontaneous on command—it ends up having the opposite effect. If the goal was to kill irony, the old version of sincerity wouldn't work. So we had to invent a new one, again and again and again" (212).

identities) are not tolerated. Such jokes are ruled unfunny by the desperately sincere. Chandler and Joey *never* took themselves seriously; rarely (and bordering on annoyingly) was there a moment of sincerity. We, on the other hand, in the twenty-first century, take everything with full-throated sincerity. Every part of our lives is taken seriously. Sincerity is the only way to keep up as a performing self who needs to achieve and achieve more. It has become the new response to neoliberal guilt. When you realize your stomachache is cancer, Tums seems inappropriate (and nothing to joke about). A little sarcastic irony is no match for the guilt of the performing self. The guilt is too sharp, its mental health dangers too acute, to not be completely sincere. Or maybe it's the other way around. Because we're so intensely sincere, policing each other, so attentively outraged by each other, we poison the air with more fumes of performative guilt.

Regardless, it is inside this transition to the sincere—in many ways on the ground that Wallace himself broke—that the memoirist becomes a mystic. Just as the late-medieval period and its budding reforms created a sincere ethos that produced its own mystics, so too the sincere times of late modernity's twenty-first century have produced their own kind of mystics and mystical pathways. It's true that Wallace was no memoirist. But his novels' sincere journeys into longing, addiction, and the search for some purpose were an invitation to a new generation of memoirists. Wallace's own journey with addiction and halfway houses was transcribed into *Infinite Jest* (characters from the novel were people Wallace met). Wallace's writing was an invitation to those who came after him to turn their prose onto themselves. And to do so with utter seriousness (it's amazing how many memoirs I read that quote or interact with Wallace). The performing self, having unlearned the tongue of irony, demanded this turn to utter sincerity.[2]

2. Or we could say it like this: David Foster Wallace argues (in his piece "A Supposedly Fun Thing I'll Never Do Again") that those in the mid-twentieth century used irony to unmask hypocrisy. The ironic and sarcastic revealed the lie of the consumer gloss. This was a moral operation. But this moral operation was taken into the mediums of the consumer system, particularly TV. Irony began to be adopted by sitcoms; Chandler replaced Ward Cleaver. Irony lost its moral reach. Inside the sitcom, irony became a twisted way to uphold the objective of fixed gloss, of selling. Wallace thought irony needed to come to an end. It did post-2015. Earnestness has replaced irony. The intent to unmask hypocrisy remains. But now without joke, shock, etc. Now with full, earnest rage. A bad marriage between the earnest and ironic is forged. The worst of each is continued, the best lost. Earnestness loses its moral vision of something greater to strive for; irony loses its playfulness, its raw countercelebrity and counterconsumerism. Earnest irony uses celebrity (social media followers) as its measure. Therefore, while it seeks to unmask, its existential need for a gaze ends up violating its deepest wishes. Those caught

Return of the Triangle

Inside our triangle, the driving sincerity (as a response to performative guilt) opens new mystical pathways. It's finally time to explore some memoirs, teasing out their shape of transformation. We'll plot them on our triangle map.

But why *these* specific memoirs? As with the people I chose to plot on our triangle map in the previous chapter, there is no systematic or methodological reason for these memoirs over others. To find these memoirs I simply sought lists of the most esteemed memoirs from 2010 to 2021. They've been broadly read and appreciated. Yet, what became clear as I examined them is that, not only were sincere transformations articulated using motifs of the mystical, but each had a place within the triangulated conflicts of modernity. These memoirists articulated their own transformation and mystical pathways from the location of the CEs, E.Hums, or Beyonders. However, it should be stated that just because a memoirist is located on one side in their writing does not mean that's where they would be in other conflicts, or even where they would see themselves. But it does mean they wrote their memoir within this disposition. Their politics may be somewhere else, but their expressed shape of transformation and therefore spirituality is either CE, E.Hum, or Beyonder.

The memoirists' expressed experiences of transcendence (which made the memoirs mystical) are either primarily T1 (external), T2 (internal), or T3 (inbreaking). The pathway of heroic action connects to T1 and locates the memoir on the side of the CEs. The pathway of inner genius connects to T2 and locates the writer on the side of E.Hums. Surrender and confession is the pathway that connects to T3 and aims the memoirist toward the Beyonders.

Another dynamic to recognize as we explore these memoirs is that, compared to the mystical thinking of other historical epochs, or even the presumption of mysticism in other periods of modernity, all three of these pathways lead not out of but deeper into the everyday. This is what makes them late-modern in ethos. What also makes them late-modern (and secular in a Taylorian sense) is that two of these pathways are able to embrace

---

inside this new sincerity are so angry because there is no way to escape these inner conflicts. The way to be is to be ironic, to unmask, but the tools are earnestness and lack of humor; the shock is now the political. It is a shock to end all shock, making the queer normative, even normal—Maggie Nelson speaks of this in *Argonauts* (Minneapolis: Graywolf, 2015), 73–75. This form of transformation is trapped in the self. Nothing from outside the self can reach the self. Eventfulness is lost.

transcendence, spirituality, and mystical sincerity without any real need for a living or personal God. They are without God. Yet, they are not without a connection to one of the three Ts and a firm location inside the triangulation of modern conflicts and dilemmas.

As we now explore some memoirs, let's start with the CE side of our triangle map.

The Pathway of Heroic Action

There are at least three (maybe four) different lanes by which to walk the mystical pathway of heroic action in the cadence of the Counter-Enlightenment. These are the lanes of (1) nature, (2) vocation, (3) sickness, and (4) exercise (though this last one needs nuance and begins to move us across the triangle). It was inside the struggle of the will to power in one of these four areas that each particular memoirist was pulled into transcendence (T1), which delivered a transformation to their life.

1. Nature

Raynor Winn is an example of someone traveling the mystical path of the heroic on the lane of *nature*. Her journey is articulated in two award-winning memoirs, which echo the mystical dimension of nature even in their titles— *The Salt Path* and *Wild Silence*. In *The Salt Path*, Winn is a Welsh woman in her early fifties who has everything in her life set and settled. Her two children are launched, and she's looking forward to settling into the next chapter of her life. Yet, in a matter of weeks everything comes undone. First, the little farmhouse in Wales that she's lived in for over twenty years—filled as much by the sacred memories of her children as her own things—is repossessed. An investment gone bad means the house that holds her past and future is stripped from her grip. Her fingers, clutching in anguish, are pried from her little farmhouse. The pain and betrayal are piercing.

There are no savings, no other options. The nest egg for the future is tied up in the beloved property. The court rules that Winn and her husband have no claim on the property; all investments are lost with the house. In a matter of weeks Winn and her husband Moth become nearly penniless. There are no funds to procure new housing. And to make matters much worse, Moth is also diagnosed with a terminal illness. He'll be lucky to live five more years.

The house and her husband are being stripped from Winn's grip. She's left empty-handed but desperately reaching for something. She can't, won't, accept the doctor's diagnosis. The doctor must be wrong. The loss of the house is painful enough. The loss of Moth is too much to bear. And even if she does face Moth's illness, how could she care for him without a house? Where are they going to go? What could possibly heal them now? Winn is utterly powerless to direct her fate.

On a desperate whim, Winn comes up with a plan. Among their remaining possessions are sleeping bags and a tent. Winn convinces Moth to walk the 630-mile South West Coast Path. England's longest footpath, winding along the rugged coastline, permits "wild camping" along its path. This will give them a place to live for the next handful of months. But more, it will give Winn a way to face the future. To find her power and some way forward. To seek an external transcendence in the salty wind and waves. She's sure this is the only way to solve their problems. The tent can be home, at least until winter comes. Nature's threats and comforts can be the salve to heal. But heal what? Not their empty bank account, not necessarily Moth's illness (though it miraculously does), but Winn's own lack of power. If she can will her way around the 630 miles, facing nature nose-to-nose, she'll overcome her guilt, find her lost magnificence, and taste transformation.

As in Cheryl Strayed's memoir *Wild: From Lost to Found on the Pacific Crest Trail*, Winn walks as the will to power that can save her by finding her and encountering an external transcendence (T1). If Winn goes nose-to-nose with the force of nature, she'll be changed. She'll find her power as her body crashes against the harsh beauty of nature itself.

Like Nietzsche before her, she claims that she doesn't believe in God, for this God whom she doesn't believe in has upended her life: "I don't believe in God, in any higher force. We live, we die; the carbon cycle keeps running. . . . If [God] exists, He had just grabbed the roots of my life and ripped them from the ground, turning my very existence upside down."[3] Her walking, her facing the pain of the trail, is her will to power. Winn and Moth face storms, heat, cliffs, and the arrival of the cold. When they tell others whom they meet on the trail that they are homeless, they're seen as guilty, losers in the neoliberal competition of selves. But when they tell others they've left everything behind to face nature in this walk, they are confirmed as doing (as being) something magnificent.

3. Raynor Winn, *The Salt Path* (New York: Penguin, 2018), 17.

But is this all too much for Moth? He is sick after all. Is Winn, unable to face his death, actually killing him? When his painkillers are gone and withdrawal sets in, she thinks so. But nature and the heroic journey heal him. The more he breathes in the salt air, with his feet on the salt path, the more miraculously he finds his strength. Winn sounds like a seventh-century mystic speaking of the miracles of the pilgrimage—but without an acting God. Nature and the walk are what heal. For both Winn and Moth the miles affirm an external transcendent experience (T1). They are alive. They are powerful. Nature is before them and they reach for it, finding themselves as they heroically face each mile and each day.

As winter comes, they find a secure place to live. They enter back into the normal flows of society. But Moth's symptoms worsen. The distance from nature, from living heroically in a tent on the trail of sea air, is kryptonite. It saps their power. The only option is to return to the trail, to walk again to save themselves. It works. Just days into facing treacherous nature, Moth is feeling better. They are living once more. It's the sea air, the salt of the sea, the salt of their own sweat against the tensions of nature's furiousness that heals again and again, transforming them both.

For Winn, the magnificence of the self is found in its will to power over and against the natural world. This is spiritual. The heroic is transcendent as the self survives and thrives next to the liminalities and even dangers of nature. Winn explains that the sea heals her. In being enveloped by the sea, she finds a way to become someone with power. Home is in herself. This is how she finds a way to live, far beyond the guilt of her failings.

Mystics have pilgrimed on such walks for centuries. But something is different and late-modern about Winn's story. This will become clear in the sequel, *Wild Silence*, where Winn touches more on the mystical, but without God.

In *Wild Silence*, Winn and Moth walk to Iona. It's the finish line of their next journey. They've found their way back into life, but Moth's death is looming. This impending death is stripping Winn of her power. She's afraid again, hiding her magnificent self once more, disappearing as she anticipates Moth's demise. She needs the salt. The sweat of the heroic walk. The transcendence of the sea air. They make it to Iona and are met by a resident of the abbey. He asks them if they are here to pray.

"No just looking," Winn responds.

The retort is direct. *This is not a place to just look. There are no tourists here, no passengers. It's a place to surrender in faith and pray.*

Moth has his own rebuttal engendered from the heroic salt path. "I know," he says, "but we've just come . . . we've had an incredible experience in the wilderness, something almost spiritual."

The Iona man responds from a very different place on our triangle map. He responds as a Beyonder. The Iona man of the abbey says, maybe too boldly in the memory of Winn, "There is no spirituality without God. You won't find a thin place out there; it's here in this building, where humans have worshipped God for centuries. This is where you'll find what you seek."[4]

But Winn and Moth are not Beyonders; their mysticism is the heroic action of the modern walk into nature.[5] Moth counters, "I don't think I'm actually seeking anything. I'm just open to what comes."[6] But Moth and Winn are surely seeking *something*, just not something beyond. What they are seeking is their own hidden magnificent power to be able to face what comes.

And what is coming is the dark days of Moth's illness. The back and forth to the hospital, the realization that he is departing, again strips Winn of her power. It buries her magnificence once more under guilt and timidity. To live through this, to grasp the transformation she seeks, she needs not to surrender, not even to find her true identity, but to remember the path. Winn says as the climax to her transformation, "The strong, fearless person who had finished the path had gotten lost somewhere in the hospital corridors. . . . Moth was right; I'd gone back to the start. Afraid of people, hiding, the child behind the sofa. . . . [That inner child] was afraid and isolated, yet she had connections to the wilderness that hadn't left her."[7]

"Connections to the wilderness" as external transcendence through nature is the engine of her transformation.

2. Vocation

The memoir *Yes, Chef* is the story of Marcus Samuelsson. Like Winn's memoirs, it begins with a walk for survival. But unlike Winn's narrative, it is *not* chosen. Samuelsson is only a child who has yet to receive the name Samuelsson. In his poverty-stricken Ethiopian village, tuberculosis has arrived. To seek treatment, he walks seventy-five miles to the city with his sister and

---

4. Raynor Winn, *The Wild Silence* (New York: Penguin, 2020), 89.

5. Charles Taylor discusses this dynamic of nature and modernity in *A Secular Age* (Cambridge, MA: Harvard University Press, 2007), 95–112.

6. Winn, *Wild Silence*, 89.

7. Winn, *Wild Silence*, 121.

mother. His mother dies. He and his sister are now orphans. Both are soon adopted by a Swedish family named Samuelsson, who lavishes them with love. Marcus feels caught between two worlds: that of Ethiopia and Sweden. But he finds his footing through food. Every Sunday, Marcus walks again. This time, it is a short distance to his Swedish grandmother's kitchen to help her prepare a Sunday chicken. The experience is transcendent. The food and her stories, being wrapped in her care, call out to him. It's the food that connects the locations and stories within him. It is the food (never the God of inbreaking) that calls out to him and changes him.

The rest of the memoir is the story about how an orphan from Ethiopia, raised in Sweden, becomes one of New York's top chefs. Eventually he opens and runs Red Rooster in Harlem, a restaurant that has won the raves of celebrities and world leaders alike. A restaurant that's made the orphan boy a celebrity (chef) himself. Samuelsson's memoir is a contemporary *Little Orphan Annie* story. But in his tale, it's his own talent and hard work—not Daddy Warbucks—that wins him riches and acclaim. Samuelsson is transformed by his own heroic action to chase his dream, to hear his true calling. This call comes not from outside him (not as T3, not like his biblical namesake Samuel) but from within, sending him passionately after a pursuit (T1). The will to overcome and accomplish the pursuit is the fuel of his transformation.

Samuelsson's heroic rise to the top doesn't come without tensions, however. He too must battle guilt. The kitchen is no soft place; it's a gladiator ring. To make it, Samuelsson will need a singular focus. Tunnel vision. He'll have to sacrifice everything else to reach his goal and win his magnificence. He'll have to breathe only for the kitchen and want nothing more than to be the best, heroically burning the boats of any other way of being. He does, burning everything else to ashes. Meeting this heroic standard, giving himself over to the task of the kitchen, transforms him. Samuelsson speaks over and over again of the transcendent quality of cooking (the external form of imposing one's will—T1). He's lost loves and hurt others all for his call to cook, to be the best. And he doesn't regret this. He wears those scars as badges of honor, like marks of conquest on a Viking spear. In Nietzschean style, the one imposing his heroic will to power cannot, should never, apologize.

For instance, earlier in his cooking life, while in Austria, as a sous chef in the Alps, Samuelsson met a woman. She became pregnant. But Samuelsson couldn't stay. The call to cook, the need for heroic action, and the external transcendence were too captivating to be with his daughter, to be a father.

His will could not be domesticated. New York called. Zoe, his daughter, was left with her mother a world away. Samuelsson sent money but couldn't give his time. He couldn't be present. Nothing could distract from his calling, from his will to be the best, to curate his action, to serve the transcendence of the meal. His attention was too directed toward his will. He willed to make something of himself. To go and conquer New York.

The inspiration of the memoir is clear. If you too can find something that calls to you, a vocation that possesses you like cooking does Samuelsson, you'll be changed. You'll be transformed from lost orphan to artist, from meek and distracted to razor-focused and powerful. You'll be admired for your passions and for how your passions and your will impose on the world. You'll find your power. *Yes, Chef* is a tale of career success. But because it's a success that is organic and artistic, it outstrips all other responsibilities and is therefore laudable. Such success is praised because it fits so squarely into the heroic actions that deliver transformation (particularly in a neoliberal epoch). Samuelsson is seen, and sees himself, as a person of depth. His heroic pursuits of his calling and vocation make his self magnificent.

The climax of the memoir, in my mind, is chapter 24.[8] Samuelsson tells the reader of going back to Europe to see Zoe for the first time. She's now grown, moving into her teens. He's been completely absent. It's painful, but Samuelsson has no regrets. He's overcome all guilt with the power of success. He left her for the kitchen, and the only way back to her and over the awkward reunion is through the kitchen. He cooks and they eat together. It heals. The talent of his heroic cooking is the device that mends, overcoming all guilt. It does so because it's the location of the spiritual, the place of his transformation. Ultimately it mends because cooking in the kitchen manifests Samuelsson's power and talent.

It's an odd logic that most readers don't question because the transformation is so boldly claimed. But the passion and singular focus on the art of cooking is both the excuse that drives him away from his daughter and now the only way to cope with the pain and space between them. His heroic passion is somehow both the poison and antidote. This is an odd contradiction that is overlooked inside the T1 of the vocation's passion and ability to transform.

It's no wonder, then, that so many late-modern people live under the uneasy drive that if they could only find their dream job, what they're really supposed

8. Marcus Samuelsson, *Yes, Chef: A Memoir* (New York: Random House, 2013), 252–60.

to be doing in the world, in turn they would find meaning, transcendence, and rest in their own magnificence. This is a transformation by the heroic chasing of passions. It's so neoliberal and performative in its claim that creative work is a transforming spirituality, a mysticism that needs not God but only one's own heroic talent (if one can find it and sacrifice all else for it!).

3. Sickness

Nature and vocation are the two primary lanes on the heroic action pathway of the Counter-Enlightenment. They are the primary ways of experiencing transformation as the will to power through T1 (external transcendence). But there are also two outside lanes that, though squarely on the CE side of the triangle, nevertheless lean toward the Beyonders and the E.Hums, respectively.

The lane that tilts (just slightly) toward the Beyonders is what I'll call the "sickness narrative." The sickness narrative, like trees bending around a building to reach the sun, leans toward the Beyonders but only because they're related to the dying narratives, such as that of Yip-Williams. These dying narratives are squarely in the Beyonder side of the triangle. While bending toward Beyonders, ultimately the sickness memoir is fundamentally different and remains CE. The dying memoir has a haunting moment when the ill memoirist surrenders and accepts death. Death is never conquered; the self is *not* able to overcome death. The self is not magnificent but dying, surrendering, confessing the impossibility of creaturehood. The sickness narrative stays in the CE camp because the person overcomes, willing a victory, rather than surrender. This keeps most sickness memoirs from the pathway of surrender and confession. Rather, the sickness narrative tells a tale of *truly* heroic actions taken to confront and overcome an illness. The memoirists find their power in looking death in the eyes and living, overcoming. They fight fate heroically, and the winning transforms them. The core of their mythical heroism (Nietzsche would smile) is the self-winning magnificence in its bravery in battle.

These sickness memoirs are usually written by a younger person. The two I explored were written by young women. In *Between Two Kingdoms: What Almost Dying Taught Me about Loving*, Suleika Jaouad tells about her life with cancer. She says, "Death never comes at a good time, but getting a death sentence when you're young is a breach of contract with the natural order of things."[9] She now needs to fight to survive. Her heroic task spans 1,500 days, over four years of treatment. It takes everything. To beat cancer, Jaouad must find a heroic power to overcome the loss and to keep surviving. She is in the bleak, harsh kingdom of cancer, fighting to exist while others live. Romance, vocation, and even nature itself are lost. She must find the will to power to survive. She watches many who are sick like her valorously lose the fight. But she wins. Now reentering the kingdom of the living, she needs to find a way to live again. Her victory and pained journey back into life are an experience of T1 transcendence. The sickness now directs her to live magnificently. The sickness, and her ability to overcome, is the impetus for a mystical journey of what it means to live.

The second memoir I explored in the sickness category is *Brain on Fire* by Susannah Cahalan.[10] Cahalan is a young woman on the fast track to success in New York publishing. She's an up-and-coming journalist for the *New York Post*. Then out of nowhere she starts hearing voices and anxiously feels like she can't hold on to reality. Things become worse. Cahalan is not herself in the most frightening of ways. Her personality completely changes, leading to violent outbursts and rude behavior. She moves home with her mom, and joining her estranged father, they together search for a reason. They need to know what is happening to her. There are many confident and assured theories but no answer. Some doctors blame it on her partying, others think it's schizophrenia or bipolar disorder. But none of their treatments work. Each failed diagnosis seems to push her further into madness. There is a mystical search here for knowledge. Cahalan's family yearns for the arcane knowledge that will save them all. They are even willing to pray, taking on mystical practices as she faces risky surgery. Prayer is something that neither of her parents believes in but that they nevertheless race toward.

Finally, the heroic appears. The heroic action is of course partly Cahalan's own. Like Jaouad she heroically survives, overcoming her illness. But the real hero is the mystical guru who brings the true knowledge, unveiling the arcane, delivering the right diagnosis. Dr. Souhel Najjar discovers that Cahalan is suffering from an autoimmune disease. Her affliction is not psychological or spiritual. Her brain is on fire with an infection. It (and only it) is the reason

9. Suleika Jaouad, *Between Two Kingdoms: What Almost Dying Taught Me about Loving* (New York: Bantam, 2021), 189.

10. Susannah Cahalan, *Brain on Fire: My Month of Madness* (New York: Simon & Schuster, 2012).

for her odd behavior. Dr. Najjar's knowledge and treatment saves Cahalan, putting her, like the demoniacs in Matthew 8, into her right mind.

As a journalist, Cahalan begins reporting on her own experience, telling her story. She magnificently describes the journey of sickness and how the heroic will of the doctor, her parents, and of course herself saves her. As a case study for Charles Taylor's description of how sin is eclipsed by sickness in late modernity,[11] Cahalan is led from her experience to assume that all odd spiritual manifestations of seeing visions or demonic possession are nothing more than brain infections.

Ultimately, what both Jaouad and Cahalan do in their memoirs is give sickness dignity. They both give the reader a window into the longings and needs of those who are struck with a debilitating illness. This is wonderful. But within this is a clear assumption that what produces dignity is bound in the self's heroic actions to face the illness. This heroic overcoming is transformational. It's an external transcendence (T1) of survival. The survivor possessing a spirituality of the will. It's a transcendence 1 that meets the limits and tension of life, seeking to heroically overcome them. We particularly celebrate (maybe rightly) the power of the will to survive, confirming its spirituality. As the iconic college basketball coach Jimmy Valvano said as he was battling cancer, "Don't give up, don't ever give up!" This "don't ever give up" is what produces a magnificent self we celebrate. The one who heroically never gives up, never surrenders, becomes transformed. Their heroic will to fight is a kind of spirituality. This is clearly a CE form of mysticism.

4. Exercise

If sickness is one of the outside lanes on the heroic action mystical pathway of the CEs, then exercise is on the opposite side. It's fascinating that both sickness and exercise, though seemingly opposite, share a mystical pathway. Both demand an external will to power that produces a concurrent transcendence (T1). What transforms a self is the external battle with sickness or your personal limits. Exercise possesses a transcendence through the self winning its magnificence by overcoming its once imagined limits. Realizing what you can do, what you can accomplish, is the essence of the experience of T1 on the exercise lane. After a great workout—a limit-traversing session—the exerciser is filled with a (near) spiritual euphoria. Exercise can wash away all

---

11. See Taylor, *Secular Age*, 618–20.

guilt, whether guilt from overeating during the holidays, from an overall loss of focus, or from the feeling of just taking too many losses.

This overcoming of limits as euphoria is also where sickness and exercise differ. Sickness bends slightly toward the Beyonders in its attention to the dignity to accept what you cannot control—that you're sick. Through the will to power you should never give up, but you do have to accept the limits of your sickness. Exercise has no place for this acceptance. You might accept that you'll never be a professional athlete. But all your limits, all your supposed "cannots" *can* be overcome. And when you overcome them it's spiritual. A full spirit and body breakthrough. There is a dual sense of both transcendence 1 (external) and transcendence 2 (internal). It starts with the will to power mobilized to overcome your own mental and physical limitations. When you keep meeting your goals, seeing your body reshaped and grasping health, you feel like you are not only taking (responsible) heroic actions but also reshaping your inner identity, finding your unique genius. Exercise as the will to overcome limits unlocks who you really are. That's powerful! No wonder Nike and Under Armour are worth billions.

Exercise leans heavily toward the E.Hum side as well. Exercise is a unique and powerful cultural construction that seems to shape the inner identity of the self directly through willed exertion. The will to accomplish your exercise goals, to count your miles, and to win your workout (having people applaud this) delivers a sense that your self is magnificent both internally and externally—spirit and body. As the exercise memoirs tell us, exercise mystically unites the two.

It's no wonder that exercising individuals and a whole exercise industry are staples of Western late modernity. Walk through a park in almost any city in the West, and apart from the grass and benches you'll see one recurring thing: people exercising—wrapped in athletic gear, earbuds in, smartwatches blinking. No one, other than children, deliberately ran in a park before the late 1970s and the arrival of neoliberalism. The first runners explain how people in cars would stop and ask them if they were okay. The driver would be confused about what this adult person was running from. The park before the 1980s was for leisure, to escape from industrial work (the very reason most parks were built in big cities in the late nineteenth and early twentieth centuries). Yet, leisure as the purpose for the park has been replaced in a neoliberal epoch by the hurried spiritual exertion of the exerciser. The exerciser in the park wants nothing of leisure. When there is constant guilt, there is no leisure. Rather than leisure, the exerciser is in the park to push to overcome their limits and to feel the rush of being (looking) magnificent.

Not surprisingly, with the arrival of neoliberalism and the performing self, the park shifts from a place to get away from work to a place to work (work out). German historian Jürgen Martschukat has drawn out this larger shift with precision in his fascinating book *The Age of Fitness*. Martschukat explains that "the last half-century may be considered the age of fitness, and it is no accident that this coincides with the age of neoliberalism. . . . Neoliberalism . . . interprets every situation as a competitive struggle and enjoins people to make productive use of their freedom." He continues, "The individual is supposed to work on themselves, have life under control, get fit, ensure their own productive capacity and embody these things in the truest sense of the word."[12]

What gives exercise its spiritual-mystical capacities is not only the euphoria that it can produce but, inside of neoliberalism, a certain form of responsibility it possesses. Exercise is given moral depth by it being the *right* thing to do. It is *your own* responsibility to attend to *your own* health, *your own* magnificence, *your own* constant performance of reaching to be better, preparing to win. Martschukat explains, "Both sides of this coin (the culture of fitness and the fear of fat) revolve around the successful self, which proves its success by mastering its own body."[13]

The mastering of the body becomes every individual's responsibility. There is a responsibility on all of us to do what is right for our self. To take the time to work on our self so that our self is fit to battle for victory, to feel good about who we are, to overcome the guilt with no source, and to move toward our own magnificence. Most exercisers work out alone, for the sake of their individual transcendent (T1 and T2) experience of improvement. Martschukat states, "What those engaged in 'getting fit' generally have in common is that they are active, but rarely organize themselves in clubs or associations. They do not participate in a specific league, and they are never out to win a competition. Yet they all want to improve themselves somehow."[14] The improvement of the self—through the will to empower the self—is a firm lane on the mystical pathway. It is a secular mystical pathway that needs no living God.

---

12. Jürgen Martschukat, *The Age of Fitness* (London: Polity, 2021), 3.
13. Martschukat, *Age of Fitness*, 2.
14. Martschukat, *Age of Fitness*, 1.

The number of exercise memoirs appearing in the twenty-first century, in the height of the neoliberal age of fitness, is legion. Michelle Marchildon offered a deeply mystical memoir in 2012. Its title firmly signals its location inside the neoliberal logic of exercise: *Finding More on the Mat: How I Grew Better, Wiser and Stronger through Yoga*. "Finding" and "wiser" in the title point to the mystical. "More," "grew better," and "stronger" signal the neoliberal drive for performed, willful, and empowering improvement. "Mat" and "yoga" reveal that this mystical journey of improvement is produced through exercise.

She starts the memoir by telling the reader how yoga changed her life by introducing her to grace. The mat is the epicenter of grace. She defines grace by asking the question, "What is grace? And how do we get it?"[15] Trying to "get grace" is an interesting juxtaposition. As she explains it, there is no sense of grace as a gift, as something that is beyond. There is no contention that grace can be tasted only when we surrender and confess. Yet, for Marchildon, grace is clearly found mystically. Even so, it has little content. Grace is a quiet assured peace that happens directly when she practices yoga well. Grace has little direct content, but it does directly impact the self. Yoga gives a feeling of grace that opens her to her own magnificence. She says, "But that is exactly what we need more of in our lives, more contentment with the moment. More acceptance of what is. More recognition for where you are, wherever that is. That is all Grace. It helps to be quiet and listen to find Grace. So before each yoga practice, in fact before each pose, I take a moment to tune in to myself. I use breath to listen up and see how I feel and where I am. I practice [yoga] to find Grace."[16] She speaks of grace as a transcendence. It's not a transcendence that breaks in but a transcendence that is both external (in the exertion of the pose) and internal (in the way it tunes her to her own self).

Another example is Alexandra Heminsley's *Running like a Girl: Notes on Learning to Run*. Heminsley was the last person to imagine she'd be a runner—let alone run multiple marathons. She couldn't even run around the block. The thought of running a 5K was too much for her to contemplate. She wasn't someone who even liked the idea of sweating. Yet within months she was making easy work of 5Ks and soon conquered a marathon.

15. Michelle Berman Marchildon, *Finding More on the Mat: How I Grew Better, Wiser and Stronger through Yoga* (Chino Valley, AZ: Hohm Press, 2012), 33.
16. Marchildon, *Finding More on the Mat*, 33.

This all changed her. And she testifies to that on every page. Every page, in surplus, she proclaims that through conquering the marathon, she changed herself dramatically. It infused her with a power. Heminsley's heroic action to better herself, to obliterate her limits, won her not only an inner feeling of accomplishment but an overwhelming amount of esteem from others. Conquering the marathon, becoming a marathoner, moves her to feel (and look!) magnificent, and leads others to see that magnificence as well:

> Through the summer after my first marathon I was basking in the shimmery golden rays of my victory. At business meetings, at weddings, at Sunday lunches, people who hadn't seen me in a while wanted to catch up on every detail of my impossible feat. How on earth had I managed it? How had I trained? How had I discovered I could do such a thing? I was the Girl Who Did, an inspiration to all! . . . People nodded thoughtfully as I blessed them with my knowledge. . . . The only advice I had for those who said they would never be able to make it farther than 5K was: "You have to decide to. You just have to want to. That was all I had done—I had wanted to."[17]

This is indeed the CE will to power, the heroic action that transforms.[18] It's so transformational to Heminsley that she calls her experience of running a "conversion."[19] Running has so changed her life that she feels the necessity to evangelize others, leading them too into the transcendent transformation of running.[20] She calls running something she believes in. Yet, this belief is not in something beyond but something within the self. It's a way of unearthing the self's own magnificence. She testifies that when she believed that she could run a marathon, when she gave herself over to her drive to heroically and

17. Alexandra Heminsley, *Running like a Girl: Notes on Learning to Run* (New York: Scribner, 2013), 86.

18. Byung-Chul Han connects the will to power and exercise saying, "Nietzsche's 'ultimate man' is remarkably relevant to our present times. 'Health,' which is nowadays considered an absolute value—almost a religion—was already 'respected' by the ultimate man. At the same time, he was also a hedonist." Han, *The Scent of Time: A Philosophical Essay on the Art of Lingering*, trans. Daniel Steuer (London: Polity, 2020), 1.

19. Heminsley, *Running like a Girl*, 128.

20. There is more to say about Heminsley's memoir, but I don't have space. Her tale is an evangelical one in the sense of the zeal for running: her testimony to running's power to transform, her use of running to do good (charity runs), and then her loss of the love of running. Her belief in running at one point is fragilized. But she finds it again by returning to evangelizing. She'd evangelized for running right after her own conversion, but she lost the zeal. In the end, though, she finds it again.

willfully overcome her limit, she was radically transformed, overcoming all inner guilt.[21] And her good news to us all is that we too can be transformed. If only we would reach for a transcendence (T1) through the heroic act of overcoming our limits and run the 26.2 miles.

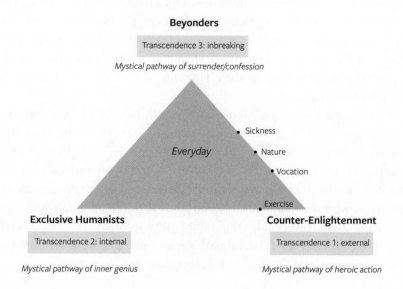

The Pathway of Inner Genius

With the CE mystical pathway of heroic action mapped, we can move across the triangle to Exclusive Humanism. As with the CEs, there are different lanes of transformation that come in the cadence of Exclusive Humanism. The E.Hum mystical pathway is bound to what William Desmond calls transcendence 2 (internal transcendence). Because this transcendence has its source and impetus internally, it is transcendence without the necessity for God. There is mysticism without God here on the E.Hum side as well.

21. Martschukat adds, "There seems to be something heroic about fitness, as is also evident from a glance at lifestyle magazines like *Fit for Fun* or *Men's Health*. But why does the hero exercise such irresistible appeal to fitness aficionados who romp around in gyms or test their limits as runners and recreational cyclists, when we supposedly live in a 'post-heroic society'? For decades, commentators on both sides of the Atlantic have branded heroes passe. Our society, it has been claimed, no longer has any need for heroes, that is to say, combat-ready individuals willing to step up and make sacrifices in order to stretch their limits, render the impossible possible, and thus to become role models demanding emulation." Martschukat, *Age of Fitness*, 106.

E.Hum mysticism follows the pathway of discovered or claimed inner genius of the self. The self's magnificence is claimed or won *not* necessarily by heroic action—as with the CEs—but by discovering the self's most true inner identity. The process becomes spiritual and transformational to the core—overcoming guilt and bringing healing—as the unique inner self expresses and receives recognition for its genius. It becomes mystically genius to find and claim who you really are. Your most true identity is a hidden, mystical city. Where the CE pathway of the mystical, and its several lanes, moves toward the will to power, the lanes of the E.Hum mystical pathway move along the modern moral order.

What makes these mystical memoirs bend toward E.Hum is that their transformation is linked with the embracing of an inner desire. Expressing your truest desire is the purest form of transformation; it unveils your self as magnificent. On the ground of the modern moral order, inside the mutual benefit to be who you really are, transformation is fused with the genuine and genius discovery that unites identity and desire as one. It finds acceptance and affirmation that delivers a dynamic, spiritual transformation. We can name these three lanes of the mystical pathway of inner genius as (1) romance, (2) child-rearing, and (3) the art of discovered talent.

1. Romance

John Glenn was the third American in space and the first American to orbit the earth. He would go on to multiple terms as a US senator from Ohio. He never wrote a memoir. But if he had, it's doubtful that the rational, commonsense Glenn would have said one word about romance. And God forbid that romance itself be soaked in the mystical. Yet, a different John Glynn tells a much different story in his *Out East: Memoir of a Montauk Summer*.[22]

If John Glenn was the quintessential post–World War II Marlboro man, then John Glynn is the archetypal millennial. John Glynn graduated from an elite university. More than any specific learning, Glynn's education taught him how to meet interesting people. Most importantly, it taught him how partying with those interesting people makes them into friends. Accruing friendships is as important as accruing class credits.

For young adults like Glynn, after graduation, those who become interesting friends by partying with interesting friends in college migrate to the

---

22. John Glynn, *Out East: Memoir of a Montauk Summer* (New York: Grand Center, 2019).

mecca of elite interesting young adults: New York City. Parts of Manhattan and Brooklyn become the big leagues of interesting, elite young adults. Those boroughs are where interesting people keep the party going, broadening their friendship networks with more interesting people as they seek their own genius (think the HBO show *Girls*). New York City is the place where the right social life is worth gold, the place where those friendships—not class credits—are cashed in for the good life. Meeting interesting people and deepening existing friendships are the key to living well in millennial New York City. Your elite university degree is the mixer that connects you with the right people.

Glynn is doing very well. So well that, as summer approaches, he's invited to join a share house in Montauk on the Atlantic coast, in the Hamptons, a train ride away from the city. The idea of the share house is simple. The right people are invited to pay in. They are given a schedule of weekends when a room in a big beach house is theirs. The room itself is of little concern because the point is not to sleep but to party until daybreak with all your housemates. The share house is the epicenter of summer social life for these young New Yorkers. It's the place where friendships are deepened and new ones are forged over (many) drinks and (a lot of) gossip. Being invited into the share house is no small accomplishment. Glynn is honored. But not all is right.

There is a malaise (an eating guilt) that Glynn just can't shake. All the friendships with interesting people, the successful social life, are rewarding. But still, something is missing. In some way he's not fulfilled. In some fundamental way he's not found himself. His truest self is escaping him. The anxious, guilty unease comes as a two-headed monster. First, it comes on Sunday evenings as a depressive awakening to the workweek. The partying and proficient friend-making—which is what Glynn and his cohort learned in college—is over, at least for five days. When you live for the weekend, the workweek is hell. Work demands an intense performance of the self, just as the share house does. But it's a performance outside your true education—to party and to mind your social group, building your network. Glynn and his friends call this first strike the "Sunday scaries."

The other head of the monster of malaise and guilt attacks Glynn, even sadly, at the share house itself. Tragically, it strikes while he is partying. He wants to fall in love. He believes he already has, in some small ways. But not with the intensity that could transform him. There have been plenty of girls he's "loved" (or nearly loved) but not with what he calls a "mystical" kind of love.[23] He wants the kind of romantic love that his parents shared. Glynn (again, the archetypal millennial) has a close relationship with and deep respect for his parents. He retells for his readers how his parents fell in love and how steady, sure, and meaningful their romance has been over many decades. That's what Glynn is missing. He longs for the mysticism of romance (he even calls it "mystical"). He longs for the transformation of the self that a true romantic love would surely bring. An intense romance would assure him that his self is magnificent. Glynn is in a malaise that he believes only a mystical romantic love can heal. He's had all these friendships and yet no intense romance—no transformation. He has seen this mystical depth that his parents share, and he longs for it too.

Here is where the modern moral order appears, planting this story of romantic transformation on the E.Hum side of the triangle. To Glynn's surprise, he starts feeling something for someone at the share house. It has an intensity he's never experienced. This is what he's always hoped for. He figured that at some point partying and romance would mix like the ice and vodka in his margaritas. But to his surprise the unquestionable intense desires of allure are for Matt. Glynn has never felt this. He's never felt romantic passion for a man. He is certain that this is the mystical love he has sought. But can he really embrace it? What would his friends, especially his gay friends, think? Most importantly, what would Mike think, one of his closest friends from college and the leader of the share house? Glynn fears that his intense desire for Matt will be interpreted as interloping, as ultimately not authentic. Yet his feelings *are* intense. Without Mike's recognition (and approval), Glynn is not sure he can follow the beckoning of this mystical call of romance. The modern moral order demands mutual equal regard. Glynn should be able to love whomever he desires, but this gets tricky if it offends Mike. If Mike thinks, and therefore rules, it to be inauthentic (and thus offensive), Glynn cannot move forward. Mike is the equivalent of the monastery prior or master who can affirm or resist Glynn's reach for the mystical life.

The central transformational moment in the memoir comes when Glynn tells Mike of his intense desire for Matt. Mike approves! He'll even be Glynn's wingman, helping him share his feelings with Matt. Mike's approval and support within the modern moral order allows Glynn to embrace his truest desire and to find out who he really is, entering the numinous city of his true identity, the mystical place where self-definition and desire merge into one.

In the end, things are up and down with Matt. Matt shares that he too has feelings for Glynn. This could indeed be a mystical romance. But the timing is off. Matt has just entered another relationship. But Glynn has had his breakthrough regardless. He's been transformed; he has embraced his truest desire and thereby found his real identity. He knows who he is and he has received the recognition necessary for it. A romance with Matt might not have taken him as deep into the mystical as he had hoped. But now he is ready, prepared for the journey. Desire and identity have fused, and therefore Glynn knows his self as magnificent. Going forward, Glynn believes he could love a woman. But what Matt taught him is that it would never be as intense as his love for a man—it would never move him to the mystical level he seeks, never fully transubstantiate desire into core identity. The intensity is the key. For romance to deliver the mystical transformation Glynn seeks, it must bear the intensity to wield a transformation. The self must be drawn deep into its passions to bring forth the inner genius. The intensity is transcendence 2. Its origination is fully interior. The experience of desire and the experience of identity become one, an intense internal transcendence. Glynn discovers he's made not for any ordinary love but for the intensity of mystical romance. Mystical romance, Glynn tells his readers, can heal all anxious malaises (all guilts of the self).[24] All you have to do is follow your desires, find some good friends for support, and tell that other person who gives you the intense feelings that no matter who they are, you're into them. Then you'll discover your magnificent self. Intense romance is the place where the everyday bears the mystical depth of transcendence 2.

2. Child-Rearing

There was no reason in conventional times, such as the late 1950s and the days of firm gender roles in the nuclear family, for there to be child-rearing memoirs. Ward and June Cleaver had no need to write about their child-rearing experience. There was little mystical weight to child-rearing in these

24. For theoretical reflections on romance and its deep philosophical and sociological purchase, see Eva Illouz's most recent significant contribution, *The End of Love: A Sociology of Negative Relations* (London: Polity, 2021). See also Illouz, *Why Love Hurts: A Sociological Explanation* (Malden, MA: Polity, 2012); and Illouz, *Consuming the Romantic Utopia: Love and the Cultural Contradictions of Capitalism* (Berkeley: University of California Press, 1997).

conventional epochs (in the medieval period, only those who denied child-rearing could enter the mystical). In conventional times, socialization and enculturation were powerful (even helpful) but not conducive to mystical reflections. There was no reason for any real reflection because there was little sense that child-rearing could interrupt or shift your freedom or desires, could bring a radical shift to your identity. There was little sense in the 1950s, for instance, that child-rearing could impose a contradiction in yourself that the modern moral order and its calls for mutual benefit couldn't resolve.

It's the friction between the assumed conventionality of parenting and the unconventional ways of obeying your inner desire that produces dozens of mystical memoirs of child-rearing in the twenty-first century. The spiritual memoirs of child-rearing are most often written by rebels of conventionality, people who have discovered their inner genius by throwing off the normal. Such memoirs are often written by people who have infused the modern moral order with an unconventionality. Since the late 1960s the modern moral order has turned toward the freedom to be who and what you are. From inside the modern moral order, what's conventional is often assumed to be gross, even violent. Conventionality, then, is an enemy of the modern moral order and its mutual benefit. Conventionality is presumed to attack inner uniqueness and to police desire. Conventionality puts order, patterns, and restrictions on people, which originate somewhere other than those people's own inner magnificent selves and the self's desires.

But what happens when the rebels who reject conventionality (which is all of us, on one level or another) become parents? How do we stay honest to our inner desires and freedoms and yet give ourselves over to our children? How do we balance the recognition that our conventionality is, on some level, good for our children and the feeling that it is repulsively oppressive to us? What do we do with competing desires? With the fact that the last thing we want to become is our parents and yet here we are now a parent? The guilt of being untrue to the self, or being a bad parent, demands a spiritual-mystical way into and through parenting.

Coping with these questions of contradiction demands a mystical guide—a memoirist (who often starts as mommy blogger). Finding a way to raise children without violating the modern moral order and your truest "badass" identity will call for real inner genius. It will require a genuine and magnificent way of attending to the needs of your child without losing your own unique identity; it demands a spirituality. Finding a way through this contradiction, coming out on the other side, is transformational. And the memoirist testifies to how. To be a good parent *and* a magnificent self, the memoirist shows, is an accomplishment of inner genius. It's a profound way of balancing identity and desire. Surviving and thriving inside the contradictions of conventionality and rebel desire (while supporting the modern moral order) requires a spirituality that calls for internal-bound transcendence (T2).

Jenny Lawson's memoir *Let's Pretend This Never Happened* is a good example of this category.[25] Lawson is hilariously edgy. With genius wit, she shares her stumbles and failures as a parent. She is always a bumbling rebel, but in the end a good parent. She owns her failures through edgy, rebel humor such that it ultimately allows her to speak of her successes, but more how she could remain this rebel *and* be a mom. She can do this by embracing an "oh f—k it" attitude. The "oh f—k it" is a humorous and spiritual way of coping with the contradictions of desire. Saying "oh f—k it" allows her self to find transformation in its own inner, edgy genius. It allows her to do the mystical: connect competing desires, uniting them into a single nonconforming identity (she can be both mom and authentic rebel—she can be it all).[26] Transformation occurs as she is able to be a self who stands outside the contradictions by laughing at them. She says "oh f—k it" to both the standards of conventional parenting and the ideals of resisting conventionality. Lawson offers a child-rearing spirituality bound in the self's inner genius that through humor is able to say "oh f—k it" as a form of transcendence (T2), emulating the modern moral order's drive to fully embrace the self's desires.

There are other examples. A much different memoir is Neil Thompson's *Kickflip Boys: A Memoir of Freedom, Rebellion, and the Chaos of Fatherhood*.[27] The subtitle highlights elements of the modern moral order. It's a memoir of freedom and rebellion. The rebellion is dual. Thompson's boys rebel first by falling in love with skateboarding over other (conventional) sports. And second, those boys choose to live all of life in rebellion. Thompson tells heart-wrenching stories of his boys' struggles with school and drugs. But the rebellion is also Thompson's. He rebels against the scripts of the absent, abandoning father. He takes every step to be emotionally present and

25. Jenny Lawson, *Let's Pretend This Never Happened: (A Mostly True Memoir)* (New York: Putnam, 2012).

26. The movie *Where'd You Go, Bernadette* is also a great example of a mom as an authentic rebel.

27. Neil Thompson, *Kickflip Boys: A Memoir of Freedom, Rebellion, and the Chaos of Fatherhood* (New York: HarperCollins, 2019).

supportive, even inside the chaos. He even embraces the chaos as a way of parenting. The chaos becomes its own spirituality. The resolve of his presence is bound in his inner genius to see himself as a father, without pretense but with complete presence, which is transformational. And not just to him but to his boys as well. His inner genius is central to his ability to give up on the conventionalities and the rules that his boys should live under. As a present father, he resists those rules for the sake of being with his kids. Thompson and his boys are transformed by pure acceptance. Acceptance, if you can get to its pure form, delivers transcendence (T2) inside the modern moral order. The inner genius is the resolve of Thompson to just hang on. It's beautiful and mystical. This very resolve transforms him and his boys.

The richest and most groundbreaking child-rearing memoir, in my reading, is undoubtedly Maggie Nelson's *The Argonauts*. Not only is the writing enchanting, but unlike Lawson and Thompson, Nelson is a philosopher. This makes her reflections deep and nuanced. Where Lawson and Thompson are more tacitly committed to the modern moral order, Nelson is explicitly so. For Nelson, there is much riding on the mutual benefit of individual desire and its uniting with identity inside the modern moral order. Therefore, the memoir tells the story of the birth and raising of her son as well as the intense (spiritual) romance that brought her boy into the world. Nelson tells us how she fell in love with the transgender artist and intellectual Harry Dodge.

Nelson writes about her love and decision to have a child as Harry transitions. She explores what it means to carry and birth a boy in a queer family. What does it mean to mother as a queer woman? The conventional and unconventional collide for Nelson. She was once like Glynn, even experiencing the transformation of romance. But she is now pulled somewhere even deeper, somewhere more challenging inside the modern moral order of desire. She's pulled into asking what it means to carry and mother this child. She can't parent this child in any way other than as a queer woman. But that doesn't eliminate the way her pregnancy and parenting connect her to millennia of other conventional mothers, even to her own mother, to other bodies that have borne life and yet knew nothing of her own identity. She explores with depth the thought of Donald Winnicott and Judith Butler, seeking what it means to mother inside her gender-bending reality. Nelson asks about parenting:

> But what about it is the essence of heteronormativity? That my mother made a mug on a boojie service like Snapfish? That we're dearly participating, or

acquiescing into participating, in a long tradition of families being photographed at holiday time in their holiday best? That my mother made me the mug, in part to indicate that she recognizes and accepts my tribe as family? What about my pregnancy—is that inherently heteronormative? Or is the presumed opposition of queerness and procreation (or, to put a finer edge on it, maternity) more a reactionary embrace of how things have shaken down for queers than the mark of some ontological truth? As more queers have kids, will the presumed opposition simply wither away? Will you miss it?[28]

Parenting this child leads Nelson to explore what is normal and what is radical. In the struggle between—in the struggle to parent as part of a long history and yet in a new way inside the embraced desires of the modern moral order—Nelson speaks of transformation. She touches something spiritual in embracing both her desires and the demands to rear this child. She touches something transcendent in herself, ignited to express her inner genius by and through the contradictions that birthing and raising this child brings to the surface. She is her desires, but she is also desiring to raise this boy. How she balances these desires is filled with inner conflict but also transcendence (T2). For Nelson that is enough. It sweeps her into something spiritual. She continues wrestling with conflicting desires and her identity, making them into one. Nelson's inner genius is unveiled. As she embraces the tension, her spirituality is animated and transcendence (T2) is experienced. She allows the tension to feed her own identity by accepting all of her conflicting desires. Nelson is awakened to live fully in the everyday, being both queer and conventional, a mom and so much more. The tension is embraced as a spirituality.

3. The Art of Discovered Talent

Earlier, on the CE side of our triangle, we explored vocation as one lane on the mystical pathway of heroic action, using Marcus Samuelsson's *Yes, Chef* as an example. Samuelsson's memoir is a mysticism of chasing your dreams. Its transcendence (T1) is bound in the will to power to burn your ships and live for your singular goal. Samuelsson's dogged commitment made him into a celebrity chef (the celebrity is a mystical priest in our late-modern neoliberal age of performance; the celebrity is a celebrity because their performance has won attention). If Samuelsson's perspective—vocation as a mysticism

---

28. Maggie Nelson, *The Argonauts* (Minneapolis: Graywolf, 2015), 13.

of heroic action—has an E.Hum frenemy across the triangle, it is the art of discovered talent. This lane is best represented in singer-songwriter Brandi Carlile's memoir *Broken Horses*.[29]

Carlile's wonderful memoir has been well received and lauded by many, particularly by those who tacitly inhabit the E.Hum side of our triangle. This makes sense because Carlile's memoir inhabits all the lanes of inner genius mysticism. She discusses intense romance, a unique discovered sexuality (coming out), and even child-rearing. All of these do their work to usher Carlile into transformation. But never in a flat way. Here the memoir is fully mystical. She speaks of many spiritual, even enchanted, experiences. She writes of miracles she's experienced. Religion itself isn't something discarded or ignored but wrestled with deeply. Throughout the memoir, however, Carlile remains on the E.Hum side. She touches beautifully on all the E.Hum lanes. The ability to highlight all these lanes gives *Broken Horses* its wide reach and impact. Yet, ultimately *Broken Horses* moves on a different lane than the others we've explored on the E.Hum side so far. Carlile walks what is perhaps the primary trail on the E.Hum side: the lane of the art of discovered talent.

Carlile's story, which we pick up at the beginning of her life, is clear. The memoir explains in detail how she doesn't fit (here is the guilt). Even as a child, she knows herself only as mismatched, standing against the flow. Not fitting means something profound: she is without acceptance. This lack of acceptance comes on many levels. Her family is peculiar. They are rural people, never accepted in the growing suburbs of Washington. Their (near) poverty is isolating. Their weird beliefs are ostracizing. Their lifestyle and political ways are not normal. This feeling of not being normal wraps itself around Carlile from her earliest days. She knows that deep in her own self she is atypical. She's a tomboy, a girl who is not girly. A girl who likes girls. This produces more unacceptance. Not only is her family not accepted, and not only are their ways of life odd, but her own budding identity and her deepest desires are unacceptable. Further and deeper goes her *not* fitting. She wonders if even her unaccepted family can accept her now that her deepest desire, and therefore identity, is expressed. She knows her church cannot accept her. The church had been one of the places she learned to sing. But sadly, the church can't, won't, accept her desires that unveil her truest self. Carlile gives us a multidimensional picture of not fitting.

---

29. Brandi Carlile, *Broken Horses* (New York: Crown, 2021).

Inside the commitments of Exclusive Humanism and its modern moral order, this not fitting is a big problem. It violates the mutual benefit for those who cannot fit—particularly if this not fitting is because of their own inner desires. Not fitting is a violence done to the self. Carlile doesn't fit because her desires cannot find union with her self-definition. She cannot find the acceptance of her expressions. Therefore, she is at a loss in seeking acceptance for the magnificence of her self.

Yet, unlike Samuelsson, Carlile finds her way, entering transformation, though not by burning her boats and willing herself to victory. Transformation happens not necessarily through finding her vocation but by finding her art, her unique talent. Something nascent and potent within her changes her; it's not what calls out to her that changes her. This is how she overcomes the guilt of not fitting and finds acceptance. Once you find your magnificence, inner art or talent becomes the fuel that rockets you to the moon. The art of your inner talent can profoundly deliver you from not fitting. Ultimately, Carlile's art opens up her inner talent, transforming her, producing an acceptance first of herself and then from others (even Elton John!).

Tara Westover's *Educated* would also need to be plotted here. Westover's transformation, much like Carlile's, is deliverance from the *not fitting*. The not fitting is overcome by the artful discovery of an inner hidden talent. The disheveled mountain girl unfit for school finds within herself an academic savant. Hidden within the girl who never went to school is a Cambridge scholar. The art of discovered talent radically transforms Westover.

In E.Hum form, and its mystical pathway of inner genius, Carlile and Westover find transcendence (T2) by discovering their unique talent, by staying true to their self, by embracing the art within and slowly but surely letting the small flame of talent grow. Carlile's memoir is clear: She is not just crassly racing for success like Samuelsson. The more she's true to her own voice, to her own inner genius, to her own talent, the more the flame of her talent grows (and yours can too!). Eventually it brings the acceptance (and recognition) your magnificent self deserves.

Carlile finds this acceptance not by the will to power but by more attentively tending to the talent of her inner genius, by finding the artist inside. The expressions of art form the talent of the inner genius, bringing a union between her self and her desires. The art of finding your talent allows for the self to be accepted for its true identity. The art of your unique talent excavates your truest identity. When Carlile accepts her own identity, not only does her art shine

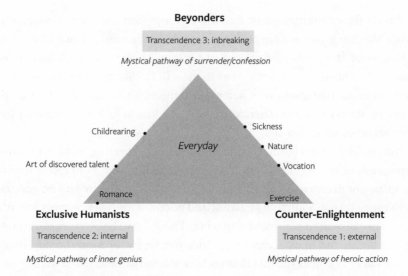

brighter (bringing Grammys) but she also receives the acceptance the modern moral order says she deserves. Like Samuelsson she wins this acceptance by performance. But unlike Samuelsson she wins by tending to her inner genius, not the will to power. When she finds her inner genius, all else falls into place (love, romance, career, even religion—the miracles point to the depth of the art of her talent that was always within). She is transformed; the art of her talent is a doorway into a spirituality of transcendence (T2). The art of her talent produces the acceptance that her self needs to embrace its magnificence.

This appears to me to be the most common lane not only on the E.Hum side of the triangle but maybe overall in late modernity. Inside the everyday drive for performance in neoliberalism, there is a constant invitation to find your self by discovering your talent and to recognize that your talent can be a spirituality if you make that talent into an art. You can be transformed, can be healed from *not fitting*, can find your magnificence, if you can just find the art of your unique talent that will unearth your inner genius. "Find the one thing you're good at," we tell young people as the core neoliberal wisdom. Any talent can become an art.[30] This art can deliver you to a transcendence (T2). All you have to do is find an authentic performance that reaches into your own magnificent inner genius.

30. For much more on this, see Andreas Reckwitz, *The Invention of Creativity: Modern Society and the Culture of the New* (Malden, MA: Polity, 2017); and Andrew Root, *The Church after Innovation: Questioning Our Obsession with Work, Creativity, and Entrepreneurship* (Grand Rapids: Baker Academic, 2022).

The Pathway of Surrender and Confession

It is now time to turn to the mystical pathway less traveled in late modernity. This pathway is much less traveled because it can respond to, but never support, the performative self of neoliberalism. Yet, as we'll see, though less trafficked than the other two pathways (and their seven lanes we've just discussed), this pathway is still walked. And not just by backward religious leftovers but by some very good and insightful memoirists.

It's not an easy path to walk, however. Its lanes, as we'll see, are not as worn and wide, and so they don't support neoliberalism. There are some reasons for this. First, unlike the pathway of heroic action (CE) or the pathway of inner genius (E.Hum), this is a mystical pathway ambled by Beyonders. The term "Beyonder" is a reference *not* just to a metaphysical commitment but to a way of life. The "Beyond" in Beyonder refers to the commitment that life is lived to the fullest or truest when we acknowledge something beyond strictly human flourishing. In our suffering, we might be met by a numinous redemption. And connected to that, there is something beyond death. This something beyond death leads those walking this path to paradoxically attend more directly to death, journeying with it, seeking its mysteries, through its concrete reality as part of everyday life. We'll see this more clearly below as we explore Beyonder memoirs. Like the apostle Paul, all the lanes we will explore on this Beyonder pathway wrestle with some kind of death experience.[31] The shift in what makes up the core struggle on this pathway makes for a much different spirituality. Where the lanes of the other two pathways seek to conquer or to cope with performative guilt, on this pathway the struggle is rather with impossibility, nothingness, and forms of negation.

Which leads us to the second reason this is not an easy path to walk. Ultimately what makes this Beyonder mysticism less traveled is that it's a pathway of surrender and confession. The Beyonder pathway claims that transformation and healing does not come through heroic action or a mined inner genius but through surrender and confession to the impossibility, nothingness, and negation in the self and the world. Surrender and confession keep the beyond bound to the everyday. The Beyonder surrenders to something beyond and seeks an encounter with some kind of inbreaking transcendence. This transcendence is encountered when, up against a death experience, we are led to confess and

---

31. For much more on this, see my *Faith Formation in a Secular Age* (Grand Rapids: Baker Academic, 2017), part 2.

surrender. The confession is that in our sufferings and joys inside the everyday, the everyday itself is unveiled as the place where an inbreaking transcendence arrives. Transformation comes through a profession that "at once I knew I was not magnificent" (to again quote Justin Vernon). The transformation that heals and changes a life is delivered when the self surrenders to its limits and confesses that it has no power within itself (no genius or heroism) to save it from impossibility, nothingness, and all sorts of forms of negation. It's a confession that the transcendence needed to transform a life can have no origin in the self—not in the self's external action (T1 of the heroic) or internal constitution (T2 of inner genius). Rather, the transcendence that transforms a life, the mysticism that brings union with life, is experienced as completely inbreaking. It must be, the Beyonder path contends, because the self is too bound in impossible nothingness to save itself from within its own magnificent performance.

The Beyonder pathway of mysticism as surrender and confession is bound completely in transcendence 3. It's a transcendence that comes from completely outside, meeting a particular self in the self's moment of surrender and confession. When the self surrenders its actions and confesses its unmagnificence, this transcendence (T3), coming from far outside the self, totally foreign to the self, breaks in on the self, transforming and liberating the person—bringing life out of death.

This mystical pathway obviously cannot be walked (or very seldom is) without some sense of a living God. These mystical memoirists come to the realization that the source of transformation, and therefore the reality of transcendence, is beyond. This sense of transcendence (T3) being an outside, inbreaking encounter allows some (or many) to witness a divine agent at work. As Protestantism, particularly in pastoral practice, has dealt with the secular age, it has too often accommodated its own views of transformation with the pathways and lanes we've discussed above (directly or indirectly linking hands with E.Hums and CEs). While not completely without merit, doing so has confused our views of formation and minimized the centrality of divine action (T3). Our pastoral practice has become more shaped by inner genius or heroic action than by the surrender of the cross.

I personally have a great amount of respect for all the lanes of mystical transformation we've explored.[32] But I hope to show that being a Beyonder,

---

32. I sense in all of these pathways some of Hartmut Rosa's concept of resonance, which explores the kinds of actions that connect us deeply with life, leading us away from instrumentality toward a sense of being spoken to by the world. See Hartmut Rosa, *Resonance: A Sociology*

and seeking and leading others onto the mystical pathway of surrender and confession, is the shape of a ministry that attends most fully to divine action (to an encounter with a living God).[33] It's the way into a transformation in the Spirit of the crucified Christ.[34] But before I make this case, turning more directly to my normative commitments, let me continue with a description. Particularly, allow me to lay out, through more memoirs, the specific lanes of surrender and confession.

The examples of memoirs I discuss below, those who walk this path of surrender and confession, are *not* religious apologists. Rather, these memoirs are written by people who are quite the opposite. Some of these people have come to discover the traditions of religion to be helpful (encounters with an inbreaking transcendence and finding transformation within death will do that!). But ultimately these memoirists speak of a transformation that happened when they came to realize that they were "not magnificent." In these moments of confession and surrender they were encountered, finding a union with this inbreaking transcendence (T3) that changed them by the force of something outside them.

I can spot three lanes on the Beyonder mystical pathway of surrender and confession. These lanes are (1) loss, (2) imminent death, and (3) addiction. The first lane, loss, will need to be plotted twice on our map, because there are at least two different mystical events of transformation in such memoirs surrounding loss and the confession of its pain. Inside loss, and the surrender and confession it brings, some memoirists encounter the mystical transcendence 3 of transformation in encounters of friendship and others in nature. Therefore, it's best to list these lanes as (1a) loss and friendship, (1b) loss and nature, (2) imminent death, and (3) addiction.

---

of Our Relationship to the World (Cambridge: Polity, 2019). See also my *The Congregation in a Secular Age: Keeping Sacred Time against the Speed of Modern Life* (Grand Rapids: Baker Academic, 2020) and *Churches and the Crisis of Decline: A Hopeful, Practical Ecclesiology for a Secular Age* (Grand Rapids: Baker Academic, 2022).

33. There are, of course, leadership challenges here. Leading people in such a way is open to possible abuse, a demand that the surrender take the shape of surrendering to the leaders. However, this is a false form of what I'm getting at and building toward; it is the opposition of the Rhineland mysticism I explore below. The leader is called to surrender to something beyond, to humbly confess all motivations to power and performance, the temptation to judge herself by the will to power or by her inner genius. As the leader, she is to lead in the humility of the one given a gift, as a self that is un-magnificent. Abusive leaders assume that *they* are magnificent selfs and their people un-magnificent. Therefore, they must all submit to the leader's magnificence and not get in the way of the leader's performance.

34. Through the cross of the Son, who is sent into the everyday to redeem the world by the love of the Father.

1a. Loss and Friendship

Saeed Jones's *How We Fight for Our Lives: A Memoir* is hard to place, and at times even harder to read. It is beautifully written, honest on every page. But its descriptions of experiences and events are at times very graphic. For the first three-quarters of the book, it appears to be anything but a Beyonder piece. There is little to no confession or surrender. It's hard to even see the mystical. Jones tells the reader story after story of how he came to understand and live out his sexuality. With gritty beauty, he explores what it meant for him to be a big Black boy coming to the realization that he was gay. We're told of Jones's college days and the risky, at times deviant, sexual escapades he partook in.

But the memoir is not ultimately about his inner genius, not about how he came to win acceptance for himself from others. Rather, this is a story about his mother. It's about her stability, love, anger, and commitment. He tells of how a young Black single mother, facing poverty, raised and cared for him with both tenderness and aggression. Their relationship was close, tense, and complicated. There were equal times of tender care and fierce violence. But there was always commitment—Jones to his mother, his mother to him. She has been his life. But intimacy with her, and most particularly with others after her, is difficult for Jones. With others, intimacy is always wrapped up tightly with sex. And sex that is rarely tender and usually violent.

Jones is the furthest thing from a religious apologist, and yet in the last chapters a Beyonder transformation comes upon him. It's the last chapters that push the memoir into the Beyonder part of our triangle. The unmystical or antimystical gives way to the deep profession of a mystical encounter. Jones tells the reader that his mother has died. His own promiscuous sleeping around has gutted him. He's lost, floating above the world. His mother was the gravity that kept him grounded. Her loss frighteningly untethers him. His grief puts him in a vapid zero gravity. He's not sure how to go on without her. How he can return to something solid? He's now floating, aimless, and empty.

His mother's life insurance has put a little money in his pocket. He feels like the best way to honor her is to travel. Feeling like a floating stranger in the world without her, why not become a stranger in Barcelona? He's alone and lonely. That's the way he wants it. Intimacy has been warped for him. It's best to stay to himself. The best way, he figures, to spend this trip of mourning is alone, lonely, in isolation with his grief. Maybe that's what he deserves, he reasons. Maybe the loneliness will be the substance of the rest of his life.

Yet by happenstance he meets Esther at his hostel. She's a wanderer like him, much older than Jones. Esther is a late-middle-aged white woman from Canada. She's nothing like anyone Jones hung out with in college. There is nothing interesting about her at all. But that's just why he agrees to join her in sightseeing. There is no pressure. They can just see Barcelona. But one day trip turns into more. They decide to see other sights together, spending more time together. No agenda, just two lonely people wandering together. They talk, mostly about what they're seeing and exploring day after day.

And then it arrives! Transformation comes through the surrender and confession to a friend. It brings with it an inbreaking transcendence (T3). Jones says, "Our last night together in Barcelona, Esther and I went out to dinner. We ordered tapas and giggled every time she said 'sangrita,' even though she already knew it was called 'sangria.' The café we chose was in an outdoor plaza overlooking the city. In an easy silence, we watched the sunset together."[35]

The giggling, the easy sunset, these are signs of persons in relation, of life together beyond performance. It's the hidden power of just being together. Jones has not experienced much of this in his life. The power of this weak but sure moment of togetherness, of human person related to human person, moves him.

The free friendship brings to the surface a confession. The confession, surprisingly, is a vulnerable surrender to another. With the giggles still rattling gently in Jones's chest and the easy silence still lapping into his being, Jones enters deeply into confession. The friendship brings it to the surface. Jones is now ready to surrender to his brokenness, to admit his un-magnificence and his need for a friend, for otherness. Inside the gift of Esther's friendship, Jones says to her what he hadn't been able to say to anyone, not even to himself. He confesses, saying to Esther, "My mother died in May. That's why I'm here."[36] These two short sentences say so much. Jones's sunset confession is that he is broken and lost, running and scared. The loss of the complicated relationship with his mother, and the experience of nothingness and impossibility it brings, cannot be conquered; it must be confessed. He tells Esther that his mother, the great she in his life, is dead. And he is broken and lost.

35. Saeed Jones, *How We Fight for Our Lives: A Memoir* (New York: Simon & Schuster, 2019), 190.

36. Jones, *How We Fight for Our Lives*, 190.

Esther responds not with performative advice but, profoundly, with the ministry of her own confession, "My mother died this year too."[37] She tells Jones that she too is broken and lost. They hold each other's confessions. They share them and bear them together. They hold each other's hands. They admit to each other that their selves are not magnificent but broken, lonely, and grieving.

This mutual confession draws them beyond into the transformation of transcendence 3. The mutual confession leads Jones to where he hasn't been throughout the memoir, into the mystical. He ponders inside this mutual confession whether there might have been some knowing, some spirit that connected them from the start. Something drew them to each other. Did some providence bring them together? He says, "I wonder if we had, in some way, always known that we had this in common."[38] The togetherness of a common surrender to loss and its confession to a friend brings union, communion, and transformation. From far outside Jones's self he is met by otherness, by inbreaking transcendence (T3) born in the relations with a stranger-made-friend. The mutual confession is the force that births new life, leading his being into rest.

Jones testifies to this, saying, "Holding hands across the table," a kind of intimacy he's almost never experienced, "we took turns letting the words pour out of us." The mutual confessions continue, solidifying transformation. Jones testifies, "It was overwhelming, describing the women we missed so much. Words coming home like waves. It was freeing to just say it. Our mothers are why we are here."[39] We could equate this "freeing" with a transformation, coming about because they were just able to "say it," to confess the un-magnificence of the lostness. Their mothers are why they both live and why they both grieve. Together, in that shared grief of confessed suffering, the two friends are the reason that the other has experienced a transforming encounter.

1b. Loss and Nature

For Jones, the words of a confession of loss and the surrender of that loss to a friend came as a blessed wave. The words were the wave of mercy. Sonali

37. Jones, *How We Fight for Our Lives*, 190.
38. Jones, *How We Fight for Our Lives*, 190.
39. Jones, *How We Fight for Our Lives*, 190.

Deraniyagala also experienced a wave, but it had no mercy. When this wave crashed it brought only hell and devastating loss. In *Wave: A Memoir of Life after the Tsunami*, Deraniyagala tells the haunting story of returning home to Sri Lanka for Christmas 2004.[40] She lives in England with her young family. It has become their tradition to return to Sri Lanka for the holidays. She loves her home country. And she loves watching her young children, both under ten, play so lovingly with her parents.

It's become tradition on Christmas Day to go to the coast and stay in a resort right on the water. Deraniyagala, her husband, and their children stay in one unit. Her parents in another. Both units have ocean views. Boxing Day on the beach promises the giggles and the sunset that Jones experienced with Esther. There is no indication it won't happen. The sky is a stunning clear blue. The day, as it awakens, has an easy feel to it. But then strangely the water recedes. It remains out for minutes. Deraniyagala calls her husband to look at it from the balcony. They stare as the water starts coming back in. And then further in. It's closer to the building than they've ever seen. Now it's in the bottom floor. They grab their children and run. They try to escape in a car. But the water overtakes the car like a sugar cube in hot tea. The wave comes between Deraniyagala and her children. As the car flips, she can't hold them. She can't hold on to anything. She's washed away. So are her children, her husband, her parents. All of them. Somehow she finds a grip, grabbing a tree branch that unfathomably holds.

The wave is no miracle to Deraniyagala. It's a cruel hell. After days of searching, days of refusing to think the worst, it proves to be the worst. They're all dead. She is alone. Alive, but without them. Parents gone, husband gone, two small children—tearing her to the core—gone. Living with such loss, she's sure, is far worse than dying. When the doctor prescribes her an antibiotic for an infection caused by the trauma of the wave, she wonders, what's the point, I'm going to kill myself anyhow. The grief is a sinister wave that never stops crashing, pinning her to its rough, jagged bottom with no release. The grief is more merciless than the wave.

The rest of the memoir, chapter after chapter, paints the pain of loss. The guilt of living is so penetrating. Everything is haunted. Years later, she returns to their house in England, seeing Vik's (her oldest son's) friends, who have grown older. Vik never did. The wave washed away all futures for

---

40. Sonali Deraniyagala, *Wave: A Memoir of Life after the Tsunami* (New York: Knopf, 2013).

Deraniyagala. Yet she still lives. The guilt of living, the guilt of feeling joy or hope, embracing any future, with the thought that Vik would now be nearly fifteen, is too much to face.

The transformation comes in the final chapters. Deraniyagala is back in Sri Lanka years later. The ocean still taunts her. She hates it. She's barely able to look at it. It just takes and takes, and then takes some more. Her self is anything but magnificent; it is only grief-stricken and lost. She's exhausted from running and running from the grief of this death experience.

By chance, against her better judgment, she finds herself on a boat to go whale watching, in the ocean she hates. She agrees to go, but she knows she won't enjoy it. Like so many other experiences since the wave, she'll be present but not there. How could she enjoy watching blue whales? Vik loved blue whales, the huge gentle giants of the sea. Together they watched shows about them. It should be Vik, not her, on this boat. These waters should have taken her, *not* him. She anticipates that when she sees the first whale she'll need to shut down or be destroyed by the grief.

But as the first whale surfaces, it arrives with a transcendence, breaking the surface of the water, inbreaking on her very grief. Out of the belly of the hated ocean comes the beauty of the whale, beckoning her to be here, to stay, to confess her grief, to live. The beauty of the whale compels her to confess to the world, to the one who holds the world, to her broken self, that she misses Vik, that Vik should be alive but that instead she is alive, that her own self is so immensely broken. Confessing this grief allows her to be there, to be overtaken, embraced by the beauty, reminding her again, for the first time since the wave, that being alive is a gift. She surrenders to her grief. She surrenders to the beauty of the world where oceans can bring death and new life. Deraniyagala encounters something outside her, an inbreaking transcendence (T3), that transforms her by calling her to confess and surrender to her grief, to seek life in the loss and negation. The confession, her ability to not depart from her grief but instead face it, opens her to the reality that she is being reached for. Her confession, against the backdrop of beauty, helps her see that not around or beside but through the grief of loss comes promise. She discovers that when she confesses, something far outside her encounters her, ministering to her. The beauty of nature calls her to confess her loss.[41] The

---

41. Another memoir that moves on the lane of loss and nature is Helen MacDonald's *H Is for Hawk* (New York: Grove Press, 2016), the tale of how training a hawk allows MacDonald to cope with the grief of losing her father.

beauty of nature is the catalyst that opens her to a confession that meets her with transcendence (T3). The grief met by the beauty opens her to a Beyonder transformation.

2. Imminent Death

Above we saw that one of the lanes in the CE heroic action pathway was the sickness narrative. Core to these articulations is the truly brave act to "never give up." These sickness narratives are similar to the imminent-death narratives I want to explore now. Though they are similar, there is a stark difference. The sickness narrative is a form of CE heroic action because the one sick, through the will to power, overcomes. That's wonderful, and it's what anyone sick should wish for. But this overcoming keeps the sickness narrative from taking the mystical pathway of the Beyonders.

What makes the imminent-death memoirs so different from the sickness narratives is that, in the former, the sick person surrenders. They enter death. They stop fighting it. For a while, their story might look like a sickness narrative. They followed Jimmy V and tried to "never give up." But what is captivating, offering a much different shape of transformation, is that in imminent-death memoirs the one sick eventually does give up. They surrender, confessing a lack of a magnificent will to overcome. With this confession of surrender, they witness to a transcendence 3 and prepare to die. This bravery in surrendering to death is not bound in the will to power but the hope that what is left behind—children, spouses, parents, siblings—will be touched by mercy and love. There is indeed something more important than their own self (which is the opposite of the performing self of neoliberalism). Ultimately, they awaken to something beyond that reaches out to them, loving them and seeing them through. The hope and promise is that in the confession of weakness (a beautiful un-magnificence of being a creature who dies), those loved ones will be infused with life, with a connection, that is sure, though grieved.[42]

We can see this pattern clearly in Paul Kalanithi's *When Breath Becomes Air*.[43] Kalanithi, a neurosurgeon with lung cancer, is transformed by his imminent

---

42. Byung-Chul Han says prophetically, "A life without death, which is what capitalism strives to achieve, is what is truly deadly. Performance zombies, fitness zombies, and Botox zombies: these are manifestations of undead life. The undead lack any vitality. Only life that incorporates death is truly alive." Han, *Capitalism and the Death Drive*, trans. Daniel Steuer (London: Polity, 2021), 9.

43. Paul Kalanithi, *When Breath Becomes Air* (New York: Random House, 2016).

death. The top student, the high-achieving young doctor who has it all (the art of the talent, the know-how, the will to power) must confess that he is dying, that he is not magnificent but contingent and frail. His awareness to his dying humanity gives him openness, like never before, to the humanity of his patients. Facing his death, surrendering to its presence, meeting its negation, he's taken for the first time into the mystical, seeking to share in his patients' negations for the sake of union and love, not just pure solutions.

His new openness to the mystical does even more. It leads him to his own longing to have, hold, and love a child. As he dies, he's able to hold his own baby, seeing her in the world as he's leaving it. He confesses his love for her and surrenders to his death and to his absence. His letter to her as he dies is soaked in a transcendence (T3) that is bound in confession and surrender, in the facing of death. Kalanithi speaks to his daughter of the pain of not being with her, not able to witness her growth. But he also tells her of the incredible ministry she provided him as he died. Their love and connection, so short, was nevertheless transformational and mystical. It was a doorway into something beyond, a gift so radiant it just must live on beyond his death. Their love and connection wraps him tightly with the warmth of transcendence, transforming him completely as he dies. He dies fully in the union of their love. This is a fullness beyond simple human flourishing, beyond death itself. The profound passivity of their connection, the spirit of their short life together, is a deep witness to the beyond.

We've already referenced Julie Yip-Williams's *The Unwinding of the Miracle: A Memoir of Life, Death, and Everything That Comes After*. As the title and subtitle indicate, Yip-Williams, even more than Kalanithi, enters discussions of the mystical. She explores the miracle of her life as she dies of colon cancer. Life itself is the winding and unwinding of a miracle. The subtitle directly points to the beyond. Struck with cancer, with two young girls, Yip-Williams reflects in the memoir on her whole life. Confession and surrender have been part of it from the beginning. As she tells her story, it could easily be read as heroic action, maybe even the discovery of an inner genius. She's overcome much. Born legally blind in South Vietnam, she graduated from Harvard Law School and traveled the world (by herself). But for Yip-Williams, these were not performances of her magnificent self, but miracles. Traveling, particularly by herself, was a pilgrimage, a way to pray. Praying was something she had done since childhood. She cried to God. She told, confessed, to God (T3) as a child that she would surrender to God's will if God gave her love.

Now living inside that love, caring for her husband and two children, she prepares to leave them. They are the fulfillment of the miracle, of a life that reached far beyond simple flourishing. Her death is now the unwinding. But even in its unwinding there is a miracle. She surrenders again, asking God to care for her family. She receives assurance that in her loss they will live, that they will live as she has, out of the miracle of life, out of the Beyonder commitments that life is so much more than achievement. She was woven into life by the miracle of birth, and as it unwinds into her death, it remains just as much a miracle. For she knows that in the care given and received—in the gift of life itself—she and her children have been transformed. She asks them each to face her death, to surrender to it, to enter it. She is sure that they will also find the miracle that in surrender and confession of impossibility comes transformation. We can hear this all so beautifully in Yip-Williams's words to her children:

> My sweet babies, I do not have the answer to the question of why, at least not now and not in this life. But I do know that there is incredible value in pain and suffering, if you allow yourself to experience it, to cry, to feel sorrow and grief, to hurt. Walk through the fire and you will emerge on the other end, whole and stronger. I promise. You will ultimately find truth and beauty and wisdom and peace. You will understand that nothing lasts forever, not pain, or joy. You will understand that joy cannot exist without sadness. Relief cannot exist without pain. Compassion cannot exist without cruelty. Courage cannot exist without fear. Hope cannot exist without despair. Wisdom cannot exist without suffering. Gratitude cannot exist without deprivation. Paradoxes abound in this life. Living is an exercise in navigating within them.[44]

3. Addiction

Leslie Jamison's memoir *The Recovering: Intoxication and Its Aftermath* resembles John Glynn's *Out East* (which we discussed as an example of the romance lane of the E.Hum pathway). Jamison and Glynn could have been college friends, drinking together. For both, life is about the party. For both, the context begins at elite universities, where their first degree is in drinking. The difference is that Jamison sticks around these elite universities for a second degree. And gets new drinking partners along the way.

---

44. Julie Yip-Williams, *The Unwinding of the Miracle: A Memoir of Life, Death, and Everything That Comes After* (New York: Random House, 2019), 8.

Jamison begins graduate work in literature. She even makes it into the renowned Iowa Writers' Workshop, in which David Foster Wallace was both a
student and teacher. Jamison's specific research focuses particularly on those
authors championed by David Foster Wallace in the YouTube interview I
watched while jet-lagged in Tokyo. She notices that all of them drink. All the
best students at the Iowa Writers' Workshop drink hard. She's determined
to keep up. The best writers are drunks, she believes. Long before Iowa and
her studies, addiction was part of Jamison's life. While in high school and as
an undergrad she struggled with anorexia. As her graduate studies took off,
she traded all this for alcohol. She's a writer after all! As a budding writer,
she supposes booze must become an essential instrument. For the edgy, ironic
writers Jamison admires, alcohol is as essential as their typewriter. Many of
them believed drinking to be indispensable to their writing. Jamison's research
shows otherwise. But her own drinking affirms her place with them.

Soon her drinking is overcoming her life. Some form of addiction always
has, whether eating, not eating, or drinking hard. Like the authors she admires, she thinks that drinking is the way to follow desire, to unearth your
inner genius and get it on the page. Drinking *a lot* is even a heroic act that
produces crazed experiences worth writing about in the first place. Drinking
is the sacramental accoutrement to unleash the inner genius through heroic
(drunken) action. But it's destroying her! It is an empty pathway. The spirituality of drink that births inner talent is a lie.

She eventually loses everything. Romances crash and burn, opportunities
are dashed, her own ambitions become diluted. She is a bad drunk, a full-on
alcoholic. Like David Foster Wallace before her, she goes to AA. It begins a
back-and-forth, sober-to-drunk cycle on repeat. She needs to get sober, but
she also wears her drinking like a robe. It's what interesting writers do. Even
when they go to AA, they write about AA, outsmarting AA, voyeuristically
gathering stories.

At one point at AA, Jamison stands to tell her story. She knows she needs
sobriety. But she takes pride that her heroes, like her, were drunks. Drunken-
ness gives her good stories and the ability to tell them. Yet, when she stands
to tell her story, performing it for the listeners, a man in the back, a fellow
addict, shouts, "This is boring!"

It shakes Jamison. She realizes he's right! The man's confession (it wasn't
an outburst as much as an uncomfortable confession) unveils that she is
not confessing but performing. His confession that her story is no confes-

sion reveals that drinking has no magnificence. Jamison's drunk self is not magnificently interesting and talented. Through the man's confession, she must surrender to the truth that she is lost. She is in need of transformation that cannot come from her will to power or her heroic action or her inner genius. She must confess that she is lost, that she is an alcoholic. She must surrender to a higher power outside of her. The man's comment ("This is boring!") becomes the confession that leads her to see at once that she is "not magnificent."

The confession is met by surrender when she's told by an AA member that she must learn to pray. AA is a hall of late-modern mystics of surrender and confession, our late-modern monastery of constant prayer. We overlook these mystics because of the bias of the neoliberal age of performance. But they stand before us as witnesses that the performing self is a lie. Life and transformation come only by giving ourselves over to something beyond us through confession and surrender. The members of AA pray as the confession of un-magnificence and the surrender to a God (higher power) who is other, able to bring transformation out of death and chaos (transcendence 3).

Jamison resists this advice. She doesn't believe in any of this stuff. But the addict-mystics of the Beyonder pathway, living in the musty church basements, pounding black coffee and chain smoking, tell her to do it anyway. She's told to just walk the path, to pray, to become a mystic. She's told not to worry about what she believes but to just confess, surrender, and pray. She does so, awkwardly. And it transforms her.

She says, "This ruptured syllogism—if I understand myself, I'll get better—made me question the way I'd come to worship self-awareness itself, a brand of secular humanism: Know thyself and act accordingly. What if you reversed this? Act, and know thyself differently. Showing up for a meeting, for a ritual, for a conversation—this was an act that could be true no matter what you felt as you were doing it. Doing something without knowing if you believed it—that was proof of sincerity, rather than its absence."[45] "Sincerity" was the word David Foster Wallace used in those interviews. He called for a turn to the gritty sincere, seeing it so starkly and beautifully in those in recovery. But this sincerity has turned and bitten us because we've missed that sincerity must be bound not to our inner genius identities and heroic actions but to

45. Leslie Jamison, *The Recovering: Intoxication and Its Aftermath* (New York: Back Bay Books, 2018), 303.

our confession of un-magnificence and our need for something beyond. Only this kind of sincerity can create humility.

As surrender, Jamison prays. "I didn't know what I believed, and prayed anyway. I . . . got down on my knees to pray even though I wasn't sure what I was praying to, only what I was praying for: don't drink, don't drink, don't drink." And here comes the Beyonder confession: "The desire to believe that there was something out there, something that wasn't me, that could make not drinking seem like anything other than punishment—this desire was strong enough to dissolve the rigid border I'd drawn between faith and its absence. When I looked back on my early days in church, I started to realize how silly it had been to think that I'd had a monopoly on doubt, or that wanting faith was so categorically different from having it."[46] This is the sincerity of confession.

Mary Karr's *Lit* shares much in common with Jamison's *The Recovering*. In my mind Karr's *Lit* is the very top of the genre.[47] It is the most articulate description of the lane of addiction on the mystical pathway of surrender and confession (I wish I could give it the full chapter it deserves).

Karr is also a writer, though she is almost three decades older than Jamison. Karr actually met David Foster Wallace before he had become well-known. Karr met Wallace when he was just out of treatment for addiction. He tells her he's writing a novel that surrounds addiction (it will become the most important novel of the 1990s, *Infinite Jest*). Karr thinks it sounds dumb. At first, Karr finds Wallace too earnest and sincere, too pretentious for her liking. But when Karr relocates to Syracuse, Wallace follows. They fall in love and live together. These are some of the happiest years of Wallace's short, tortured life.

Yet in the years after Wallace leaves and their relationship comes undone, Karr's drinking gets out of control. She had always drunk too much. But now it's overcoming her. Her son is growing. Sadly, she has to confess that she's not sure if she's as committed to him as she is to drinking. His presence causes her to confess, to surrender, to sacrifice. She begins going to AA meetings. But she has no patience for this higher power thing. She enters detox. It's intense. She contemplates killing herself. Instead, as a last resort she decides to pray. Like Jamison, she doesn't believe, but she needs to pray.

46. Jamison, *The Recovering*, 303.
47. Mary Karr, *Lit: A Memoir* (New York: Harper, 2009).

She prays as the confession of surrender,[48] the confession that her self is not magnificent and needs an outside power to save her. In a hospital bathroom, in that desert place of death and darkness, God meets her in sheer silence. A transcendence 3 breaks into that moment and transforms her, placing her on the pathway of new life. A new life of prayer.

She prays as confession and surrender. Confession and surrender bring forth a transformation through a transcendence 3. But still, she's not sure she believes anything formally. She's not the religious type, she keeps telling herself. One day her son asks if they can go to church. She reluctantly agrees. In the liturgy of a small Catholic church, she hears and sees what she's known—that the way of confession and surrender through prayer brings forth transformation from beyond. In prayers of surrender she searches for a God she's not sure she believes in. Karr is ushered deeper by learning to pray with others, by praying with a priest, by being baptized.[49] Ironically, Karr, the deep-drinking unbeliever, joins the church, is baptized, and studies the Christian tradition. Karr is sincere, and the object of her sincerity is not her self but what is beyond. This gives her sincerity (and writing) a beautiful and humorous irony. It is veracity in sincere irony of confession and surrender. The sincerity is in the confession; the irony is in the surrender. Ultimately,

---

48. Karr says,
   But what if I don't believe in God? It's like they've sat me in front of a mannequin and said, Fall in love with him. You can't will feeling. What Jack says issues from some still, true place that could not be extinguished by all the schizophrenia his genetic code could muster. It sounds something like this:
   Get on your knees and find some quiet space inside yourself, a little sunshine right about here. Jack holds his hands in a ball shape about midchest, saying, Let go. *Surrender, Dorothy*, the witch wrote in the sky. *Surrender, Mary.*
   I want to surrender but have no idea what that means. He goes on with a level gaze and a steady tone: Yield up what scares you. Yield up what makes you want to scream and cry. Enter into that quiet. It's a cathedral. It's an empty football stadium with all the lights on. And pray to be an instrument of peace. 'Where there is hatred, let me sow love; where there is conflict, pardon; where there is doubt, faith; where there is despair, hope' . . .
   What if I get no answer there?
   If God hasn't spoken, do nothing. Fulfill the contract you entered into at the box factory, amen. Make the containers you promised to tape and staple. Go quietly and shine. Wait. Those not impelled to act must remain in the cathedral. Don't be lonely. I get so lonely sometimes, I could put a box on my head and mail myself to a stranger. But I have to go to a meeting and make the chairs circle perfect. (Karr, *Lit*, 234)

49. For a wonderful theoretical reflection on the kind of transformation that Karr experiences, see James K. A. Smith, "Continental Philosophy of Religion: Prescriptions for a Healthy Subdiscipline," in *The Nicene Option: An Incarnational Phenomenology* (Waco: Baylor University Press, 2021), 53–62.

Karr joins the long mystical pathway that centered on prayers of confession and surrender. It transforms her. The confession that all performances cannot save gives her a fullness in the beyond. The encounter in the confession is frighteningly other, but a sure beckoning into life.

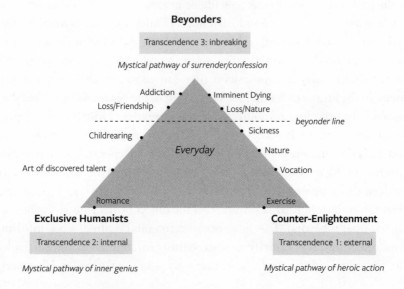

Dipping into the Normative to Conclude

We've now come to the completion of our map. It is just a map. There are details (maybe even whole lanes) missing. But coming to the capacity of my imagination and the reader's patience, we can see these eleven lanes of late-modern mysticism. These eleven lanes are laid on three different pathways. The Counter-Enlightenment pathway is constructed from the will to power, which is built around heroic action. The lanes on this pathway (which *sometimes* lean toward E.Hums or Beyonders) are nature, vocation, sickness, and exercise. Building within the stone of the modern moral order (and its mutual regard), Exclusive Humanists forge a spirituality and therefore a mystical path of inner genius. The lanes on this pathway are romance, child-rearing, and the art of discovered talent.

All these lanes of the CEs and E.Hums, I contend, are secular mysticisms or spiritualities. By "secular," I mean these are spiritual mysticisms that see no need in articulating—and therefore have little concern for or interest in—a living God. There is a transcendence (or spirituality) to them, but it is bound to the self. The self overcomes its performative guilt with little to no inbreaking of a divine reality. This transcendence has its source in the self and not in the event of an encounter with the living God.

True, some of these specific lanes at times have been part of a central commitment to life with God. For instance, once upon a time, child-rearing and vocation—particularly in the Lutheran imagination—were central pathways to walk before and with God. But such pathways have been overtaken by the neoliberal logic of a performing self. These lanes have been transposed onto very different mystical pathways, with very different anthropologies and views of transcendence. Until these differences are confronted directly, it won't matter how badly pastors, denominations, and foundations want to return to the importance of, say, vocation. Such efforts will continue to be short-circuited, as the voltage of a Beyonder desire gets mixed with CE forms of action and E.Hum views of the self. Until these realities are directly confronted, vocation will continually be caught in a CE frame of heroic action inside the will to power.

What makes it so difficult to confront (even to see) this cross-contamination is the triangle itself. In late modernity our own imaginaries are always shifting between two sides that are pitted against the other. We're always sliding around within the triangle. It's very difficult to even discuss vocation without sliding in and out of commitments to heroic action and inner genius, rarely keeping our attention on confession and surrender. It's difficult ultimately to be formed into a Beyonder. And yet there is no way to mine the depth of vocation for, say, Luther without walking the Beyonder pathway of surrender and confession. It is only after the confession and surrender of the cross and its justifying work that vocation can be inhabited by divine action, becoming the concrete shape of formation.

Therefore, I've tried to show how different the Beyonder pathway of surrender and confession is from the other two. Its difference is its confession that the self is not magnificent. In the self's confessed un-magnificence, an encounter with an inbreaking transcendence is found. Transformation on this pathway is in the shape of the cross. We can see this concretely in the lanes of loss, imminent death, and addiction. In confession of loss, death, and impossibility, the Spirit of life moves, taking what is dead and bringing forth new possibility. Transformation comes through the surrender to something beyond that inbreaks. Such transformation is very important for the pastor and Christian ministry. The objective of ministry should be to form people into Beyonders by the pathway of surrender and confession (not through triumphalist religious battles in a culture war).

While respecting all the lanes and pathways of mysticism discussed above, I believe that only surrender and confession can attend to such divine action as ministry calls for in late modernity. The pastor and minister is to call her people to walk this pathway as Beyonders. To understand transformation as bearing the shape of confession and surrender, I contend that confession and surrender must have priority over all the other pathways and views of mysticism. All mysticisms must be ordered under, even judged by, the Beyonder way. Transcendence 3 must have priority over transcendence 1 and 2. Ministry, if it's to include transformation in and by the Spirit, must be in some way shaped by surrender and confession.[50]

My task in the rest of this project is to show why and how. Particularly, how surrender and confession take us into encounters with divine action (making us Beyonders), shaping us for transcendence 3 and leading us into deep forms of transformation. Inside late modernity, next to the modern moral order and the will to power, this assertion that confession and surrender are normative will be met with skeptical concern. The concern is twofold. On the one hand, surrender and confession seem dangerous. They appear to risk the humanity of the self (indeed, they are a risk to the self but *never* to our humanity, as I will show). On the other hand, though we've explored examples above, it is hard to clearly articulate how surrender and confession lead to an encounter with God, shaping us as Beyonders. Jamison and Karr could only point to their practice of prayer. That might actually be enough. A pastor or minister who teaches her people to pray is directly forming her people. Both Jamison and Karr made it clear that prayer as surrender and confession transformed their life. It will be my task to show more intricately *why* and *how* prayer and other events of confession and surrender connect us to the life of the living God.

---

50. Benjamin Myers, in reference to Rowan Williams's theology, says, "In the same way, Williams thinks that it is often our failures that bring us closest to the well of life. It is often only in failure that the ego is dethroned and decentred: at last we are drawn out of ourselves, set free to locate the real source of our being in Christ. His power is made perfect in weakness. 'Those parts of our own individual experience that seem least pious or "together,"' Williams says, 'may be the points at which we are exposed to God, and so the points from which we most truly come to live in Christ.' It is here, in the most vulnerable and difficult dimensions of our experience, that God's kenotic omnipotence is most deeply and secretly at work." Myers, *Christ the Stranger: The Theology of Rowan Williams* (Edinburgh: T&T Clark, 2012), 80.

To address these two concerns, I'll need to enter a process of retrieval. I'll return us to two historical mystical schools. We'll examine Pseudo-Dionysius the Areopagite (Denys) from the fifth century and the Rhineland mystics (Meister Eckhart, Johannes Tauler) of the fourteenth century (as well as Martin Luther through them). To prevent us from getting lost in our retrieval, and to keep our Beyonder desires bound in the everyday (wrestling with modernity), I'll weigh the visions of these premodern mystics against the most important Beyonder thinker of the everyday in modernity—the Jewish philosopher-theologian Franz Rosenzweig (whom we met in chap. 4).

I am aware that retrieval will not be enough. For us late-modern people, seeing the long tail of the tradition, recognizing the ancient mystical pathway of surrender and confession, is not enough to convince us of anything (it might even create more skepticism). Therefore, before we can begin this retrieval, I must take another step and show you why the pathways of inner genius and heroic action are inherently flawed. While we can respect the lanes of these pathways and see how they can blunt some of the guilt of late modernity, they can only help us cope and can never free us from the performative self and the drives of neoliberalism. To show why the pathways of inner genius and heroic action cannot deliver, I'll turn first to a very different thinker from Denys, the Rhinelanders/Luther, and Rosenzweig. I'll explore the thought of the contemporary Korean-German philosopher Byung-Chul Han. Han, better than anyone, has unmasked the problems with our performative neoliberal age. His challenges to our epoch will make my retrieval both clearer and more germane.

7

Why Not All Mysticisms Are Equal

Welcome to a Smooth, Pornographic World
Obsessed with Action

The anchor city in our double summer trip to Europe in 2021 is Berlin. We came to Europe twice this summer to visit Berlin. From Berlin, we'll visit Prague, Paris, and Madrid. We traveled here once in early summer, right after the lockdowns were lifted, to film segments for a video curriculum on Bonhoeffer. We're back in August so that I can teach a class on Bonhoeffer at the historic Bonhoeffer House. We love Berlin. Tokens of the Ampelmann—the traffic light mascot of (East) Berlin—litter our house. Unfortunately, on this trip, we haven't found an Airbnb that works for us in this great city.

In 2018 we stayed in Grunewald, the forested outer area of Berlin. The place was perfect, but the location wasn't. It was closer to Potsdam than to Charlottenburg, City West, and the heart of Berlin we love to walk. As lame as it sounds, we've chosen the Hampton by Hilton as our place for these stays in Berlin. It's perfectly located just a block from the Sovereign Platz S-Bahn station, which takes me to the Bonhoeffer House and takes my family anywhere they wish. We stay at the Hampton West twice in the summer of 2021.

To cope with the convenient but dulling ease of hotel chain life, we decide to visit one of Berlin's weekend markets. Right beyond a Bahn station, just outside the Tiergarten, is a stretch of tables full of wares for sale. Mostly old beer steins, dishes, books, and records. We slowly stroll around. The history of Berlin gives this late-nineteenth and early-twentieth-century stuff a certain gravitas. It was being used during the wars, sitting in someone's cabinet when the wall went up and then came down. We each end up buying something. It seems like a much better souvenir than another Ampelmann sticker. Kara and I find a beautiful old hand-crank coffee grinder from the midcentury, perhaps earlier. It still has some old grounds in the bottom. It hangs in our kitchen now, reminding us daily of Berlin.

As we walk back to the Hampton, our backpacks filled with flea-market treasures, we happen to run into a building that reads Universität der Künste Berlin (Berlin University of the Arts). Byung-Chul Han teaches here. Inside these walls, students have heard the mysterious professor from South Korea speak of the perils of neoliberalism's digital obsessions. Art students smitten with design, technology, innovation, and performance have listened here to Han's profound warnings against all of those things. His lectures and books are becoming a staple of Berlin intellectual life.

The Backstory

A fascinating thinker, Han brings together two very interesting streams of late modernity. Born and raised in South Korea, as a boy, Han watched his country transform itself into an economic power. South Korea brought together a hypercapitalism (think Samsung, LG, and eventually K-pop) within a historic Asian honor society. In the late twentieth century, the duty and shame of the honor society merged with the hypercapitalism of neoliberalism. The measure of honor or shame, success or failure, became bound to the capitalist system of money, competition, and consumption. Recent Korean movies and TV shows like *Parasite* and *Squid Game* vividly highlight this reality. The system demands that people work harder and harder (lying or killing, at least in the movies and TV shows) to win access to the honors of the capitalist system.

As a young adult, Han prepared for this world, taking his first degree at Korea University in Seoul in metallic engineering (he examined how certain metals conduct energy—what could be more relevant in the budding digital age of chips and microprocessors?). This degree was a sensible way into the success of the consumer system. But ultimately something was amiss. On a whim, Han applied for a degree in philosophy in Germany. He would leave South Korea, knowing almost no German, to matriculate at Freiburg, the school of Martin Heidegger. Han excelled with degrees from Freiburg (with a dissertation on Heidegger) and Basel before settling in Berlin as a professor.

Throughout his career in Berlin, Han has been known for his short but potent books. His best-known book, *Müdigkeitsgesellschaft* (The tired or fatigued society), was published in English as *The Burnout Society*. In this and all of his work, Han consistently combines three elements. First, he draws from his experience of neoliberalism and the demand for the performance of competition in South Korea in the East and Germany in the West (*The Burnout Society* is a bestseller in both Germany and South Korea). Second, Han follows Heidegger's skepticism of technology. Han questions technology and its impact on our Being, something Heidegger could have never imagined—the digital age of smartphones and social media.[1] Han finds them both poisonous in that they distract us from our Being. Third (which makes Han important for us), both his Asian cultural sensibilities toward union and beauty in order and his connection to the core of Heidegger's critique of modernity bring Han to long for the mystical. But, like Heidegger before him, armed with a deep longing for Being, Han is better at critiquing the limits and shortcomings of neoliberal mysticisms than at offering an alternative. Han can help us see the limits of the mystical pathways of heroic action and inner genius. He is best at showing us why the deep commitments of our late-modern age *cannot* deliver what we long for. He vividly shows us how our mystical longings, bound in neoliberalism, are counterfeits at best.

The Core

These elements of Han's backstory give him a clear and unrelenting focus on what he sees as the core issue. For Han, the fundamental problem of late modernity is that it has shifted our attention, action, and overall imagination from *shoulds* to *coulds*. This shift is the accomplishment of neoliberalism. Following Foucault (discussed in chap. 3), Han contends that the *shoulds*,

---

1. Han is not without critique. Davide Sisto, for instance, has critiqued Han for being an alarmist when it comes to technology. See Sisto, *Remember Me: Memory and Forgetting in the Digital Age* (London: Polity, 2021), 19, 58. Other thinkers have even pointed to Han as a nihilist, finding in Han's work little hope for escaping the traps of our digital neoliberalism. This critique is somewhat legitimate, but there are openings if Han (who did study Catholic theology) could be connected with the *theologia crucis* and if we could see that naming the problem is not nihilism but is instead the mystical pathway of surrender and confession. I'm trying to develop Han's work in a theological direction.

which were central to sovereign power and the disciplinary society, have given way to the *coulds* of what Foucault calls "biopolitics" and Han calls "psychopolitics." Han uses that term because it no longer matters if you can correlate to the *shoulds* of a community, tradition, union, ethical imperative, or some other way of life.[2] Obedience has been subsumed by the project of the self. It is no longer the *shoulds* of commands that shape us. Rather, what counts now—what we obey—is how we can mine our own inner talents, abilities, desires, wants, and capacities to open a horizon of *coulds* for our own self. If we could work hard at unearthing these talents, abilities, and capacities, the *coulds* of our inner self's achievements could be limitless. Even in the honor society of South Korea, the *should* has been eroded by the *could*.[3]

What shapes our inner lives and in turn our societies (as well as what shapes our societies and in turn our inner lives) is the necessary drive to achieve. Neoliberalism's global reach brings this drive for hyperachievement and performance equally to the South Korean peninsula and to the capital of Germany.[4] Across both Asia and the West, the *should* has been replaced almost completely by the *could*. At first glance, this replacement of the *should* with the *could* seems like a great freedom. What else is freedom but the evacuation of the burdensome *shoulds* we were compelled to obey?[5] Han says, "The late-modern achievement-subject does not pursue works of duty. Its maxims are not obedience, law, and the fulfillment of obligation, but rather freedom, pleasure, and inclination."[6]

It appears to be a great freedom to only follow the self's desires, spending energy not on commands but on finding your self's talents and becoming all

2. Drawing directly from Foucault, Han says, "The prisoner in the digital panopticon is a perpetrator and a victim at the same time. Herein lies the dialectic of freedom. Freedom turns out to be a form of control." Han, *The Transparency Society*, trans. Erik Butler (Stanford, CA: Stanford Brief, 2015), 49.

3. Han says about South Korea, "When I was at school, there were slogans displayed on the classroom wall praising concepts such as patience, diligence and so on: the classic slogans of a disciplinary society. But today the country has been transformed into a performance society, and this transformation took place more rapidly and more brutally than elsewhere. . . . Classrooms are now filled with slogans like 'Yes you can!'" Han, *Capitalism and the Death Drive*, trans. Daniel Steuer (London: Polity, 2021), 94–95.

4. There are nonetheless still major differences between East and West, which Han addresses pointedly in his discussion of the differing responses to the pandemic in *Capitalism and the Death Drive*.

5. In *Two Concepts of Liberty* (Oxford: Clarendon, 1958), Isaiah Berlin discusses this negative freedom. In the neoliberalism of the achievement society, negative freedom (the emptiness to *should*, or living without any burden that one *should* do this or that) becomes assumed to be what freedom is (full stop).

6. Byung-Chul Han, *The Burnout Society*, trans. Erik Butler (Stanford, CA: Stanford Brief, 2015), 38.

you *could* be. But Han finds this deeply misguided. The *should* of obeying a command, standard, or tradition that is outside the self is indeed risky. No doubt, those who give the commands and demand obedience to the standard or tradition can be dangerously authoritarian (inside the neoliberal *could* society, we hear many stories of priests and fascists who demand icky obedience to commands). But Han believes the obsession with the *could* is even more dangerous than the risks of the *should*. The switch from the *should* to the *could* makes the self turn against itself by turning in on itself, demanding that the self perform, achieve, and possess all its *coulds* without end. The shift from the *should* to the *could*, though packaged as an advance in freedom, is anything but freedom. Han believes that this shift from the *should* to the *could* is not a gift but a Trojan horse.[7]

Whether in South Korea, Germany, the UK, or the US, we now live and breathe in an achievement society. Inside an achievement society, the impetus to work hard, giving yourself over to the performative and consumptive models of the good life, is not the burden of the grounded *should* but the dreamy state of the *could*. You must work hard because of what you *could* be, of what you *could* make of yourself. Your freedom is complete. There is no *should* that stands over you. But shockingly, we come to realize that this freedom is its own bondage. The *should* is replaced fully and powerfully by the *could*, so much so that the self and its chasing of the *could* becomes a more vicious slave master. This slave master, surprisingly, is located not outside of us but within us (the call of our discontent is coming from within the house!). We discover inside the neoliberal achievement society that we've been forced to be our own slave master, our own worst critic (as the great achievers of our epoch repeat all the time). We are our own condemning power, which demands perfection of our own selves. We demand this of ourselves so we can keep winning more and more, turning our *coulds* into accomplishments. We are free to chase any *could*, but in the end these *coulds* must be turned into magnificence. They must be turned into accomplishments that broadcast the self as magnificent (social media and the smartphone are indispensable, essential to the perpetuation of the self-obsession of chasing *coulds* for the sake of winning magnificence—the *likes* that manifest success).

7. Han says, "Desire is fueled by the impossible. But if the constant message, for instance in advertising, is 'you can' and 'everything is possible' then this marks the end of erotic desire. There is no love any longer because we imagine ourselves to be utterly free, because we have too many options to choose from." Han, *Capitalism and the Death Drive*, 98.

Han believes our "freedom" is indeed complete. So complete that it has become a complete nightmare.[8] And whom do we blame for this nightmarish freedom? Whom do we hold accountable for our discontent? The neoliberal system is so profound and powerful because it leads us to assume there are no other options but this neoliberal system of driving *coulds*. Because the *should* is gone and buried, replaced completely by the *could*, there is no one to blame. There is no one in charge to blame. There are only the selves who have won, who have cashed in the *could*, turning it into accomplishments and big bank accounts. They remind us often that they are not corrupt but instead just like us. They just turned their own *coulds*, the same *coulds* you have, into a kingdom (with a private island!). We could too, it's supposed, if we *could* just do better, find our talent, and perform it with a magnificence that wins. Ultimately, the only one to blame is yourself. Your discontent, the failures in the system, are your (individual) fault alone. Your *coulds* failed. Don't blame anyone else! Plus, the thinking goes, we can't punish or restrict (there is no *should* to even do so) those who have "worked" hard to turn their *coulds* into accomplishments. That would be harsh. Those who are lacking aren't smart enough to see and chance their *coulds* in the first place. "It's a shame," we say, "she could have been so much more, but she just couldn't get it together."

While the logic of *could* is sold as the highest good, it does produce a deep, existential fear. Inside the shift from the *should* to the *could*, you surprisingly must live with a heavy guilt (we explored in the chapters above how this arrives and produces secular mysticisms). No matter how much you accomplish, win, and achieve, you're aware you've failed to be all you *could* be. Han says it this way: "The performance-oriented subject is compelled to achieve ever more. It thus never reaches a satisfying point of completion. The subject lives with a permanent lack, and with feelings of guilt. Because it is competing not only against others but—primarily—against itself, it tries to get ahead of itself."[9] The *could* has no bottom. The deeper you go and the more you accomplish, the more you realize it. If you feel unhappy, it's not something fundamental about the system or your Being inside the shift from the *should* to the *could*; it's because you've failed and wasted your *coulds*. All you can do, up against

8. Han states, "Freedom is a counterpart of compulsion. If you experience the compulsion to which you are subjected, and of which you are not aware, as freedom, then that is the end of freedom. That is why we are in a crisis. The crisis of freedom consists in the fact that we perceive compulsion as freedom. In this situation, no resistance is possible." Han, *Capitalism and the Death Drive*, 129.

9. Han, *Capitalism and the Death Drive*, 45.

this discontent, is get yourself off the mat and reach for more *coulds* again and again. Work harder in chasing your dreams.

This embedded and embodied logic running through the West and the East, Han believes, is the incubator of the mental-health crises we face. Depression, ADHD, and especially anxiety all have their cultural origins, Han believes, in the dawn of the achievement society and the obsession with a self who chases the *coulds*.[10] An achievement society built on *coulds* asks us to always (nonstop) compare ourselves, compete, and chase the *coulds*.

Han's attacks on technology, particularly the smartphone and social media, cannot simply be iconoclastic. Rather, Han thinks these are the perpetuating tools, the steroids, of the neoliberal achievement society of performing selves. These technologies, the chasing of the like button—while seeming mystical in their offered freedoms for seeking the *could* and broadcasting your achievements—are actually, at their essence, acidic. They destroy any real connection to the world and its Being, flattening the mysticism we yearn for. Han understands that the achievement society and the tyranny of the *could* has so metastasized in the bones of our societies that we can hardly see beyond it. To cope with the guilt of the *coulds*, new spiritualities and mysticisms have arrived. But these mysticisms (of heroic action and inner genius) have no ability to confront the cancer of the *coulds* in the performative drives of the achievement society and the obsession with likes.

The pathways of heroic action and inner genius are mystical spiritualities made specifically for the could. They are made for a society built to achieve likes. Therefore, these mysticisms can be strategies for success only inside the *coulds* of the achievement society. If we are not very careful, they can malform, instead of transform, us. These mysticisms, because they're so bound in the performing self and its chasing of or coping with the *coulds*, cannot reach the transformational depth that our spirit seeks. They fail to give us an encounter with true otherness—they become too locked in the self, too fixated with the self, too concerned with the self turning its *coulds* into magnificent victories. The self-fixation in these mysticisms cannot deliver a freedom to

---

10. "The process of repression or negation plays no role in contemporary psychic maladies such as depression, burnout, and ADHD. Instead, they indicate an excess of positivity that is, not negation so much as the inability to say no; they do not point to not-being-allowed-to-do-anything . . . , but to being-able-to-do-everything. Therefore, psychoanalysis offers no way of approaching these phenomena. Depression is not a consequence of repression that stems from instances of domination such as the superego. Nor does depression permit 'transference,' which offers indirect signs of what has been repressed." Han, *Burnout Society*, 41.

just *be* through the very gift of the event of encounter with otherness. The *could*-based mysticisms of inner genius and heroic action in the end are for the benefit of more performance, more achievement, more chasing of the self's *coulds*. Surrender and confession, on the other hand, demand that we stop and receive, turning away from the self, opening to an otherness (transcendence 3) that can transform us *not* into all we can be but into what we are not (into the Spirit, into Christ, into union with the triune God).

Drawing from Han, we can see why the mystical pathways of inner genius and heroic action, while understandable, cannot be ultimately fulfilling— never getting to the deep transformation we long for and need. Han helps us see why pastors should not look to follow these pathways (avoiding the temptation to religify or Christianize either inner genius or heroic action). The pastor and minister must avoid allowing their imagination to be shaped by these neoliberal mystical pathways of the *could* (something we've been unable to do thus far). Following Han's critique will help us see why surrender and confession is necessary, even if Han doesn't quite go to the same theological depths as the concluding chapters of this project.

What Han can help us clearly see is the contrast between the mystical pathways of the *could* of inner genius and heroic action and the mystical pathway of surrender and confession. This contrast bears the weight of a versus, or either/or. Han takes no trepid steps in drawing out these juxtapositions. We will examine three of these bold contrasts that Han walks us into: (1) positivity versus negativity, (2) transparency versus veiled, and (3) *vita activa* versus *vita contemplativa*. Examining these three contrasts will help us see why the mystical pathways of heroic action and inner genius cannot reach the transformational depth we seek. More pointedly, doing so will reveal why Christian forms of (trans)formation need to be imagined beyond these pathways, centering instead on surrender and confession.

Positivity versus Negativity

Leave it to a professor of philosophy at the art university to begin one of his best books, *Saving Beauty*, with discussions of the sculptures of Jeff Koons, the iPhone, and (classic Han!) Brazilian waxing. These are all examples of the late-modern neoliberal aesthetic obsession with the smooth. We want everything smooth. We are happy when our day and our travel are smooth. We are drawn to all sorts of smooth surfaces because we wish to experience only the smooth throughout our lives. Therefore, the smooth is assumed to be beautiful (though, as we'll see, Han thinks a smooth beauty is a hollow beauty).

The smooth, Han says, "embodies today's *society of positivity*. What is smooth does not *injure*. Nor does it offer any resistance. It is looking for *Like*. The smooth object deletes its *Against*. Any form of negativity is removed."[11] Han's statement on the smooth here is packed with meaning. We'll need to touch on each of his italicized terms. Each word or phrase reveals why the smooth (particularly a smooth mysticism or spirituality) is shallow. But let's unpack this further by examining Han's examples of our misguided obsession with the smooth. Luckily (or not), Han spends most of his time with the sculptures of Jeff Koons and not Brazilian waxes.[12] By examining Koons's art, Han seeks to show why the smooth is assumed to be beautiful but in the end is banally gross. The smooth is gross because it lacks the *against* and *otherness* we need for transformation. Smooth beauty—like the glossy, photoshopped pictures of a model's perfect skin—is just a safe but devious faux beauty that eliminates otherness.

Jeff Koons's pieces go for millions of dollars (like $58 million!) and seem to transfix the viewer. But his pieces are all sculptures of the everyday, and not really the kind of everyday life that births the mystical or could open us to transcendence (T3). There is no *Against*, no negativity, in Koons's everyday. Koons, like Andy Warhol before him, makes the disenchanted consumptive product, the flat and disposable, the object of his art. He's a pop artist. Han explains that Warhol, like Koons, sought to master smooth surfaces. But Warhol kept a wink toward negativity—toward limit and impossibility, death and loss—even in his smooth depictions of consumer surfaces. Han says, "[Warhol's] surfaces are not entirely smooth. The series *Death and Disaster*, for instance, still lives off negativity."[13]

But not so much with Koons. He has foreclosed on smooth positivity, completely exorcising the negative. Koons's sculptures of the everyday are smooth

---

11. Byung-Chul Han, *Saving Beauty*, trans. Daniel Steuer (London: Polity, 2020), 1 (emphasis original).

12. Here is a sense of what Han says about Brazilian waxing: "Brazilian waxing makes the body smooth. It represents today's compulsive hygiene. The essence of eroticism, for [Georges] Bataille, is soiling and, accordingly, compulsive hygiene would be its end. Dirty eroticism gives way to clean pornography. Depilated skin, in particular, gives the body a pornographic smoothness which is felt to be pure and clean. Today's society, obsessed with cleanliness and hygiene, is a society of positivity which feels disgust at any kind of negativity." Han, *Saving Beauty*, 9.

13. Han, *Saving Beauty*, 2.

Van Gogh, *The Siesta* (1890–91)

and positive without fail (and thus they lack depth). There are no human beings struggling in the beauty and pain of the everyday—such as in Van Gogh's *Peasant Character Studies*. Rather, the everyday that Koons sculpts is bound completely in smooth consumer objects. He captures only the smooth, positive surface and therefore only the most disposable of these consumer objects. He sculpts what often becomes trash. And he does so with pure sincerity (it would rupture the positivity to not do so). There is no hint that he knows that the object he sculpts is itself disposable trash (that'd be too negative). There is no ironic wink that a sculpture of a bright blue balloon animal is worth $58 million. Rather, the balloon animal is so smooth it avoids any threat of negativity.[14]

14. We could place this discussion on Koons next to our discussion of David Foster Wallace from the previous chapter. Wallace believed that irony in the mid-1990s had lost its ability to move the reader into reflecting and wrestling with negativity (with the limits and yearning of humanity). Irony became a consumer disposable product or distraction—a balloon animal. Wallace called for a move to the sincere to return to the necessary negativity of beauty (which Han explores profoundly). What Wallace couldn't imagine is Koons, who uses pure sincerity

Jeff Koons, *Balloon Dog* (1993)

Sculpting the object of a balloon animal is interesting in itself. It reveals further avoidance of all negativities and an equal obsession with the smooth. A balloon animal is a consumer good that has a very short life before it becomes trash. Its short life allows the balloon animal to be absent of all negativities. Its quick move into trash is a comfort. A balloon animal cannot, for example, bear the weight of history. No one passes on a balloon animal to their child, saving their childhood balloon animal for the next generation. Rarely (and never for long) is a balloon animal the comfort a child uses to sleep, help-ing her through the difficult negativity of her finitude and its scary demand to surrender to sleep. A balloon animal, unlike a teddy bear, even lacks the negative weight of history. The balloon is without the negative beauty of the Being of the one who is no longer a child. A teddy bear passed on to a child, however, unveils how everyday life is soaked in the tragedy (again, negativity) of time itself. We suffer time. Now that we are no longer children, we pass on the treasure of our childhood to our own children, knowing that they too are growing up so fast. The beauty in the pain of the child's growing up transforms us, striking us with a revelation of the child's otherness.

---

to fence off all negativity, even the negativity of seams. Everything becomes sincerely smooth so that we can more quickly turn our *coulds* into performative magnificence.

Yet, the smooth does something else in its fetishizing of the positive over the negative. Han says, "Jeff Koons's sculptures are as *smooth as a mirror*, so to speak, allowing the observer to see him- or herself mirrored in them."[15] Han explains that there is no inner reality to Koons's sculptures. No hidden depth. His sculptures resist all that. They want no infinite mystery, no *absconditus*, nothing hidden. The smooth mirror resists any penetration to a depth. The smooth mirror finish, like that of the iPhone, keeps you always on the surface—touching a flat, smooth surface as a distraction from depth. What keeps this surface life livable is that the smooth mirror reflects yourself back to yourself. It keeps you, like Narcissus, transfixed on a smooth version of yourself.[16] There is no longer anything resembling depth, only a reflection, a rebound to the self of the self. The smooth makes the self the only thing that is important. The self's reflection paints the self's achieved magnificence on a smooth surface. We love smooth surfaces, finding them beautiful because we are obsessed with our self. The supposed beauty of Koons's sculptures is that you see yourself. You are on top of the object, becoming the object, because yourself and your performance is most important—the ultimate. The self needs the smooth to perform in this world of *coulds* (more on this soon). Han says, "The *alterity* or *negativity* of the *other* and the *alien* is eliminated altogether. Jeff Koons's art possesses a *soteriological* dimension. It promises *salvation*. The world of smoothness is a culinary world, a world of pure positivity, in which there is no pain, no injury."[17] There are no edges, no encounters with otherness, that might upend and interrupt, reminding you of your Being, proclaiming that you need something outside of you to save you.

Han contends that Koons's work is a vivid representation of our cultural obsession with the smooth, for the sake of the removal of (due to the disgust with) all negativities. We wish for no resistance. Inside the neoliberal *coulds* we fearfully hate any and all negativity (unless it comes to those we are competing against). We hate negativity because it's a resistance or drag to our performance. Therefore, negativity is deeply threatening. ("This company—this

---

15. Han, *Saving Beauty*, 5.

16. "Selfie addiction has its roots not in self-love but in narcissistic self-reference. A selfie is the beautiful, smooth surface of an emptied, wholly insecure self. Today, in order to escape torturous emptiness, one reaches either for the razor blade or for the smartphone. Selfies are smooth surfaces that, at least for a moment, present the empty self in a favourable light. But when we turn them over we find them covered in bleeding wounds. Thus, wounds are the reverse side of selfies." Han, *Capitalism and the Death Drive*, 48.

17. Han, *Saving Beauty*, 5.

church!—wants no negative people in it!") Our own experiences of negativity disgust us—even traumatize us—because negativity threatens to slow us down, even blocking us from chasing our *coulds*. Any negativity threatens us with the neoliberal horror of failure. It threatens us with failing inside all the "freedom" of our *coulds*. Because the shift to the *could* makes our self the measure of everything, all failures strike hard against the self, unmooring the self, attacking the self existentially. There is so much talk of resilience and accepting vulnerability in our late neoliberal age because we are so frightened by all the threats of failure. Failure, as the manifestation of negativities, is a travesty, because it delivers an acute antipositive experience of un-magnificence to our performing self. We cannot accept un-magnificence because we cannot believe that out of negativity could come beauty, otherness, and transformation (we've swallowed that neoliberal lie). We are scared of the depth, feeling safer on the smooth surface.

Negativity, in all its forms, becomes forbidden because it is assumed to *injure* severely. Negativity abuses because it's assumed to destroy and ravage. Destroy and ravage what? People are often too undone by negativity to know. But clearly what is injured is the self, the energy to chase the *coulds* jeopardized. Negativity strikes against our *could*-based, self-created possibilities. Negativity upends the self from performing magnificently.[18] The self—if it experiences too much resistance, too much drag, too many snags—can be corrupted by negativity and therefore become unable to perform by finding energy for the heroic or access to the inner genius. With no achieved magnificence through performance, there is only the trauma of failure.

The negativity becomes abusive. All such experiences of the negative are now labeled as trauma. There is so much trauma in the discourse of our experiences because inside a society of obsessive positivity, *any* form of negativity becomes a burden too heavy to bear. Institutions, particularly schools, are asked to keep all negativity out of the curriculum (which makes studying history, literature, and certain sciences nearly impossible). When the guilt of failing to be all you can be with all your *coulds* is always surrounding you

18. Han's insight here is so germane to our lives: "In a society in which everyone rates everyone else, friendliness is commercialized. People become friendlier in order to receive better ratings. Even at the very heart of the collaborative economy, the relentless logic of capitalism still rules. Paradoxically, despite all this wonderful 'sharing,' no one gives anything away. Once it begins to sell communism itself as a commodity, capitalism has reached its culmination. Communism as a commodity: that spells the end of any revolution." Han, *Capitalism and the Death Drive*, 20.

with threats, the last thing you can stand are the snags of negativity. You want it smooth. As is true with all performances, negativity is unproductive in achieving success (even the days of the negative, yelling coach are over). Performers want it smooth because negativity is the opposite of the applause that will validate your performance. When you live for the smooth life of applause, negativity is anathema.[19]

Yet, there is more: There is not only an inability to deal with negativity inside our obsessions with the smooth, but our obsessions with the smooth and our repulsion for negativity block us from essential realities. Han believes that without the negative we lose what we most long for. We lose the distance necessary for encounters of beauty, otherness, and transformation. We choose *like*, deleting anything that stands over and *against*. Anything but *like* is all too negative, too risky. We'd rather stay on the smooth surface than risk the negative distance of real beauty, otherness, and transformation.

For instance, true otherness, an inbreaking transcendence (T3), cannot be smooth. It cannot come without a death experience. It cannot occur without a rupture of what is and what will be (it must be apocalyptic). True otherness cannot be possessed; it remains at a distance even as it envelops and possesses you. True otherness cannot be covered with a warm blanket of the same. It cannot be covered even with the comprehensible. The true otherness of God or our neighbor comes with the judgment that neither God nor our neighbor is our *like* (never our possession). They encounter us from a distance. They are other and thus ultimately unknowable. We can only love them and respond to them in the negative confession of their unknowability, with respect to the negative distance between us. To encounter them we must refuse the smooth temptation to possess them as objects. We must bear the negative reality that otherness (divine or human) is pure subject. Their beauty is in their *against*. They stand against our possession of them, our categorizing them, turning them into a smooth *like*.

There is no inbreaking transcendence (T3) without negativity. Indeed, there are only counterfeit mysticisms without the negative. Han says, powerfully, "Without [the negativity of] distance, there can be no mysticism."[20] As we'll see in the chapters below, since the sixth century, the Christian tradition has

---

19. On Twitter, for instance, users go on the negative attack as an act of performance. They want to be the windshield of negativity, not the bug. The negativity is so ripe on Twitter because of the centrality of and obsession with positivity.

20. Han, *Saving Beauty*, 4.

claimed, following Pseudo-Dionysius (Denys), that there is no way of know-ing God but by the way of the negative (the apophatic). The smooth and the apophatic cannot cohere. The mysticisms of the *could*—heroic action and inner genius—are opposed to the apophatic, for both heroic action and inner genius resist negativity, denying that the negative (otherness) is the invitation into the mystery of transformation. The *could* mysticisms want instead to win *likes*, to stay with the like, to ride the smooth.

Yet, when we seek the *like*, desiring only the smooth and opposing any *against*, we embrace forms of mysticism without the beyond. We walk the mystical lanes that avoid, solve, or quickly move us past the negative. To deal with the negativity of our guilt, we too often seek a mysticism that refuses to rest in the negative, to follow the negative way, to seek transformation in and through the negative. We seek only a mysticism of inner genius and heroic action that refuses to surrender to the negative by pursuing the smooth. But to eviscerate the negative is to run to a mysticism that is ultimately too flat (too self-protective and self-obsessive) to encounter transformation. It becomes a coping mysticism or spirituality, not a transformation.

Unfortunately, Protestantism (both mainline and evangelical) has followed the mysticism of heroic action and inner genius because it has no stomach for the necessity of the negative (the cross!). We assume that the best congre-gation, best ministries, and best pastors will be smooth, giving off the same vibes as Koons's sculptures. The supposedly best churches of our late-modern times are so smooth, built with seamless glass and that new car smell. It is assumed that if the congregation and the pastor are to be attractive, they must be smooth, positive, and likable. That's how you get people to show up and commit. That's how you build a ministry. Yet, as we've seen of late, these congregations that glorify the smooth, avoiding all negativity, form (young) people who demand only safe and secure positivity, even smooth perfection, from their congregations. They eventually turn from the church and the Chris-tian message because their congregation gave them the assumption that the church is not a body of persons in messy confession and surrender to a God who is other. Instead, they imagined the church to be a place to smoothly and perfectly support the performance of their self. What is obvious is that this only creates congregations obsessed with the surface. It creates congre-gations that lack inner depth, with little yearning for transcendence, having no place for confession and storytelling of surrender. Only in embracing the negative, reaching for the distance, dwelling on the seams and rough edges of actual communities of persons, can we lean into the mystical encounter with divine action. The negative opens our ministries to real encounters of beauty, otherness, and transformation.[21]

All the memoirs we examined in the previous chapter, of course, discussed negativity. But ultimately, in their own way, they tell the reader how the memoirist found the smooth and overcame—magnificently defeating—the negative. The four lanes on the Beyonder path (loss and friendship, loss and nature, imminent death, addiction) all surrendered to the negative, finding new life within the negative. The pathway of surrender and confession moves not around but right into the negative, finding new life inside negativity, distance, and otherness. These memoirists who walked the lanes of loss, dying, and addiction articulated a transformation that was imbued with a beauty and otherness born right inside negativity.

Having unpacked Han's first juxtaposition—positivity versus negativity—we can see that the mystical pathways of modernity are not equal. The Counter-Enlightenment mystical pathway of heroic action and the Exclusive Humanist pathway of inner genius are both *coulds*-based mysticisms shaped for and by smooth positivity. Han has shown us why smooth positivity is a problem. Only the Beyonder mysticism of surrender and confession is able to proceed into the necessity of negativity. The church father Denys will help us see how essential negativity has been to the Christian confession for two thousand years.[22] Negativity is necessary because, unlike the smooth, it opens us not to our own *coulds* but to an encounter with otherness, to transformation not engendered from the force of our own self but through encounter with the acting God. The negative moves us from the surface to the depths. With this discussion of negativity versus positivity in place, we can turn to Han's second juxtaposition, which picks up where the first left off.

---

21. "[A] society of positivity [can't] tolerate negative feelings. Consequently, one loses the ability to handle suffering and pain, to give them form. For Nietzsche, the human soul owes its depth, grandeur, and strength precisely to the time it spends with the negative." Han, *Transparency Society*, 5.

22. Jason M. Baxter explains, "Throughout the early Christian centuries, in which authors were sensitive to the 'darkness' of God, delighting in it and drinking it in like the blackness of the night, there was no Christian who had yet formulated a method or path through such negativity—a path that would come to be known as the *via negativa*. This is exactly what Dionysius did, equipped with his Platonic learning, and this is how he secured for himself the role of 'the mystic's mystic.'" Baxter, *An Introduction to Christian Mysticism* (Grand Rapids: Baker Academic, 2021), 79–80.

Transparency versus Hidden/Veiled

When we're obsessed with smooth positivity, evicting the negative, we're moved to venerate transparency over the hidden or veiled. Han thinks our obsession with transparency is a problem. Wait, what?! I'm sure you need to read that sentence again. Yes, it's correct, Han thinks transparency signals a major problem with our achievement-based, performance-based, *coulds*-based society. Our obsession with smooth positivity creates the conditions for us to assume—without much doubt and with little reflection—that transparency is always welcome and good. As with chocolate, few of us can see any downside to transparency. We demand that our institutions, leaders, brands, even children and friends be always (and ever more) transparent. Saying that transparency might be a problem is like saying water might be a problem. But Han thinks this very assumption that more transparency is always good reveals a shallowness. This shallowness with smooth positivity turns us in on ourselves, destroying otherness, creating flat spiritualities and mysticisms. Our obsessive desire for transparency signals further that we are surface people. It exposes, I believe, that the smooth positive mysticisms of the E.Hums and CEs cannot reach the depth we need. For there is no longer depth, only attention on ourselves. The smooth and its link to the transparent reveals that our secular mysticisms and spiritualities are without the transcendence (T3) and therefore without the otherness needed for transformation.

To show why transparency is actually bad, Han returns to Jeff Koons and his picture series *Easyfun-Ethereal*. The pictures in this series are trippy, to say the least. But they give off a constant feeling. Each picture is a collage of consumer goods and objects disparately flying through the air with no rhyme or reason, no real meaning other than their entering and exiting our purviews. A cookie, a wig, and a cartoon face make up one. In another, a soft pretzel, a woman's fishnet-laced breasts, and a ladle of soup. In a third, a bunch of women's legs and toes with bagels and scones (yum!). It's easy, fun, ethereally light and transparent. It signals that everything is before us, everything is consumable and attainable. All *could* be. Nothing is hidden. Han says, "[Koons's] pictures mirror our society, which has become a department store. It is stuffed full of short-lived objects and advertisements. It has lost all otherness, all foreignness; thus it is no longer possible to marvel at anything."[23]

23. Byung-Chul Han, *The Expulsion of the Other: Society, Perception and Communication Today*, trans. Wieland Hoban (London: Polity, 2020), 59.

The smooth and transparent strips us of living in a world that can stir us by an encounter with the foreign and the other.

Transparency is equated to the clear, seeable, and coherent. Clear and seeable, sure, but Han thinks transparency is the opposite of coherent. In a neoliberal consumer society, transparency delivers chaos. The transparent, like Koons's art, makes all available and all chaotic, overwhelming us with objects and images that are meaningless, causing us only to bob on the surface. The transparent is a tidal wave of exposed stuff, knocking us off balance with all the availability. Transparency lets us see it all. But seeing it all, we are left with no meaning. As with Koons's pictures, the only meaning is in the meaninglessness.

Where we most often hear about the need for complete transparency is in relation to our data. We think it absolutely necessary that companies like Amazon, Facebook, and Google (any website with cookies) be transparent with what they'll do with our data. They even need to make our data transparent and accessible to us. But these claims for the need for transparency—lifting transparency as a solution and necessary objective—often come from the very ones who possess our data.[24] They promise us transparency because they know that transparency is no threat to their business. Transparency is not a threat because it cannot participate in transformation.[25] Transparency cannot produce any real meaning.[26]

When tech companies comply with their own recommendations to be transparent and make our data available (this particularly happens in the European

24. "The regime of digital surveillance, taking on proto-totalitarian traits by now, is already undermining the very idea of freedom. The individual has been transformed into a data set and exploited for profit. Capitalism has developed into surveillance capitalism. Surveillance generates capital. Digital platforms subject us to constant surveillance and manipulate our behaviour." Byung-Chul Han, *The Palliative Society*, trans. Daniel Steuer (London: Polity, 2021), 57.

25. Han states, "Information, by definition, cannot be veiled. It is transparent by nature. Information simply is given. It repels any metaphor, any veiling dress, it speaks straight out. This is also what distinguishes it from knowledge which can retreat into secrecy. Information follows an altogether different principle. It is directed towards revealing, towards the truth. Information has a pornographic nature." Han, *Saving Beauty*, 31.

26. Han gives some insightful texture to this discussion on data as information but not knowledge. He says, "Even the largest accumulation of information, Big Data, possesses very little knowledge. Big Data is used to find correlations. A correlation states: when A occurs, B often also occurs. It is not known, however, why this is so. Correlation is the most primitive form of knowledge, being not even capable of ascertaining the relationship between cause and effect. It is meaningless. The question of why becomes irrelevant; thus nothing is understood. But knowledge is understanding. Hence Big Data renders thought superfluous. We surrender ourselves without concern to the it-is-so." Han, *Expulsion of the Other*, 4.

Union, where by law all cookies must be disclosed and a user can request all the data that a site or app has harvested from them), they *expose it all to us*. Like a deviant flasher in the park, they go transparent, exposing it all to overwhelm us. They make our data so transparent that we can only assume it has no real meaning. Or at least no meaning we can assess. We are made to assume that there is nothing veiled, hidden, or symbolic left in the world. Therefore, while having access to everything, we are kept far from meaning. With its all-out open access, with everything transparent, there are no mysteries. Nothing is hidden and yet, despairingly, there is no meaning at all. Inside the full, all-out transparency, all interpretation, all hermeneutical questions, and all inquiries of what it all means come to an end.

The tech companies' compliance with their own rules of transparency, their own open access, looks and feels a lot like Koons's art. Transparency is so overwhelmingly noisy, the information so extensive and busy, that the delivery of transparency becomes a victory for surveillance. Complete transparency is a win for control, for the ownership of data, for the articulation that the world we inhabit has nothing hidden and therefore nothing really to encounter. Most people are so overwhelmed with all the transparency that they just don't care; they're happy to repeat the need for a transparency that is so cluttered there is nothing clear about it. Therefore, it's better, they assume, to stick on the surface, not asking too many questions of meaning, instead riding the smooth transparency in our chase for all the *coulds*.

Transparency cannot lead to confession. It actually opposes confession. In its attack on the hidden, transparency destroys otherness with its all-out pursuit of exposure. Transparency is safe for these companies because the data is so extensive. The promise of transparency can only produce a data dump. The overload of data disorients any meaning. When everything is transparent, its depth is lost. Information (even transparent information) has no transformational power without interpretation. Transparency, Han believes, is the death of interpretation. What is there to interpret? It's all supposedly clear in its transparency. Transparency claims that the world is such a desert of meaning that the symbolic is dead. There is no symbolic— that is, depth—to anything. Han contends that transparency is the enemy of the symbolic. Without the symbolic—without a sense that there are hidden, truly other realities in the world that demand interpretation—mysticisms and spiritualities must turn completely to the magnificence of the self. The self and its pursuits of conquest (heroic action) or a unique identity (inner genius) are the only oasis in a desert made bone dry of meaning by the winds of obsessive transparency.

The symbolic—the sense that what is most important and most true to us is revealed in its hiddenness, veiled in its nearness, and other and unknowable the deeper we know it—floods us with meaning. The hidden births the symbolic, which sends us searching for ways of knowing and therefore being. The need to interpret, to penetrate into the symbolic, places our being next to mystery. But transparency attacks the hidden, strangling mystery. Transparency holds nothing sacred, nothing at a distance. The everyday is never veiled or hidden but always vulgarly exposed and available. Transparency makes the demand that we brazenly expose it all. It does so because it assumes there is nothing sacred in the world, nothing mystical or spiritual, even transcendent, outside the self. The pathways of heroic action and inner genius become strategies inside the dry desert of meaninglessness, weighing down the self with the burden of being the *only* source of meaning and significance. In a transparent world of smooth positivity, with nothing hidden and therefore nothing other, all but the self's (spiritual) obsessions with making the self magnificent is evaporated. The memoirs of the E.Hums and CEs are exercises in turning self-obsessive transparency into spirituality. E.Hum and CE memoirists find meaning in themselves (in their acceptance of their unique identities, as in Carlile's *Broken Horses*, or strength to act heroically, as in Samuelsson's *Yes, Chef*), not in the hidden mystery (otherness) of encounter.

We find these E.Hum and CE mysticisms compelling, even authentic, because of our chasing of the *coulds*. This smooth chasing of *coulds* is why we still love the idea of transparency, though it is chaos. Transparency fits so well—aesthetically, emotionally, and ideologically—with the smooth. (When aesthetics, emotions, and ideology come together, as they have in neoliberalism, we find ourselves inside psychopolitics.) We valorize transparency because we adore the smooth positivity. Han says, "The transparency society is a society of positivity. Things become transparent when they shed all negativity, when they are smoothed and levelled out, when they allow themselves to be enveloped by smooth flows of capital, communication and information without offering any resistance. Actions become transparent when they subordinate themselves to a calculable and controllable process. . . . Images become transparent when they are deprived of any hermeneutical depth, even of meaning, and thus become pornographic. The positivity of the transparency society makes it a hell of the same."[27]

Inside the overexposure of transparency, the whole of our *coulds*-based society becomes pornographic (from top to bottom). The pornographic is a hatred of the apophatic, of a mysticism that seeks otherness. The pornographic can produce a self-obsessive spirituality in its glorification of the self's own magnificence. But the pornographic has no place, no allure, inside the confession of un-magnificence and the necessity of otherness. The pornographic, next to the spirit of real encounter with otherness, becomes so flat that it's foolish (even embarrassing). Inside our demands for transparency, we receive an ocean of access, though with no meaning. For Han, this access is the height of pornography, the pornographic writ large. In a transparency society, you can see everything, but the "everything" destroys the depth of mystery, the texture of personhood, the nuance of personality, even encounter itself. The pornographic wants no otherness. It avoids all meetings of the mystery of the hidden. It wants only the meaningless titillation of exposure. It wants transparency so it can have control, so it can possess. It's too frightened of the depth of meaning in otherness, of what transformation that depth of encountered otherness will deliver. The pornographic lacks the imagination and verve to seek the symbolic through interpretation. Transparency is the pornographic because it wants everything accessible, to have *all* exposed and available (even consumable), completely absent of any real meaning. Transparency wants to form a self that is free of any demands from outside the self that make a claim on the self. The pornographic is repulsed by surrender because it hates true otherness.[28]

The overexposure of transparency wilts, even destroys, the mystery that produces meaning. Inside the panopticon—inside the open-floor, fully glassed Apple Store—everything is transparent. There is no call, no demand, to

27. Han, *Capitalism and the Death Drive*, 33.

28. Han adds, "Only machines are fully transparent. But the human soul is not a machine. Inwardness, spontaneity and eventfulness, the very constituents of life, are opposed to transparency. Human freedom, in particular, makes total transparency impossible. Apart from that, a transparent relationship would be a dead relationship, without any attraction. Only what is dead is transparent. The acknowledgement that there are positive, productive spheres of human being and being-with that are utterly destroyed by the compulsion of transparency would be a moment of enlightenment." Han, *Capitalism and the Death Drive*, 37. He continues, "The compulsion of transparency is ultimately not an ethical or political imperative but an economic one. Exposure is exploitation. The one who is fully exposed is subjected to limitless exploitation. The over-exposure of people maximizes economic efficiency" (39).

interpret anything or even to ask, "What does it all mean? *What is beyond?*" Yet, transparency is not in the lexicon of the Beyonders, because transparency has no concern for symbolism, no interest in the deeper mystery of our being and its experiences in the world. The world is exposed, transparent; its images and actions have no inner depth. It is all just porn.

"No, no," you might protest, "transparency is necessary for the sake of trust. Transparency builds trust. We need transparency because we lack trust!" But this equation of transparency plus more transparency equals trust shows how transparency is closely connected with the smooth and its anti-negativity.[29] We make shouts for transparency when negativity has arrived and we wish for only the smooth. We want a quick way back to the smooth through the performance of transparency. We demand transparency as a way of smoothing our anxiety or satisfying our anger. We often don't want confession. Confession is too bound in spirit, moving us too directly into transformation. Confession turns enemies into friends, hate into love. Confession demands a surplus of meaning, of interpretation, of symbolic acts next to hiddenness. Confession enters the arcane, dwelling in the realm of real otherness. Confessing or hearing a confession connects spirit to spirit through otherness. In confession you must walk into the negative and bear tension, as in Saeed Jones's memoir and his confession to Esther of his mother's death, becoming part of it, entering a surplus of jagged meaning. Not so with transparency. When I demand transparency out of distrust, even hurt, I demand a return to the smooth, not life together. I demand to know so that I'm not surprised in my performance, so I know who is against my chasing of my *coulds*. (That seems only fair in this all-out competition.) I refuse to surrender to something bigger. Rather, I demand that my negative, uneasy feelings of distrust be appeased by a nakedness, by an exposure, that vindicates my self. I demand, as with the onlookers of Cersei's naked walk of shame in season 5 (episode 10) of *Game of Thrones*, to see all and shout, "Shame, shame, shame!"

Honesty, however, is different from transparency. Honesty moves by the force of fidelity and commitment, for the sake of union with otherness. Transparency is a work-around for honesty. It is the quick way to avoid the negativity of bearing a rugged communion with another in vulnerability and to

---

29. "The motto of the public for a transparency law is: 'Transparency creates trust.' This motto contains a contradiction. Trust is only possible in a state that lies somewhere between knowing and not knowing. If I know everything up front, trust is redundant. Transparency is a state in which all not-knowing is eliminated. Where transparency reigns, there is no space for trust. The slogan should thus run: 'Transparency destroys trust.'" Han, *Capitalism and the Death Drive*, 34.

instead receive assurances that you will not be surprised. Love is never bound in transparency. Love is never smooth. It is nourished by the hiddenness of otherness and the continued mystery of encounter with what is outside you.

An example: The staff at a school feels the administration has broken trust. Over the last decade the staff has demanded that the administration and board be transparent. The administration and board have agreed. They've been as transparent as (legally) possible. Yet all the transparency has not healed the distrust. The distrust festers because transparency eliminates the conditions of confession and surrender that would lead to transformation. Transparency alone can never produce community, never lead to confession and union, because without a larger story, without a new symbolic way of being together, transparency is just pornographic. The staff yearns for an urge that can never be fulfilled. Where the administration has failed is not in its lack of transparency but in the inability to give the staff a story of the institution that wraps it in enough symbolism that it floods them all with meaning.[30] The same reality has happened in many congregations. When distrust arrives, we imagine that transparency will heal it. But it never does because what is needed is confession, which invites us into interpretation. We need to be led into a hermeneutical process of seeking a narrative of meaning, leading us into encounters with otherness.

Confession is never transparent. Rather, confession is openness to otherness; it is surrendering to what is near but veiled. Confession is the opposite of the pornographic. It is filled with meaning and it delivers a union with mystery that can never be subsumed or owned. Confession is the opposite of exposure. While confession delivers a union, it does so not through the transparency of possession but through the gift of the mystery of otherness. The memoirs of inner genius and heroic action are often pornographic. There is no mystery or meaning outside the self; there is only meaning through the performance of the self. The memoir itself becomes the act of the self's exposure. The memoir becomes a kind of transparency that wins recognition. It loses the necessary veil of the apophatic. The form of mysticism that follows in the footsteps of

---

30. Han says prophetically, "The general denarrativization of the world is reinforcing the feeling of fleetingness. It makes life bare. Work itself is a bare activity. The activity of bare laboring corresponds entirely to bare life. Merely working and merely living define and condition each other. Because a narrative thanatotechnics proves lacking, the unconditional compulsion arises to keep bare life healthy. Nietzsche already observed that, after the death of God, health rose to divine status. If a horizon of meaning extended beyond bare life, the cult of health would not be able to achieve this degree of absoluteness." Han, *Burnout Society*, 18.

Denys, however, finds the power of transformation not in the transparency of the self but in the hiddenness of the otherness of the wholly other God.

Vita Activa versus Vita Contemplativa

Societies that glorify the transparent, titillated by the pornographic reflection of the self in the smooth, are without smell. Han believes neoliberal societies are pornographic from top to bottom because time itself no longer has a smell. Sight (and sound) overtakes all else. Neoliberal societies are pornographic because their obsession with speed is a type of sex without smell, a way of life without the depth of encounter.[31] It's all about activity without being there, consumption without encounter. In his book *The Scent of Time*, Han jumps headlong into the mystical. He discusses clocks in ancient China that were based on smell.[32] These clocks, like all early clocks, were used *not* to accelerate activity but to order and direct contemplation—to lead into prayer.[33] But now, in our societies, there is no time to smell (no time to stop and smell the roses, as the expression goes) because too much activity is called for—the clock is ticking. As Han explains in *The Scent of Time*, smell often demands some contemplation, some hermeneutical interpretation.[34] When

31. "Pornography destroys not just eros, but also sex. Pornographic exhibition causes estrangement from sexual desire. It makes it impossible to live desire. Sexuality dissolves into feminine simulations of pleasure and masculine performances of performance. Pleasure on display, in an exhibition, is not pleasure at all. Compulsive exhibition entails the alienation of the body itself." Han, *Transparency Society*, 12.

32. "*Hsiang yin* is the name of the whole incense clock, which consists of several parts. . . . As a medium for measuring time, incense differs in many respects from water or sand. Fragrant time does not flow or trickle away. Nothing is emptied. Rather, the scent of the incense fills the room, even turns time into space; it thus gives it a semblance of duration." Byung-Chul Han, *The Scent of Time: A Philosophical Essay on the Art of Lingering*, trans. Daniel Steuer (London: Polity, 2020), 56–57.

33. Han explains, "In the Middle Ages, the *vita activa* was still altogether imbued with the *vita contemplativa*. Work was given its meaning by contemplation. The day began with prayers. And prayers ended it. They provided a temporal rhythm. An altogether different significance attached to the festive days. They were not days off work. As times of prayer and of leisure they had their own significance. The medieval calendar did not just serve the purpose of counting days. Rather, it was based on a story in which the festive days represent narrative resting points. They are fixed points within the flow of time, providing narrative bonds so that the time does not simply elapse. The festive days form temporal sections which structure time and give it a rhythm. They function like the sections of a story, and let time and its passing appear meaningful. Each section of a story completes a narrative section, and this provisional completion prepares the next stage of the narrative. The temporal sections are meaningful transitions within an overall narrative frame. The time of hope, the time of joy, and the time of farewell merge into each other." Han, *Scent of Time*, 88.

34. Han expounds, "The society of positivity has taken leave of both dialectics and hermeneutics. The dialectic is based on negativity. Thus, Hegel's 'Spirit' does not turn away from the

we smell something good or bad, we are often drawn into hermeneutics, into contemplation, aware of our being in a place. We ask, "What is that smell?"

What we smell is veiled, it is hidden, it must be searched for to be discovered. Smell hits us, but we must search for what or where it comes from. Smell is not ready at hand like an image; smell is not transparent. It is not a click away. A particular smell, often more than sight or sound, can take us deeper into our here, moving us into the contemplation of the place our being is *now* in. Smell resists acceleration. Smell demands attention to a place in a time. You can accelerate images and sounds, but not smells. You can intensify a smell (by never washing your workout clothes), but you can't accelerate a smell. You can speed up the consumption of images, double-time the pace of the sound of a podcast, but you *cannot* hurry smell.

Han, the prophetic mystic of neoliberal discontent, finds disease within this drive to accelerate everything and ignore the importance of smell. Even so, Han admits, it's logical. Societies built on *coulds*, while denigrating *shoulds*, will always laud activity (particularly hyperaccelerated activity) over contemplation. In such societies of smooth positivity and pornographic transparency, sight will always be emphasized over smell, activity over contemplation. In a society of *coulds*, there is little value in states of contemplation, but there is a great deal of value in constant activity.

Social media is the constant availability of networks of constant activity built around images. The internet has proliferating images but no (zero) smells. In turn, because social media, and the internet as a whole, has no smell, it is a directionless place. It is neither here nor there. The internet has many sites but no heres in which to be. It has many (exponential) places or sites to visit but few to encounter. Smell, Han contends, is essential to the encounter with otherness in time. Smell is a major part of the pilgrim's journey into a new here, beyond the same of all the sites.[35]

---

negative but endures and preserves it within itself. Negativity nourishes the 'life of the mind.' Spirit has 'power,' according to Hegel, 'only by looking the negative in the face and tarrying with it.' Such lingering yields the 'magical power that converts it into being.' In contrast, whoever 'surfs' only for what is positive proves mindless. The Spirit is slow because it tarries with the negative and works through it. The system of transparency abolishes all negativity in order to accelerate itself. Tarrying with the negative has given way to racing and raving in the positive." Han, *Transparency Society*, 5, quoting Georg Wilhelm Friedrich Hegel, *Phenomenology of Spirit* (Oxford: Oxford University Press, 1977), 19.

35. Han says insightfully, "The *peregrinus* [pilgrim] feels a stranger in this world: he or she is not at home Here, and is thus always on the way to a There. In modernity, it is precisely this difference between Here and There which disappears. The modern human does not progress

Han contends that there are no pilgrims in the internet age because there is no place to go, no heres to enter. There are sites (transparent sights) but no smells. There is no here because there is no direction, no invitation to bring your body into a state of contemplation in a place. There is no place where my being is drawn deeper into contemplation. There is only a smell-less site of images and prompts that push for constant activity. This constant activity is won at every level by the loss of contemplation. Social media becomes a confusing place to contemplate anything that might stretch you into an encounter with otherness. People use social media as a way of pacifying any dissonance with otherness. They return to the smell-less site of the internet to put away the discomfort of contemplation and return to constant (often pointless) activity. Han believes that for us, sight and constant noise overcome all other senses. The noisy activity of the consumption and creation of images overcomes all demands to stop and smell, contemplating otherness and beauty. Smell interrupts positivity and transparency. So instead, we decide to cover the smell of life with the perfumes of consumptive *coulds* that demand constant activity.

Drawing on themes from Heidegger, Han contends that it is smell, far more than sight or sound, that reminds us that we are *thrown* into the world.[36] Smell tells us that we are beings in time, that we are in this time in this place, inescapably in our bodies, searching for depth more than distance, resonance more than acceleration.[37] A strange smell is the surest sign we're in a strange place, unable to escape it, forced to contemplate what it means that our being is here in this now. Sound, particularly music, can move us across time (hearing that song from high school takes us back). This no doubt has a *thrownness* to it as well. But scent most powerfully moves us into contemplations of a

---

towards a There, but towards a better or different Here. For the peregrinus, by contrast, there is no progress associated with a Here. Further, his path is neither 'orderly' nor 'secure.' Rather, the desert is uncertain and insecure. As opposed to the pilgrim who follows a prescribed path, the human creates a path him- or herself. He or she is more like a soldier who marches towards a goal, or like a labourer. The peregrinus is thrown into its facticity. The modern human, by contrast, is free." Han, *Scent of Time*, 29. He continues, "The new media abolish space itself. Hyperlinks make pathways disappear. Electronic mail does not need to conquer mountains and oceans. Strictly speaking, it is no longer something 'ready-to-hand.' Instead of 'hands' it immediately reaches the eyes. The age of the new media is an age of implosion. Space and time implode into a here and now. Everything is subject to de-distancing" (61).

36. The echo of Heidegger in *Being and Time* is clear here. Han says, "Thus, the age of haste and acceleration is an age of forgetfulness of being." Han, *Scent of Time*, 74.

37. In *The Scent of Time* and *The Disappearance of Ritual* (London: Polity, 2020), Han references Hartmut Rosa. Han is more a mystic than Rosa, meaning in part that Han's thought is more opaque. This is nowhere more true than in his dialogues with Rosa, which can be hard to understand in Han's affirmation and nuancing of Rosa.

here, moving us deeper into a particular place, to stop and maybe even to pray. Scent grounds us, it takes us to the ground, as the father of our other mystical school, Meister Eckhart, says.[38]

Han's discussion of smell makes the point that societies that have embraced neoliberalism all emphasize sight over smell. In doing so, inhabitants of these societies are often caught in a life of activity (*vita activa*) over a life of contemplation (*vita contemplativa*). Such societies eviscerate contemplation, drowning it in more and more activity. Activity becomes all there is. Neoliberal societies are made of sight and sound, of images and noise. Those living in these societies of activity can easily fall into boredom. Societies such as ours are even plagued by boredom (even with our unending, streaming entertainment). Though there are transparent and pornographic images everywhere, and everything is shaped for smooth positivity, boredom fearfully proliferates. Han contends that our societies of activity become plagued with boredom because our way of life is void of contemplation. Boredom strikes when (hyper)activity loses its direction, making the (hyper)activity that is the shape of life pointless and aimless.[39] Schoolchildren get bored on summer vacation because they are free from the practices of contemplation to accelerate their activity. This free activity is at first a paradise—it's all smooth and positive—but after a month (even a week) the boredom comes. And it's often heavy. Heavy enough to flatten the world. All the free activity is unable to reach a transcendence worth contemplating.

The mysticisms of the E.Hums and CEs are similar. They are mysticisms of the *vita activa*. They are about a transcendence (T1 or T2) that calls for no contemplation. These kinds of transcendence are found only in more and more activity, like exercise—more and more pursuits of inner genius and heroic action. The mystical breakthroughs of the E.Hums or CEs are almost always born in action, almost never in contemplation. What is there to contemplate after all?

38. In *The Scent of Time*, Han draws mostly deeply from Heidegger, whom he wrote his dissertation on at Freiburg. One of Heidegger's heroes is Meister Eckhart, who represents (is even the father of) the mystical school I'll draw from in my retrieval starting in the next chapter. Eckhart discusses the ground in almost all of his work, but a good example is his treatises called "Counsels on Discernment." See Meister Eckhart, *Meister Eckhart: The Essential Sermons, Commentaries, Treatises and Defense* (New York: Paulist Press, 1981), 269.

39. Han says, "Profound boredom is the flip side of excessive activity, of a *vita activa* that lacks any form of contemplation. A compulsive activism keeps boredom alive. The spell of profound boredom will only be genuinely broken if the *vita activa* incorporates the *vita contemplativa* into its critical pole and once again serves the latter." Han, *Scent of Time*, 84.

The lanes of these mystical pathways venerate and rarely escape the *vita activa*. Unlike the mysticism of the Beyonders, almost never is their transcendence experienced as a force to stop and to confess, leading to prayer. The Beyonder pathways all invite prayer. The memoirists who represent the Beyonder pathways almost all prayed—even before believing—because the pathway of surrender and confession is not a *vita activa* but a *vita contemplativa*. The centrality of contemplation calls for prayer. Rarely, or never, do the mysticisms of E.Hums and CEs call for a surrender of activity.[40] Rarely do these memoirists recognize, like the addict, that activity itself is deconstructive. Rarely is this spirituality built around stopping. The mysticisms and spiritualities native to the societies of neoliberalism—which accelerate sight and sound—are grafted completely to the *vita activa*. E.Hum and CE mysticisms and their many lanes are bound to hyperactivity, rejecting contemplation. These mysticisms become a way to give some moisture to hyperactivity, which dries out all the depth of meaning. These mysticisms exist to give hyperactivity spirituality. But the moisture from such mysticisms bound in *vita activa* can only dampen the soil. It can never reach the roots.

In societies of sight and sound, nothing lasts. In those societies, place (being here) is not deep enough for things to last. Both experiences and objects are disposable. They are objectified for the sake of the hurried transcendences of T1 and T2. These kinds of transcendence are intended to render my hyperactivity episodically significant. Yet, Han believes it's contemplation—the *vita contemplativa*—that imbues experiences and even objects with meaning. Places become holy and routines become rituals when we are forced to smell them, to contemplate our being in and through them.[41] A transcendence 3—an inbreaking transcendence—demands contemplation because its source is not the self but rather what is outside the self, meeting the self in a place with a smell, a place where being meets being. A place like Bethel, where God is discovered in contemplation (Gen. 35). The mysticisms of the *vita activa*, which grasp for a transcendence 1 or transcendence 2, are bound—even caged—

40. "The *vita activa* remains a term of compulsion as long as it does not incorporate the *vita contemplativa* within itself. A *vita activa* that lacks any contemplative moment becomes empty and turns into pure activity, leading to franticness and restlessness." Han, *Scent of Time*, 99.

41. Han adds, "Rituals and ceremonies, in contrast, are narrative processes; they elude acceleration. It would be sacrilegious to seek to accelerate a sacrificial act. Rituals and ceremonies have their own temporality, their own rhythm and tact. The society of transparency abolishes all rituals and ceremonies because they do not admit operationalization, that is, they impede the accelerated circulation of information, communication, and production." Han, *Transparency Society*, 30.

completely in the self. The self's internal or external actions are the source and obsession of these kinds of spiritualities. Inside these mysticisms and these kinds of transcendence (T1 and T2), there is no reason to contemplate because being and transcendence have their source only and finally in the self. Contemplation has no aim other than the self. And the self has no mystery to contemplate because the self is only its accelerated activities; the self is only sight (appearance) and sound (interesting performances). Transcendence (T1 and T2) inside the *vita activa* becomes instrumentalized. T1 and T2's purpose is not to connect your being to what is beyond but to free the activity that starts and ends with the self not becoming a flat bore. Han's point is that without smell, we lose the beyond.

Conclusion

Byung-Chul Han shows us vividly and provocatively that there are deep problems in the mysticisms of the E.Hums and CEs. These mysticisms, while deserving some respect, are too bound to the *coulds* of a performing self and the drives of neoliberalism. I've begun to assert that only the Beyonder pathways avoid these traps by directly embracing negativity (over the smooth), otherness (over transparency), and contemplation (over activity). Yet, Han can only take us so far. We've been able to follow his prophetic trail far enough to see that all the mysticisms and spiritualities of our triangle are not equal. But we now must depart from Han and enter retrieval. We enter this retrieval not with nostalgia but propelled by Han's critique, ready to explore how the Beyonder way of surrender and confession is an ancient mystical pathway that might lead us forward, helping us understand the shape and depth of transformation. We'll start this exploration by stepping beyond Han, seeing that contemplation, though much better than activity, has its own problems.

This leads us to the ghost of Martin Luther.[42]

---

42. Han himself gives a sense of where I'm going: "What is needed is a particular kind of passivity. You need to let yourself be concerned with that which evades the activity of the acting subject; 'To undergo an experience with something—be it a thing, a person, or a god—means that this something befalls us, strikes us, comes over us, overwhelms and transforms us.'" Han, *Scent of Time*, 104, quoting Heidegger, "The Nature of Language," in *On the Way to Language*, trans. Peter D. Hertz (New York: Harper & Row, 1971), 57.

8

Why Passivity Is the Path

We leave the Hampton by Hilton in Berlin just after breakfast to make our train to Wittenberg. With just twenty-four hours until our flight to Madrid, on our way to Wittenberg, we learn we'll need to switch Airbnbs in Madrid, and fast. Even with the Airbnb hiccup, we have just enough time to take the fast train to Wittenberg, see Luther's fair city, spend the night, and get the fast train back to Berlin for our flight to hot Madrid.

On this late-summer day, when the heat in Germany is not even close to what will meet us in Spain, it makes the most sense to walk from the Wittenberg train station into town, which is less than a mile away. The walk serves as an unintended pilgrimage, ushering us from Berlin's bustling capital to the quiet, small, medieval hamlet of Wittenberg. The walk helps us transition. But the walk, like a true pilgrimage, is also filled with negativity and a little suffering. The mile feels long while hauling our luggage. Our bags, like our late-modern psyches, are made for the smooth floors of airports, train stations, and other zones of acceleration, not for the bumpy, antiquated brick roads of small-town Germany. My teenage children are filled with complaints.

When we arrive it's clear: Wittenberg is beautiful, and Luther's ghost is everywhere. At first, it's hard to experience his haunting. There's too much branding. Luther's name, his face, is everywhere, selling everything. We stay at the Luther Hotel and see gift shops selling Luther bobbleheads, shot glasses, playing cards, and underwear. It's all the remaining residue of 2017. That year was the five-hundredth anniversary of Luther's nailing of the Ninety-Five

Theses to the door of Wittenberg's All Saints' Church (the castle church). In 2017, Wittenberg became a hot tourist destination for church nerds, bringing a surplus of souvenirs still being sold years later. At first it feels like Luther is more on par with Tony the Tiger or Fred Flintstone than a Reformer who opened the mysteries of the living God to the world.

But that all changes when we enter All Saints' Church. The summer sun is splashing through the Gothic windows. It's spilling onto the floor, illuminating the two bronze caskets that permanently rest between the pews and the pulpit.[1] Those caskets are Luther's and Philip Melanchthon's. We sit in their presence remembering that just outside the door to the left, Luther nailed his Ninety-Five Theses, and now here he lies in this beautiful space. The haunting sweeps us down the street, less than a thousand yards, to Saint Mary's Church. Luther's bones are sitting in All Saints' Church, and the walls of Saint Mary's are metaphorically stained with Luther's words. He preached hundreds of sermons from this very pulpit. Behind the pulpit rests a beautifully painted altarpiece with Luther himself depicted preaching on the bottom front panel.

Kara and I stare at the altarpiece for a long time. We walk from side to side examining it slowly, trying to take in every detail. Our teenage children, not so much. They walk up to it, say, "Cool, I guess," and walk to the back of the church. They sit in a pew and look at their phones as intently as Kara and I look at the altarpiece. The deeper Kara and I become transfixed by the altarpiece, the heavier the annoyed boredom becomes that overtakes our teenagers. Soon we're being shot looks of impatience. We realize it's time to shift from St. Mary's five-hundred-year-old altarpiece to cheeseburgers at the WittenBurger restaurant.

Where We're Going

The objective of these final chapters is to make a case for the Beyonder pathway of surrender and confession. I want to make this case for confession and surrender because without its explicit articulation, our Protestant senses and imaginaries, and therefore pastoral practices, of transformation and spirituality (particularly inside pastoral ministry) will take the form of inner genius or heroic action. The spiritualities and mysticisms of inner genius and heroic action, as we've seen, lose the necessity for the divine act and being. The self

1. Truthfully, Melanchthon's casket was more in the sun than Luther's, which might be more fitting.

becomes so weighted by the pursuits of magnificence that even God is eclipsed by the self's importance (we have no time to seek God's glory because we must perform our own glory). The self becomes our full occupying idol in this late-modern secular age. The self is our myopic focus such that inner genius and heroic action become spiritualities and mysticisms without any real concern or interest in God. When ministry, directly or indirectly, adopts these forms of spirituality and mysticism, ministry too operates with views of transformation without God. These forms of ministry, following these mysticisms, fall into the apotheosizing of the self.

In the previous chapter, Byung-Chul Han, not a theologian but a cultural philosopher, helped us see why a spirituality made for the magnificent performing self is no spirituality at all. Han explained why the late-modern apotheosizing of the self is a treacherous lie. Building off Han, I pointed out that the pathways of inner genius and heroic action—while commendable at one level—at a more fundamental level are pathways that rest on a rotten foundation. Inside the apotheosizing of self, both pathways of inner genius and heroic action are obsessed with smooth positivity, transparency, and ultimately a contention that the self is magnificent (and yet needs to continually achieve magnificence). We (necessarily) create spiritualities and mysticisms without God when negativity, hiddenness/otherness, and the impossibility of the self are lost in illusions of the self's grandeur.

The long tradition of confession and surrender as a mystical pathway (and an imaginary for ministry), however, sees and experiences all this very differently. Instead of positivity, the Beyonder pathway of confession and surrender enters negativity or negation (the focus of the next chapter). Rather than transparency, it seeks to encounter what is other through what is hidden in emptiness. Ultimately it claims that transformation begins not when the self finds its magnificent genius or heroism but rather when it honestly confesses its un-magnificence—that the self is broken, in need, and up against impossibility (the self needs to be saved by something outside the self that can free the self from its own self-obsession). Confession and surrender claim that transformation comes and faithful mysticism rests on the confession of a revelation that "at once I knew I was *not* magnificent."[2] What this "un-magnificence" means will be our pursuit in this chapter.

---

2. This mysticism is built on faith. I use "faith" here to signal to Luther's turn to faith. Luther had a critical stance against some forms of mysticism, which I'll unpack below. To say

This centering on the un-magnificence of the self feels a bit icky, even quite heavy, to our late-modern ears. It's heavy because it runs counter to our formation in a neoliberal achievement society of performing selves. Jürgen Moltmann's words could not be more true than now in the third decade of the twenty-first century, inside a raging neoliberalism fueled by ubiquitous social media: in the social-media-driven neoliberalism of an achievement society of performing selves, the theology of the cross (the *theologia crucis*, which claims that God is known in the hiddenness of the losses and suffering the self encounters) indeed "cannot be much loved."[3] It can even be disdained and painted as nefarious. Therefore, to unpack what I mean by the confession of un-magnificence[4]—which embraces distance and hiddenness in emptiness—we need to return to the altarpiece in Saint Mary's Church in Wittenberg.

Two Uneducated Observations of the Panels

The altarpiece in Saint Mary's Church in Wittenberg was painted by Lucas Cranach in 1548. It was not that long after Luther's nailing of the Ninety-Five Theses to the All Saints' Church door and right in the midst of the battles of the Reformation. Cranach's panels are a catechism. They're meant to teach. Mainly, they're designed to open up the mysteries of the theology that Luther preaches. His theology doesn't shy away from distance and hiddenness in the emptiness and need (un-magnificence) of the self. All four front panels are centered on Luther's commitment to his reworking of the sacraments. The sacramental drips from each panel, witnessing to the mystical. But this mystical reality of the sacraments is imagined in a new way.

I'm no art major, but I notice two things before my meditation is interrupted by the surly teenage demand for cheeseburgers.

---

it simply, Luther did not wholeheartedly embrace mysticism, and he often had critical things to say about it. He believed some forms of mysticism violated the centrality of faith (as the rich theological category Luther imagines).

3. Jürgen Moltmann, *The Crucified God* (Minneapolis: Fortress, 1974), 1.

4. John Stoudt says, "For Luther, faith meant resignation and repentance, a conflict of penitence in which God becomes justified in us. Here Luther's basic dialectical idea appears, namely, that with God's justification in us our own justification in God takes place. This mystical heart of Luther's doctrine of justification implies resignation, repentance, humility here in this world, for with Luther as with Eckhart and German mysticism one act of faith unfolds itself both as man's justification by God and God's justification in man." Stoudt, *Jacob Boehme: His Life and Thought* (1957; repr., Eugene, OR: Wipf & Stock, 2004), 29.

Lucas Cranach, *Reformation Altarpiece*, 1547–48

Observation 1: The Community

First, I notice that in each panel there is a group of people, a community. They are depicted as ordinary people gathered to participate together in the mystery of Christ's real presence in the sacraments. The message is clear: the sacraments are for ordinary people, the mystical encounter with Christ through the sacraments is a communal reality. The days of the lording priest

and monastery are over. The mystical (or, better, sacramental) can no longer
be caged by the cloth or bound in the cloister. The community is now central.
This means it's no longer what you *do* that draws you into this mystical reality
but the necessity of *being* together, of receiving this gift of Christ's presence
in faith with and for others.

The community in the far left and right panels witnesses directly to this
mystical and sacramental reality. The community witnesses and testifies to a
baby's baptism and peers around the edges of a nobleman's confession. In the
bottom panel they receive Luther's preached word, which proclaims that the
fullness of God is revealed in the crucified Christ. The negativity of the cross,
the hiddenness and emptiness of the crucifixion, is central and essential to the
encounter with this real presence of Jesus Christ himself. The cross of negativity,
distant nearness, and hiddenness in emptiness is the central manifestation of
who God is, how God acts, and what it means to be human before this God made
known in the cross. The community lives through and out of this theology of
the cross. In the bottom panel, Luther preaches this gospel of God made known
in suffering, as some in the community sit and others stand. But all take in the
hiddenness of the mystery and beauty of the cross, of this body broken for us.

The center panel is Cranach's depiction of the Last Supper, the community par excellence, the place where Jesus gives his broken body fully to the
community. The disciples—some of them looking very much like sixteenth-
century Germans—partake of the cup with Jesus. They partake of the cup
that mystically is Jesus. This, too, signals how the sacramental is for everyone.
Before the Reformation, ordinary people took the host but only the priest
took the cup. Cranach depicts the cup being passed liberally. Yet, ultimately
what Cranach shows is the disciples together in conversation, sharing in Jesus
as they share together in the communion of the meal. But here too negativity
and hiddenness are present. Judas is at this table, scheming. Ultimately this
is Jesus's *last* supper before his body is broken like the bread so that all the
world can receive his body as a gift and a feast in the community of salvation.
The sacramental is inextricably for persons in relationship. It is a communal
reality built around shared suffering. This community is made up of ordinary
and broken people who share in one another by sharing in this meal that is
magnificent as it gathers and saves the un-magnificent.

This is the first thing my untrained eye notices in the altarpiece. But there is
something else I see as well, something that takes us further in understanding
this claim of un-magnificence.

Observation 2: Passive Receiving

As I look at the altarpiece with my untrained eye, my second observation is even more important for our pursuits of making a case for the Beyonder path of confession and surrender. It appears that each panel filled with communal participation in Luther's new sacramental reality (panels for baptism, the Lord's Supper, confession, and preaching) is centered on a state of passive receiving. The main mood in each panel is passivity. It's the direct receiving of something from outside the self. The self is asked to be in—even placed into a state of—passivity.

Cranach contends in these panels that the sacramental does not take the shape of, and the mystical is not encountered through, activity (*vita activa*). That would be in direct opposition to Luther's vision of justification by faith alone. Nor, however, is the sacramental a contemplative reality (*vita contemplativa*).[5] Rather, the sacramental—as a mystical experience of Christ's real presence—is encountered inside passive surrender (*vita passiva*). Each panel seems to represent this *vita passiva*. In passivity we are opened to an inbreaking transcendence (T3) and paradoxically led onto the Beyonder pathway of confession and surrender. Whatever the acknowledgment of unmagnificence means, it is bound to passivity (passivity is the best, dare I say only, medicine to performance).

We can see this passivity directly in each panel. All four front panels communicate that it is in *receiving* alone that we are transformed by Christ's real presence. In the left panel the baby can neither act nor contemplate for the sake of her own salvation, for the sake of her own self. There's no assumption (it would be absurd) that the self of a baby can seek to perform her own magnificence, competing with all the other infants for status and recognition (cue a Will Ferrell bit). It's ridiculous to assume that the baby's won magnificence is what qualifies her for baptism. Rather, she must simply and solely receive. Her infant passivity to the mystery is a blessed gift. She must just be, as the water and the words wash over her and the community holds her. The baby's very being (the fact that she is an infant) is a witness to us all that it is in the self's passivity, not the self's performance, that the self is transformed. In the self's childlike surrender we truly receive what is outside us that will save us. The baby is loved and treasured as the community holds her. But her need to be baptized, wetted by the death and resurrection of Jesus, is a sure

5. Now we begin to move beyond Han's vision.

confession that she, that her self, is not magnificent. Indeed, brokenness and impossibility surround her, and therefore only the negative death of the cross and the hidden glory of the resurrection can save her.

In the right panel the nobleman is in confession. His bearded face communicates that he is, of course, not an infant. Unlike the infant, the nobleman is willfully kneeling to receive. It is not the will of others but his own that takes him into the sacramental. The nobleman is putting aside his actions and contemplations in order to confess. He is a nobleman: if anyone in this sixteenth-century room is a magnificent self, it's him. But this nobleman is on a knee before a pastor who looks a lot like Luther (but is actually John Bugenhagen). Before this pastor, who speaks the word of God, the nobleman is passively receiving the gift of forgiveness. The nobleman is passive because the source of forgiveness is not within him but comes from beyond him. It is pure gift that he can never act or think his way into but can only receive through confession (through the negativity of spoken un-magnificence). In faith, the community wills that the infant be baptized. In the same faith the nobleman confesses so that he might receive the real (mystical) presence of Jesus Christ in forgiveness.

In the bottom panel, there is no ambiguity, no question whether that is Luther in the pulpit. It is unquestionably Luther who is preaching. Luther's pointed finger of proclamation witnesses to the very passivity of the being of God, who enters death and distance in Jesus's nearness to our own suffering and death. The gift of salvation, the most direct unveiling of God's own being, is revealed in the surrender of the cross, in the paradox of God's nearness in the distance and hiddenness of death. The whole of Luther's theology begins and ends with the cross (*theologia crucis*). All eyes of the community are on the cross. In the cross God is most active in passivity, bringing salvation to all selves, not through their magnificent action or contemplation but directly in their faith to trust that God is present, bringing life out of death. This is God surrendering to death so that death can be overcome by God's own action. The mysticism of the cross believes that while the distance and hiddenness are always distant and hidden, the God of the cross enters them, bringing life and community directly out of them.

If we happen to miss this theological point, the central panel makes it even more clear. To my untrained eye, the scene of the Last Supper is quite busy. It is clearly a community full of life. Some disciples are in contemplation, others seem to be plotting action. But interestingly, Jesus's own attention is on neither action nor contemplation but on the one who is passive. John, the beloved disciple, passively lies on Jesus Christ's chest. Jesus's attention is fully on him. Jesus embraces the one who is passive to receive: this one is transformed. The one who abandons busyness and competitive ranking, for the sake of being in faith by way of surrender, is the one who receives the presence of Christ. Jesus's own being is given to the one who passively receives, not the one who performs.

This second observation of passivity beckons us further in explorations of the self's un-magnificence. The centrality of passivity in Luther's *theologia crucis* and sacramentality connects us to the final of Han's three critiques from the previous chapter.

From Burgers to Bayer

As I eat my cheeseburger and fries at WittenBurger, less than a hundred yards from Saint Mary's, I find myself thinking again about Byung-Chul Han. I wonder what Han, the philosopher of the art university, would think of Cranach's panels. "Has Han seen them?" I wonder to myself as I dip my fries in an excessive amount of ketchup, signaling that I'm an American. Jeff Koons's late-modern pieces disgust Han, but what would Han think of Cranach's late-medieval (or early-modern) panels?

As we saw at the end of the previous chapter, Han is concerned that inside a neoliberal achievement society of performing selves, the life of action (*vita activa*) swallows up, bones and all, the life of contemplation (*vita contemplativa*). We are no longer reflective people but obsessively (hyper)active ones. This, Han believes, imposes a spiritual disease across all our late-modern societies. Our hyperactivity strips the world of its spirit of otherness, beauty, and scent. There is no time to interpret, perceive, or *be* at all. There is no time because we must act, and then act some more, or perish under the burden of the *could*.

My point, building off Han, is that the late-modern mysticisms of the E.Hums and CEs (inner genius and heroic action) are built directly for this hollow hyperactivity. These spiritualities are bound in the *could*, making the self the only and final place of significance. This ultimately leads us to divinize the self. What is outside the self has been flattened to meaninglessness, making only what is inside the self important. These hyperactive mysticisms are constructed to be smooth and transparent so the self can be quickly apotheosized as magnificent. These mysticisms and spiritualities must make the self into something magnificent, helping the self cope with the guilt of the *coulds*, because it is the only way to keep the noisy hyperactivity of late-modern life—which is vapid of spirit and without otherness—from obliterating us in the guilt of our own meaninglessness.

My guess is that Han would agree with the way Cranach's panels turn from a life of activity. Or maybe he would assume that all the depictions of the sacramental life were simply religious forms of this same (hyper)activity.[6] I imagine Han, following in the tradition of Hegel, would probably prefer panels that depict an ancient Greek ethos of a life of contemplation. He'd want something like men sitting under a tree contemplating the horizon. Like a good student of Heidegger, however, he would see contemplation, even under a tree, as being not just about contemplation itself. It wouldn't be about contemplating what it means to contemplate, but rather what it means to *be* at all, to be thrown into the world.

Luther could affirm some of this. Cranach's panels have some sense of this being thrown into the world, *being* inside of communities and practices. But what Luther could *not* affirm is the ancient Greek ethos of a *vita contemplativa*. Luther found the ethos of the ancient Greek philosophers and the drive for a life of pure contemplation problematic (as we'll see, speculation becomes an enemy for Luther). Luther found Aristotle's unique way of fusing this ethos of contemplation with action—what Aristotle called praxis—particularly devilish.[7]

In my uneducated interpretation, Cranach isn't depicting a *vita activa* or *vita contemplativa*. I wonder if Han would pick up on this. As the great contemporary Luther interpreter Oswald Bayer has argued, Luther denies both the *vita activa* and *vita contemplativa* for the sake of the *vita passiva*.[8]

---

6. He wouldn't be completely wrong. The (hyper)active society has its origins—in part—in the Reformation. We've discussed this above. I've also discussed this in other works. See particularly Andrew Root, *The Church after Innovation: Questioning Our Obsession with Work, Creativity, and Entrepreneurship* (Grand Rapids: Baker Academic, 2022), chap. 4.

7. I discuss this in depth in my *Christopraxis: A Practical Theology of the Cross* (Minneapolis: Fortress, 2017), chaps. 4 and 6.

8. Sarah Coakley also discusses passivity, doing so in a different theological tone than Bayer. She says, "What then does this particular life and example tell us about the relation of beliefs and 'practices'? What it suggests, and is now to be spelled out, is that the most purified Christian 'practice' (from whence a theology 'of the deep end' may 'be enunciated'), is one of being 'like God [in Christ] . . . handed over to the world, to wait upon it, to receive its power of meaning.' It is a passage into a peculiarly active form of passivity in which the divine pressure upon us meets not blockage but diaphanous clarification. And this—discreetly, quietly, and often even unconsciously in the recipient—through the long haul of repeated 'practices' of faithfulness." Coakley,

The *vita passiva*, I figure as I eat my cheeseburger, is what Cranach is trying to depict in his sacramental panels. It's about receiving, the reception of, the gift of Jesus's real presence to the self from outside the self. The self confesses its un-magnificence so it can receive a gift, so the self can be receptive to God's own act. The cross is too painted in distance and hiddenness to be encountered as a gift without the confession of the self's own un-magnificence, without the stopping of all activity and contemplation to just receive, to live in a mode of reception. The cross is the ultimate gift, for the crucified Christ turns death into life, giving us complete release from all performances to just *be* with and for others in community.

The necessity of confessing the self's un-magnificence isn't for the sake of flagellation. Confessing un-magnificence isn't a dire performance but an articulation (an honest admission as confession) of the true state of the self. *To perform a flagellation on the self is bad religion.* The confession of un-magnificence, which is central to Luther, is never for the sake of beating up the self. The self is *not* to go from the project of apotheosization to a punching bag. (The legitimacy of beating up the self is bound in the same logic as the divinizing of the self. The self beats itself up when it fails to win in performance.) Luther has no hate for the self. Luther is an Augustinian; the self is the place where God meets us. But for this to happen, the self must confess its un-magnificence as the way to remember that the self is a creature, called to stop and receive. The self confesses its un-magnificence—that all its obsessive performances in act and thought, even its religious ones, must end—so the self can just be, entering a state of passivity (attentive waiting[9]) for the sake of receiving God's presence in God's own action. (For Luther, God is active; we know God only through God's life of action—*vita activa*—but the human creature has its being not in action but in the reception of God's own action.)

Ultimately, the self must confess its un-magnificence so the self is freed from being a performer to being a receiver, given community with God and one another. The life of faith in the crucified Christ—the life that receives

---

The New Asceticism: Sexuality, Gender and the Quest for God (London: Bloomsbury, 2015), 110, quoting W. H. Vanstone, *The Stature of Waiting* (London: Darton, Longman & Todd, 1982), 115.

9. "The 'practices' of prayer that have all along sustained this process [of communing with God] may, if the contemplatives are to be believed, be purified and simplified into silent responsiveness, into an empty waiting on God which precedes 'union' in its full sense. This 'practice' of contemplation is strictly speaking God's practice in one—a more unimpeded or conscious form of that distinctive human receptivity to grace which has sustained the process all along and which is itself a divine gift." Coakley, *New Asceticism*, 125.

the mystery of the sacraments of Jesus's real presence—is a life that stops and waits to receive. It is a life lived in reception to the otherness of God and neighbor.[10] It is a life that has its goodness not in the self's magnificent performance but in the gift of Jesus's own person, which the self is invited to receive. Jesus particularly gives his own person to our experiences of death and loss, to the very places of impossibility, where we are only able to receive in passivity. Here impossibility and passivity are connected.[11] The death of the cross is the beckoning for the self to stop and receive the only thing that can save and redeem the self—the gift of God's own action.[12]

Oswald Bayer believes that this attention to passivity is what connects Luther's theology of the cross with a life of faith.[13] The cross and faith are held together, as the deep realities they are for Luther, by passivity. Bayer contends that Luther turns to passivity over activity and contemplation because of his reading of the Rhineland mystics. The Rhineland mystics (Meister Eckhart, Johannes Tauler, the Mysterious Frankfurter of the *Theologia Germanica*) assert that the self is in deep need of receiving something from outside the self to save the self.[14] The self is never a performative project but a receiver, a creature of reception. The self receives what can save it, thereby connecting

10. Rowan Williams unpacks some of this very nicely, saying, "The Lutheran 'conversion to the world' has little to do with the fashionable notion that God is to be found in the world or in the service of others rather than in prayer and the conscious attempt to direct our reflective and imaginative life Godward. If conversion does not begin in each person's private hell, in the meeting with God the crucifier and the crucified in the depths of the heart, there is no ground for the second level of conversion. But once the self has been dethroned in the interior victory of God's righteousness, there is only one possible 'translation' of this into bodily life, and that is the service of the neighbor. The self that is killed by God in order to be made alive must experience this death in the social, the public world at the hands of other human beings." Williams, *The Wound of Knowledge: Christian Spirituality from the New Testament to Saint John of the Cross* (Lanham, MD: Cowley, 1990), 165.

11. Eberhard Jüngel develops this theme in *Theological Essays* (Edinburgh: T&T Clark, 1989), chap. 4.

12. Philip Ziegler draws this out further through his discussions of Paul and Kierkegaard. See Ziegler, *Militant Grace: The Apocalyptic Turn and the Future of Christian Theology* (Grand Rapids: Baker Academic, 2018), 156.

13. See Oswald Bayer, *Theology the Lutheran Way* (Minneapolis: Fortress, 2017), 25–28.

14. "In the logic of German mysticism, man cooperates in the attainment of his salvation by simply freely doing nothing (i.e., *Gelassenheit*). Weigel dismisses the synergistic controversy with a mystically influenced reciprocity of divine and human activity—a reciprocity . . . which springs from the most basic presuppositions of his theological thinking. His last words on the issue are: Man must bring forth sheer passivity, resignation, a surrendered will, a dying to self, and hold himself still. For as soon as man goes out of himself with his own will, just so does God enter with his will." Steven E. Ozment, *Mysticism and Dissent: Religious Ideology and Social Protest in the Sixteenth Century* (New Haven: Yale University Press, 1973), 47.

the self to the divine being, by stopping (not by doing or thinking).[15] The self must stop and let go of all activity and contemplation, embracing the self's emptiness and distance from God, so it can receive the magnificent birth of God directly inside the self's own empty un-magnificence.[16] Eckhart even wants us to forget all we know about God (a major turn from *vita contemplativa*) so that we can enter more deeply into nothingness and to find in our nothingness the God who transcends all contemplation. Eckhart means something very similar to Luther's passivity when Eckhart says that we find God in nothing, that God is (in) nothingness.[17]

15. "The Rhineland tradition, which was also a major influence on the devotion movement, and therefore on Erasmus, stressed the presence of the divine within each human being, and proposed that this presence is not only the core of the human self, but also something that can be realized by a process of self-emptying and detachment." Carlos M. N. Eire, *Reformations: The Early Modern World, 1450–1650* (New Haven: Yale University Press, 2016), 277.

16. Johannes Tauler says, "If you want to be taken up into God's inmost nature, to be transformed into him, then you must free yourself of yourself, of your nature, your inclinations, your actions, your self-opinion, in short of all the ways in which you have had of yourself. For with these it cannot work. Two bodies, two entities cannot occupy the same space. If warmth is to enter, then the cold must leave. Is God to find a way in? Then created things and all that which is in your possession must make a space for him. If God is really to be active in you, then you must enter a state of true passivity. All your faculties must be stripped of their action and their self-assertion and you must maintain yourself in a pure denial of yourself, deprived of all force, dwelling in a pure and absolute nothing-ness. The more we become nothing, the truer and more essential is our union with God. And if it ever became as pure and as essential as is the case with the soul of our Lord Jesus Christ—which of course is not possible—then our union with God would be as great as is Christ's union with him. We become God in so far as we lose ourselves. If God is truly to speak to you, then all the energies of your soul must be silent. It is not a question of learning to do, but of learning not to do." Tauler, "Sermon 31," in Oliver Davies, *The Rhineland Mystics: An Anthology* (Eugene, OR: Wipf & Stock, 1989), 71.

17. I don't want to oversell how connected Luther is to Eckhart. Luther never quotes Eckhart. Ozment draws from Heinrich Bornkamm in showing the significant difference between Luther and Eckhart. There are ten distinct differences Ozment lists:
1. Less bold and speculative than Eckhart, Luther confined himself to Scripture and biblical terms.
2. He believed that religious intellectus was the special insight of faith, not, as Eckhart taught, a latent ability in the ground of man's soul.
3. Luther could find no "still point" in the depths of the soul which served as a medium for divine purity.
4. Luther conceived man as a whole being, not as a composite of contradictory natural and supernatural essences.
5. Luther saw man's union with God to bring a new understanding of his distance from God, while Eckhart believed it removed all sense of distinction.
6. Luther did not believe that union with God came by ascetical exercises, as the final state of contemplation, as Eckhart taught the nuns of Cologne.
7. Critical of external works and religiosity, Eckhart held that the inner work of humility performed in quest of mystical union was meritorious of grace.

On the Beyonder pathway the self becomes receptive to the gift of trans-formation that comes from the cross of Christ by surrendering to nothingness and confessing impossibility. Surrender and confession are the shape of a life of reception. They are the marks of passivity that open us to receive the transcendence of God's own act of the ministry of love for, and communion with, the self. The Beyonder pathway of surrender and confession is a mysti-cism bound in the *vita passiva*.[18]

Han has helped us see that the mysticisms built for the *vita activa* of the E.Hums and CEs are bankrupt. But to move beyond this critique we need to explore more in-depth not the *vita contemplativa*, as Han wishes, but the *vita passiva*. Han seems to believe the *vita contemplativa* can be a mysticism in itself. The Rhineland mystics, and Luther following them, aren't so sure.[19] To see further the importance of the *vita passiva*, and how it's the substance of the confession of un-magnificence and the surrender to creaturehood, we need to recognize how fundamental passivity is to a Beyonder pathway.[20]

---

8. For Luther, people were as divinely called into worldly vocations as into clerical ranks.

9. Whereas for Luther preaching and the sacraments were the only media of God's spirit and truth, Eckhart considered them external aids to the individual's retreat 'into the depths of the soul' where the inner word and spark of the soul served as the true media of the Spirit.

10. Luther did not share the mystic's disdain for the world as something unreal and to be surrendered—"the world was more filled with God for Luther than for Eckhart." (Ozment, *The Age of Reform, 1250–1550: An Intellectual and Religious History of Late Medieval and Reformation Europe* [New Haven: Yale University Press, 1980], 241n57)

Rowan Williams adds context, saying, "What Luther (and the classical Protestant world in general up to the present century) objects to is the perversion of the contemplative approach into a 'mysticism' which imprisons God again in a set of human experiences. Eckhart's insistence that no particular, special religious experience mediates God unambiguously, that there must be no seeking after 'inwardness or peace' for its own sake, is very close to Luther's thinking. And if Luther can be read in the light of Eckhart (and of Eckhart's disciples, Suso and Tauler, whom Luther studied extensively), it is clear that the reformer cannot simply be interpreted as an enemy to contemplative theology and practice: he is, rather, an uncompromising champion of the innate iconoclasm of contemplation." Williams, *Christian Spirituality: A Theological History from the New Testament to Luther and St. John of the Cross* (Atlanta: John Knox, 1980), 147–48.

18. Louis Dupré says powerfully, "In denying passivity and dependence we have excluded a deeper level of existence." Dupré, *Transcendent Selfhood* (New York: Seabury, 1976), ix.

19. Here again, Han is much like the German idealists. Hegel, Schelling, and others believed there was a way back into the mystical by recovering the *vita contemplativa* of ancient Greeks.

20. Rowan Williams adds, "What is clear is that during this period Luther realized that the righteousness of God was not 'active'—that by which God condemns—but 'passive'—that by which he finds us acceptable by making us righteous. God's *justitia* is what God gives us in order

All the memoirs of the Beyonders found the gift of redemption not in activity or contemplation but in passivity, in the receptive life of prayer, even before the ability to believe (Jamison and Karr). For Deraniyagala it was in embracing her depth of sorrow and receiving the beauty of the whale in the same waters that took her family. For Yip-Williams it was in dying well, receiving death too as a miracle of life. For Jones, it came in sitting with a new friend in the glow of a Barcelona sunset, confessing that his mother is dead and he is broken, receptive to the moment of shared suffering and rich friendship. A Beyonder mystical pathway that confesses the un-magnificence of the self rests squarely on passivity. This passivity runs counter to our neoliberal formations in an achievement society of *coulds*, and so we need to explore passivity more deeply so its theological and ministerial profundity can be grasped. To do so, we'll follow Oswald Bayer's lead further into the heart of Luther.

The Land of Passivity

In his book *Theology the Lutheran Way*, Oswald Bayer explores the *vita passiva* in a section called "Luther's Understanding of Theology."[21] It could just as accurately have been called "Luther's Understanding of Faith and Life" or "Luther's Understanding of the Mystical Preaching of Johannes Tauler." We'll explore this piece to see how passivity—not flagellation—is what rightly moves the self from curving in on the self in pursuit of magnificence to receiving the act of God (T3) and walking the Beyonder pathway. Yet, to explore the importance of passivity we first need to follow Bayer's lead and understand why Luther forcefully refuses the *vita contemplativa* and the *vita activa*. Doing so will allow us to perceive the texture and depth of passivity.

How Contemplation Becomes Speculation and Kneels to Action

In his piece, Bayer explains that Luther is somewhat caught. Luther has no patience for Scholastic theologians who are preoccupied with, and fixated on, theory. Luther is a Psalms professor and preacher. As such, Luther is drawn to

---

to make us his. It is grace and not condemnation. Luther writes movingly to Staupitz about the 'paschal' quality of this experience, the overwhelming sense of a deliverance from bondage. This was his metanoia, the conversion that made new the whole world, which revealed a new God. A God who could be loved, prayed to and trusted even as he smote and killed. A strange and a terrifying God; yet a source of life and hope." Williams, *Wound of Knowledge*, 157.

21. See Bayer, *Theology the Lutheran Way*, part 1. I'll particularly be exploring pages 21–30.

(ordinary) people crying out to God. Luther believes this crying out to God is both the most poignant picture of faith and the best way to do theology (his *theologia crucis* and the Psalms are indivisible). Whatever Luther means by passivity, it is *not* without a searching, a crying out, a seeking God, as with the psalmist. The psalmist is in the lament of passivity because the psalmist needs, demands, and cries out to receive God's act. The psalmist's act is the passivity of prayer, that in praise and pain the psalmist stops to receive God's act. As a preacher, Luther's task is to address a community with the Word that speaks to their lives—hence Cranach's gathered community in each panel. Therefore, Luther must read and study for the sake of prayer and proclamation, not contemplation. Theory for theory's sake, contemplation for the good of more contemplation, doesn't appeal to Luther, who reads the Psalms and bellows the Word from Saint Mary's pulpit.

But this rejection of contemplation goes deeper. Luther denies that theology and faith are about contemplation because he worries contemplation offers the poison of speculation as a fruity punch. Luther finds particularly the obsessive contemplations of the Scholastics and other theologians to be poisonous. What makes contemplation noxious is that in the hands of theologians, contemplation becomes a game of speculating about God. It becomes about trying to get behind God, making God's hiddenness transparent. Speculation, for Luther (and Han), doesn't respect, and therefore accept, God's hidden otherness. In pride, the (Scholastic) theologian believes his dexterity in contemplation can completely unveil God, making God transparent. To give Luther Han's cutting and shocking language (which I think Luther would love), theologies of contemplation are pornographic. Such theologians are titillated by speculation. In the end, they want speculation more than they want encounter with the living God, who makes Godself known in the cross.

In Cranach's bottom panel, Luther points to the cross as the center of the community—as he preaches to the community—because Luther refuses speculation. Like Paul, Luther preaches only Christ and him crucified (1 Cor. 2:2). The crucified Christ is God revealed, and concretely so. But the fact that God is revealed in the cross means that this revealing remains always veiled and hidden. The cross opposes in all ways the idea that God can ever be transparent, that theology and faith can ever be pornographic (the pastor who is sure that he knows God's will, that God's will is transparent to him, is a pastor with a pornographic theology that has rejected the cross).

Yet while the cross opposes transparency, the cross affirms concreteness. The cross gives us *not* speculations about God but the direct encounter with the living God, who acts (backwardly) in the world, at the very ground of our lives. The cross concretely reveals God while allowing God to remain hidden in the world in a very particular way. The cross is the shape of God's direct encounter with us. But this direct encounter through the cross evades all transparency. The cross rebukes the temptation of the self to turn in on itself to seek its own magnificence through its own speculation—we know only Christ and him crucified.

For Luther the *vita contemplativa* is too contingent on the self. Its relationship to the self is too dependent on the magnificence of the self to accept the gift of God's hidden otherness. A magnificent self is too turned in on itself, obsessed with its own thoughts, to stop and recognize that it is in absurdity and weakness that God is made known, that hiddenness and otherness are essential. Indeed, as with Paul in the Corinthians letters, to speak of this God made known in the hiddenness of the cross is not to be magnificent in contemplation but a fool (1 Cor. 1:18). Proclamation is witness to the cross, as God's own veiled unveiling, pulling us out of ourselves to encounter the event of the cross in its absurdity. To behold the cross is to find God present in the places we cannot overcome by our contemplation—our suffering and deaths. The self cannot, through its own magnificent speculations, move itself (perform its way) near to the otherness of God. But the otherness of God comes near to us in our need for a minister next to the self's impossibilities.

For Luther, the pastor doesn't speculate about God, making God transparent, becoming addicted to a pornographic theology. Without the cross as central it is possible for human beings, through overattention to actions or contemplations, to eliminate God's otherness and hiddenness from our imaginations. Luther believes the pastor gives attention to the cross as the witness to God's own unveiling, as an event of revelation. This revelation is an inbreaking transcendence (T3) that remains hidden, particularly in the fact that this unveiling is bound in negativity—in the suffering of the cross. Luther fuses theology and the life of faith together by attending only to the God revealed, the God made known in the veil (in the hidden unveiling) of Jesus Christ crucified.

The *vita contemplativa* cannot do this. The *vita contemplativa* too quickly inflates the self, drawing the self into itself in the performance of the self's speculation. Speculation, as opposed to an encounter with the event of reve-lation, inflates the self. Inside the *vita contemplativa*, faith becomes defined as the virtues that the self performs, as a righteousness located and produced by the magnificent self.[22] The righteousness the self seeks is self-made. This self-made righteousness keeps us performing. It makes us too active in our contemplations to stop, wait, and receive the foreign righteousness of Jesus Christ, who comes to the brokenness of the self by means of his own broken-ness on the cross.

Han misses that, ironically, the *vita contemplativa* slides so easily into the *vita activa* (which can be traced historically as the Greek ethos of contempla-tion shifted into a Roman life of action, and this historical shift finds its way into the veins of modernity). Han worries that our late-modern (hyper)activity swallows contemplation. But what he doesn't see is that when contemplation demands the self's speculation, it opens the back door to the *vita activa*, al-lowing it to take over the whole house. Luther's point—and his response to Han if they were to stumble into each other at WittenBurger—is not only that the *vita contemplativa* is problematic for its obsession with speculation but that in the end the *vita contemplativa* cannot stand against the *vita activa*. The *vita activa* will conquer and colonize the *vita contemplativa* (as Rome does Greece). The active life will consume the contemplative life.

If late-modern life is overcome by (hyper)activity, strangling us with *coulds*, in the end, contemplation will be no alternative. Luther believes the *con-templatio* cannot stand against *actio*; contemplation cannot withstand the strength of action. Both the *vita contemplativa* and the *vita activa* rest on the same high anthropology of the self's magnificence. In turn, both *contemplatio* and *actio* direct the self's attention away from the cross, away from the self's *need* to receive what it is not, to search and become dependent on a foreign righteousness that can bring redemption from guilt. Instead of attention being on the cross, the *vita contemplativa* and the *vita activa* put attention on either the self's speculation or the self's works. If Luther opposes the *vita contem-plativa* because of the poison of speculation, he resists in every way the *vita activa* because of the infectious disease of works. Luther thinks the temptation of works is so full-on that eventually even contemplation becomes a work the self uses to wall itself off from God's revelation that calls us to stop and receive through suffering.

22. This is how the Scholastics think of faith. See Bayer, *Theology the Lutheran Way*, 23.

It is not necessary to say much more about Luther's revulsion for works righteousness, which rests squarely on the *vita activa*. His view on this is well-known (even unfortunately to the point of caricature). Yet, seeing Luther's revulsion toward works through our discussions in the chapters above gives his distaste a different dimension. Luther's revulsion toward works anticipates what Luther couldn't possibly imagine: the corrosive realities of the late-modern performing self of an achievement society of neoliberal *coulds*. Luther anticipated what he couldn't see, a world obsessed with and rendered lifeless or spiritless by (hyper)activity. Yet, what Luther could see, and the shapers of modernity should have seen through him, is that there is no way to hold a productive tension between contemplation and activity. Many, even before Luther, tried to hold this balance. They, like Han after them, thought that if contemplation and action could be held in a kind of yin-and-yang correlation, we could "avoid giving one preeminence over the other."[23] Han helpfully points out that this correlation has been lost: activity has swallowed contemplation in late modernity. But Han wants to reestablish the importance of contemplation. Like a Jedi, he wants to return balance between the *vita contemplativa* and *vita activa*. But Luther helps us see that Han is wrong in assuming that this is even possible. If Luther were sharing a beer with Han at WittenBurger, now swigging his third pint, Luther would remind Han of Meister Eckhart's failed sermon on Mary and Martha.[24]

The Sister Battle at Bethany

Luke's story of the two sisters in Bethany (Luke 10) has been a favorite of mystical writers in the Christian tradition since Origen in the third century. Why it's been a favorite makes good sense. The text is set up for allegory. Here is Martha, the epitome of the *vita activa*. And Mary is the manifestation of the *vita contemplativa*. And there is Jesus, clearly stating that Mary has chosen the better way (Luke 10:42). Score one for the mystics! The company line for

---

23. Bayer, *Theology the Lutheran Way*, 23.

24. Han would be interested in Eckhart. He probably has even read Eckhart because of Han's study of Heidegger. As I've said in chapter 4, Heidegger was drawn to Eckhart. The truth is, however, that Luther was not a big fan of Eckhart. It seems clear to me, though, that this Rhineland/German mysticism was very important in assisting Luther in his theological breakthrough. It is fair to say that Luther was impacted by Eckhart (and more than likely, Luther read some Eckhart), but Luther doesn't quote him much, and even when talking about the German mystics, he doesn't name Eckhart. It is Johannes Tauler, Eckhart's student, whom Luther appreciates, as we'll discuss below.

mystics since Origen has been to laud Mary. They have made the case that Mary from Bethany is a protomystic herself, concerned not with the activities of the house and therefore the world but with being in the presence of Jesus. The mystical life of refused activity for the sake of contemplation is endorsed by Jesus himself. The priests, bishops, and cardinals (not to mention the merchants, princes, warriors, and laborers) are Marthas. But the mystic in the desert, the monk in the monastery, is a Mary. And Mary has chosen rightly; she has chosen contemplation over action. The clear assumption here in this text is that Jesus is affirming the *vita contemplativa* over the *vita activa*. Jesus's words in Luke's text allow the mystics to dunk on everyone else.

But Meister Eckhart can't follow this. In the fourteenth century, Eckhart, the father of the Rhineland mystics, isn't interested in dunking on anyone. He sees no need to flex for Team Mystic. Eckhart is now a preacher, overseeing praying nuns, preaching to ordinary men and women who wander in from their activity to hear him preach. Eckhart is no longer locked in the monastery, and he is right in the middle of developing his own mysticism for the everyday. Therefore, he reads this Mary and Martha story in a starkly different way.[25] He has to read it differently because, as we saw above, Eckhart has no trust in the self's contemplations.[26]

Eckhart does not believe the self's contemplations are able to access the magnificence necessary to place the self in the presence of God. Eckhart teaches all the Rhineland mystics, who teach Luther, that the self can never access God through the self's own magnificent capacities, but only through the self's acceptance of absence and need. For Eckhart, finding union with God, participating in God's very life, is not an operation of contemplation at all. Rather, contemplation must be crucified. Eckhart believes we find ourselves (the self is found) in the presence of the living God not through the edifices of the self's thoughts and reflections but by nothing. It is only by confessing and surrendering, asserting in this confession and surrender that we know nothing of God (detaching and letting go of all our contemplations about God), that we find our self on a ground where, through nothingness, God is born in us, meeting us with life. The Rhineland mystics find the pathway to union with God (a transformation of T3) not through contemplation but through

25. Not that differently from other mystics before him—they too try to rework Martha—but not quite with the directness that Eckhart does.

26. John Caputo discusses Eckhart's use of this story in *The Mystical Element in Heidegger's Thought* (New York: Fordham University Press, 1986), 137–38.

nothing, inside of nothingness. (Luther will strip all the remaining patina of speculative Scholasticism from Eckhart's words, naming this nothingness as, concretely, the cross.[27]) This causes Eckhart (in *Sermon 86*) to read Luke 10 very differently from how we've traditionally read it.

In this sermon Eckhart flips everything on its head. It takes some hermeneutical gymnastics, which I honestly don't believe Eckhart really pulls off. But it's not without trying. Eckhart, like Han after him, is trying to bring balance between the *vita contemplativa* and the *vita activa* (Eckhart is the Yoda of the Rhineland). Eckhart seeks a balance, which Luther believes is a futile task. And Eckhart's failed attempt seems to me to be a point in Luther's case. To try and find this balance, Eckhart inverts our usual reading of Mary and Martha. Eckhart believes that it is Martha, not Mary, who is the favored one. Jesus's words are still true. Mary has chosen rightly. Not because contemplation is ultimately better than action but because Mary is a novice. Mary must enter the *vita contemplativa* and sit in "sweet solace and joy"[28] at Jesus's feet because she is not ready to enter the nothingness as a way of life. Mary is too young, too green, in Eckhart's mind, to get to the ground of her being that is necessary.

But, to Eckhart, Martha is mature. She is mature because her connection to God is not bound to feelings of sweetness that come and go like thoughts of contemplation. Rather, Martha's union with God is in the muscle memory of activity. Martha's seeking of God is unthought. It has become natural to her, needing no contemplation. Or better, the contemplation is so deep, so grounded in her, that she can just act. Like an American football player who has studied and memorized his plays, she can just react and stop thinking. Contemplation has shifted into habit. Martha serves Christ and others as a reflex. The *vita activa* has become a God-formed reflex. Eckhart finds the balance between *vita contemplativa* and *vita activa* through habitual reflex (he's not that far from Aristotle here, though he is radical among the mystics for his refusal of the *vita contemplativa*).[29] Mary has not advanced as far as

---

27. In many ways it is Eberhard Jüngel who puts the cross and nothingness back together. See his *God as the Mystery of the World* (Grand Rapids: Eerdmans, 1983), 33–35.

28. Meister Eckhart, "Sermon 86," in *Meister Eckhart: Teacher and Preacher* (Mahwah, NJ: Paulist Press, 1986), 34.

29. Eckhart's nearness to Aristotle makes some sense. Eckhart was the student of Albert the Great, who was also the teacher of Thomas Aquinas. It was Albert and Aquinas who did more than anyone to bring Aristotle (who was recently rediscovered) into the life of the church. Eckhart would have known Aristotle's and Aquinas's works very well.

Martha, so she must sit at Jesus's feet and contemplate, learning the plays. But Martha can just live.

For Eckhart, the fact that it is a reflex means that Martha has made it to the ground—the very ground of her own being—which is the direct place where God meets us in union. For Eckhart, the key is always making it to the ground, for God is found at the very ground of our being, the very place of self-emptying. Eckhart says in the sermon, "The ground of [Martha's] being was so fully trained that she thought none could do the work as well as she." The most generous reading of this line is to interpret it as Eckhart saying that the ground of Martha's being is so well formed through right contemplation that she can hear the clear call to act for God and others. This would balance the *vita contemplativa* and *vita activa*. But that interpretation massages the line quite a bit. Ultimately, this tough line, to my mind, reveals Eckhart's stumbling as he tries to land his gymnastics flip. Competition and comparison creep in, showing the dead end of trying to balance action and contemplation. This line reveals that Eckhart's landing lacks the steady stick of a Simone Biles flip.

The Receptive Life

Watching Eckhart's gymnastic flips to keep the *vita contemplativa* and *vita activa* in balance, twisting Martha into an exemplar, leads Luther to deny the whole sport. Luther decides that a life of faith cannot rest on the *vita contemplativa* and surely not on the *vita activa*. Balance between these two options is not possible, helpful, or necessary. Luther refuses the two as the ground of faith. Instead, Luther turns to an entirely third option as the place where faith and theology must rest. This third option, which moves us beyond a life of contemplation and a life of action, is a life of reception. As Bayer says, "Luther . . . sees theology and faith having their own unique life: the receptive life (*vita passiva*)."[30]

Faith does not rest in *thinking rightly* or *acting rightly*. It rests solely and only in a life of reception, in an openness to receive. Faith is only and finally a gift; faith can only be received. Faith is never anything other than the gift of the person of Jesus Christ, who comes to our person from far outside our self. Faith, for Luther, has no source in the thinking or acting of the self.[31]

---

30. Bayer, *Theology the Lutheran Way*, 23.

31. "Faith for Luther plays the same essential part, *mutatis mutandis*, as knowledge and love for the earlier mystics: it is the unique power of the soul, the *adhaesio Dei*, which unites

The self only receives faith, never producing it by thought or action. Faith is not a way of thinking (not even a way of believing, which is the typical American evangelical definition of faith) or a way of acting (not a way of social or political action, the typical American mainline definition of faith).[32] Rather, to have faith is to enter a state of reception; it is to live a life open to receiving. This life of reception stands in direct opposition to the neoliberal life of achievement and performance.

The mysticisms of the E.Hums (inner genius) and CEs (heroic action) become so alluring to both evangelicals and mainliners (pulling them down our triangle away from the Beyonders) because they are mysticisms still inside the tension between contemplation and action. Therefore, in these late-modern mysticisms, attention is first on the self (what the self thinks or believes, how the self acts). In turn these mysticisms' attention is not on the God who acts to give to the self what the self is not. Their attention cannot be on what is outside the self because inside of neoliberalism, contemplation and action are black holes where the event horizon is only and finally the self. (But as we'll see, the receptive life escapes this. For the self to receive, its attention must be outside the self—action and contemplation place attention on the self's capacities; reception focuses on what is outside the self.)

The mysticisms of the E.Hums and CEs (and the Protestant forms that follow them) can so easily be without God because their center of attention is on the self's thoughts and actions, not the self's empty hands. The attention

---

man with God: and unity is the very signature of the mystical. So that when Luther says that Faith makes man one cake (*ein Kuche*) with God or Christ, or holds him as a ring holds a jewel (*sicut annulus gemvuim*), he is not speaking any more figuratively than when Tauler says the same of Love. 'Faith' for Luther, as 'Love' for Tauler and the mystics generally, is a something that cannot be exhaustively comprised in rational concepts, and to designate which figures and images are a necessity. To him 'Faith' is the centre of the Soul—the *fundus animae* or 'basis of the soul' of the mystics—in which the union of man with God fulfils itself." Rudolf Otto, *The Idea of the Holy: An Inquiry into the Non-Rational Factor in the Idea of the Divine and Its Relation to the Rational* (n.p.: Pantianos Classics, 1917), 81.

32. Ironically, these misguided views of faith come together in anxieties around participation. Therefore, most faith formation material assumes that decline is a sign of lack of faith and that the biggest issue facing Protestantism is lack of participation. Therefore, divergent groups come together to try and solve this faith problem, groups such as the Fuller Youth Institute and the Evangelical Lutheran Church in America (ELCA). But the ELCA should know better. They should know that Luther would never define faith in this way—seeing it locked in the *vita contemplativa* and *vita activa*. Rather, faith is bound in the receptive life of the *vita passiva*. This puts a focus not on participation (and belief) but on openness to the hiddenness of God's action, receiving Jesus's real presence through the negativity of suffering and death. Discipleship is to die with Christ, not to commit to participate and believe.

on thoughts and actions makes the self the center of gravity. It keeps the self from being open to receive (to live in reception of) what the self is not, from the God who is other in hiddenness, coming near in brokenness. A view of faith not freed from the *vita contemplativa* can easily be without God as the self slides into obsessively seeking to think rightly about the self's own inner genius. In a similar way, a view of faith not moved beyond the *vita activa* can also be without God, because what matters is the self's heroic actions—the ability of the self, not God, to change the world.

As we saw in the memoirs, a Beyonder mysticism cannot be without God because the self is moved into confession and surrender. All the memoirists on the Beyonder pathway enter a life of reception. Confession and surrender, unlike inner genius and heroic action, shape the self not for the *vita contemplativa* or *vita activa* but for a receptive life. Confession and surrender open the self to be in a state of reception. Confession and surrender position the self to seek what is outside the self to meet the self where the self is up against impossibility and brokenness. The mysticism of confession and surrender is fundamentally different (and more faithful—more full of faith—and therefore should be at the center of pastoral imagination) because confession and surrender place the self in a position of reception. Only in a life of reception can the immanent frame be opened and the self made attentive to the arriving of revelation.

Luther completely rejects Eckhart's desire to balance the *vita contemplativa* and *vita activa*. Yet, ironically, it's from the sermons of Eckhart's student Johannes Tauler that Luther draws inspiration for the life of reception (*vita passiva*).[33] Bayer says, "This revolutionary new definition emerged from Luther's critical engagement with a *particular form of mysticism* that he came to know and appreciate from the sermons of Tauler."[34] This form of mysticism, which dates two hundred years before Luther, is the Rhineland form that again and again asserts that the self needs to be empty, not magnificent, in order to receive (and live a life of reception before) the act of the living God. This form of mysticism sees the practices of confession and surrender as the way to shape the self for an encounter with the God of the cross. In Bayer's words, it is only in the receptive life "that God is the active subject and the humans simply 'suffer' (*passio*) or undergo [God's] work."[35]

---

33. For a rich picture of Tauler's dependence on Eckhart, see Davies, *Rhineland Mystics*, 10–12.
34. Bayer, *Theology the Lutheran Way*, 23 (emphasis added).
35. Bayer, *Theology the Lutheran Way*, 23.

Tauler taught Luther that the shape of faith is a life of reception, which for Luther meant that "the cross alone is our theology."[36] The cross alone is our way of conceiving of God's acts in the world, for the cross is sunk not only into God's way of being but also our own. Both God and humanity know dying. The cross is the place of union between the divine and the human. But the cross is the experience of being rendered passive, receiving life out of death. For Tauler, the self is not un-magnificent because the self is awful in its performance. The self is un-magnificent because the self will die, because death is all around the self. What Luther learns from Tauler's mysticism, and what becomes concrete in Luther's own ministry, is that it is right inside this very experience of dying (in big and small ways) that the self receives life. In dying, the self takes on the very shape of the God who dies on the cross. As Bayer says, "The crucial thing about the receptive life (*vita passiva*) is that it is connected with a particular experience: an experience that I do not primarily produce but suffer or undergo."[37] Luther says, "It is by living—no, not living, but by dying and giving ourselves up to hell that we become theologians, not by understanding, reading, and speculating."[38] There is no earning or contemplating our way to transformation, no do-it-yourself spirituality, for the salvation of transformation arrives when we receive God's ministry of life inside our death. Faith is simply but profoundly the surrender and confession that death is before you, and you—your self—cannot stop it. In turn, faith is confessing that you do trust that when death comes howling, so too does your God, because God has bound Godself to all broken selves, by the cross, giving them the gift of Jesus's own life out of Jesus's own death. It's here that the un-magnificent self receives the deepest of unions (a transformation that moves into *theosis*) with the very magnificence of Christ. The self confesses and surrenders to the un-magnificence within, so the self can attend to the without, receiving the magnificence of Jesus's life as the self's own.[39]

---

36. "Crux sola est nostra theologia." Luther, *Dr. Martin Luthers Werke: Kritische Gesamtausgabe* (Weimar: H. Böhlau, 1883–1993), 5:176, quoted in Bayer, *Theology the Lutheran Way*, 23.

37. Bayer, *Theology the Lutheran Way*, 23.

38. Luther, *Operationes in Psalmos (1519–21)*, in *Dr. Martin Luthers Werke*, 5:163.28–29.

39. Bayer adds, "Those who are born anew are no longer entangled with themselves. They are solidly freed from this entanglement, from the self-reflection that always seeks what belongs to itself. This is not a deadening of self. It does not flee from thought and responsibility. No, it is the gift of self-forgetfulness. The passive righteousness of faith tells us: You do not concern yourself at all! In that God does what is decisive in us, we may live outside ourselves and solely in him. Thus, we are hidden from ourselves, and removed from the judgment of others or the judgment of ourselves about ourselves as a final judgment. 'Who am I?' Such self-reflection never

Bayer says it this way: "Faith is not a theory, nor is it the practice of self-realization or self-fulfillment, but it is passive righteousness. In other words, faith is God's work in us, which we experience by letting God work this faith in us. We do this by dying to justifying thinking and acting. This does not mean that faith is unthinking and inactive. On the contrary, it renews both thinking and acting."[40]

My contention is that all the memoirists on the Beyonder pathway of confession and surrender do this. They find faith—their spirituality cannot be without God, at the very least not without real otherness—because in their confession and surrender to the many faces of death, they encounter the arriving (T3) of the God who is present and at work in death. This brings forth union with God through the Spirit of life. The Beyonder memoirists' confession of the self's un-magnificence is the reception (the receptive life) of God's working in them, ministering new life to them out of death. The sure sign that they've entered the receptive life is the stance of prayer that many of them enter. Prayer, of course, has some elements of action and contemplation to it, but ultimately prayer is a passive stance of entering the life of reception. This is what the psalmist shows us, and Luther, the Psalms professor, cannot turn away from suffering and death.

But isn't this all too negative? Actually, we haven't gotten negative enough.

Conclusion

Following Luther and the Rhineland mystics, we've responded to two of Han's critiques in this chapter. We've seen particularly how the Beyonder pathway of confession and surrender avoids these two critiques. In relation to the first critique, we've seen how the Beyonder pathway of confession and surrender (as opposed to the E.Hum pathway of inner genius and the CE pathway of heroic action) opposes transparency and embraces hiddenness. It does this by espousing a type of low anthropology: the self must confess its un-magnificence. This un-magnificence keeps the self from falling into obsessive (hyper)activity—which is Han's second critique we've confronted in this chapter, though we've addressed this concern of (hyper)activity by moving past

---

finds peace in itself. Resolution comes only in the prayer to which Bonhoeffer surrendered it and in which he was content to leave it. 'Who am I? Thou knowest me. I am thine, O God!'" Bayer, *Living by Faith: Justification and Sanctification* (Minneapolis: Fortress, 2017), 25.

40. Bayer, *Theology the Lutheran Way*, 27.

Han. Luther and the Rhineland mystics (particularly Tauler) taught us not to re-embrace contemplation, as Han wishes, but to conceive of faith as passive reception. This embrace of passive reception is prophetic in a world of the performing self in an achievement society of *coulds*. The Beyonder pathway of confession and surrender avoids the spiritual diseases of transparency and (hyper)activity (which the other mystical pathways cannot). In turn, it can avoid self-flagellation by placing the self on the ground of reception, giving the self a spiritual life of passivity (*vita passiva*).

Yet, as we end this chapter, we need to recognize that we've only touched on Han's main diagnosis of an achievement society's spiritual disease—the obsession with a smooth positivity and the aversion of all negativity. To see if the Beyonder pathway of confession and surrender, resting on *vita passiva*, can embrace negativity, we need to turn to Luther's frenemy and one of the founders of Christian mysticism, the man of shadows, Pseudo-Dionysius. Luther's focus on suffering and the cross moves us far into the embrace of negativity. Pseudo-Dionysius will help us see why this embrace of negativity is so necessary for encountering the transformation we seek: a transformation (and spirituality) that has a living God at the center.

9

The Headless Man of Shadows

Into Negativity

There is almost a taste to my memory. I can't quite say a smell, though Byung-Chul Han would prefer that. When I think about the first months of the pandemic, I can taste something that I can't quite place. If I were to try, I'd say it tastes like the odd, dull flavor that comes upon you after you've collided hard with something you weren't anticipating. The taste of having your head rattled. If you've played sports, or slipped and fallen on ice, or been in a car accident, you might know the taste I'm trying to describe.

I have this taste every day of the first five months of the pandemic. It particularly comes in the late afternoon when Kara and I go on a walk. I taste the collision we were all in, I feel the heaviness, and I sense in everything how weird it all is. The taste of the collision comes because it's on these walks that we face our doomed plans—everything we'd been looking forward to for the spring, summer, and fall. There are so many slips and falls on these walks that, even when there isn't one, my brain nevertheless returns to the dull taste.

This ravaged hellscape of destroyed plans makes it so that I can't make new plans. I don't want new plans. I want to do what we'd been looking forward to for over a year. I want to take my mom to Amsterdam. As late spring moves into early summer, Kara keeps insisting that we need to get away. We need to leave the house and our neighborhood. We need to walk somewhere other than this route littered with the debris and carnage of our 2020 plans.

"Go where? Do what?" I rebut. "How can you relax and enjoy being away when you don't know how to get food or whether you should touch the gas pump?" It's better to stick to the stale ponds I'm used to than go chasing potentially polluted waterfalls (yep, that's a TLC reference).

By midsummer, Kara is no longer making suggestions. She informs me that she's booked an Airbnb on the Gunflint Trail. It's a remote cabin near the Boundary Waters that separate Minnesota from Canada. It's almost as north as you can get in the continental US. The Gunflint Trail is one of the most remote places in Minnesota, if not in the lower 48. There is no cell phone coverage. The closest grocery store is an hour away. A person can disappear on the Gunflint Trail. As we drive to the Airbnb, I picture murderers and fugitives hiding away in the cabins. I'm sure a few of these cabins are the backdrop to a few *Fargo*-like scenes. I see a few woodchippers.

It's almost a four-hour drive to get to the Airbnb. We take Highway 35—the 1,500-mile highway that runs right down the middle of the whole country like a spine—to its most northern end. And then we drive another two hours north. The first hour past Highway 35 we trace the coast of Lake Superior. The massive lake is always out my right window. The second hour is nothing but remote lands. It's just tall pines and small lakes and taller pines and smaller lakes. It's beautiful but getting long. As I drive this last stretch into the remote land, I watch eagles soaring in circles perpetually (that's a Ben Howard callout, to make up for my TLC reference).[1]

We've added a teenager to our car. We're taking along our nephew Vincent. He's an extrovert joining four introverts in the car. The boy never shuts up. I mean, never! Vincent has theories and observations about everything, particularly movies. He talks the whole four hours, almost without a breath. It's engaging the first hour, and in the second hour it becomes soothing, like AM talk radio or a sound machine. The third hour it's annoying. The fourth is torture. I start to wonder, even hope, that our Airbnb has a woodchipper.

The Airbnb is perfect. It's on a small, cold lake surrounded on every side by thick woods. There is no one around and a large pile of firewood. The place is big enough to sleep all five of us. There is also a detached sleeping shed bunk house about five hundred feet from the main house. After four hours of Vincent's theories, and to protect him from me, I make Owen and Vincent sleep in the shed. The quiet is glorious.

1. I'm referring to Ben Howard's song "Nica Libres at Dusk." Howard and this song specifically have served me in writing this project by being a kind of mystical muse.

While we were still driving on Highway 35, when I was engaging Vincent's banter and not wanting to pull my brain out of my ear, I ask Vincent if he's seen *Fight Club*. He's never heard of it. My 1990s soul is wounded. "Never?" I keep asking. He assures me he's never even heard of the movie. The self-proclaimed movie buff hadn't seen a classic.

We rectify this the third night. Kara, Owen, Vincent, and I watch the classic mind-bending film. Byung-Chul Han I'm sure is a fan. The film raises many of the themes of the spiritual disease that neoliberalism thrusts upon us. This spiritual disease ravages the consciousness of the main character and narrator, played by Ed Norton. The only way to escape the deadening malaise of the achievement society of neoliberalism is to create an alter ego, beyond Norton's will, named Tyler Durden (played by Brad Pitt). Yet for almost the entire film, the viewer has no idea that the narrator and Tyler Durden are the same person, both part of Ed Norton's character's split consciousness. Ed Norton's character doesn't even know this. Tyler Durden is a mystery and a sage. Durden seems to come from nowhere with a new vision and (harsh) spiritual wisdom. Durden appears out of the shadows, teaching lost men a new way to be.

As soon as Tyler Durden arrives on screen, Vincent starts theorizing on who he is. The talking is insistent. New theories pile on top of new theories as the film rolls. We shush him constantly. To my sadistic pleasure, each of his theories is proven wrong as we watch. But the swinging and missing doesn't stop Vincent from continuing to theorize and chatter. I take an aspirin with my popcorn. After each theory hits a dead end, Vincent throws himself back in his chair and says in pleasured exasperation, "Then who is Tyler Durden? Who is this guy?"

The Man of Shadow

In Christian mysticism, Pseudo-Dionysius the Areopagite (or Denys, as he is sometimes called) plays the Tyler Durden character. Like Tyler Durden, Pseudo-Dionysius is a shadow, a mystery man. No one really knows who he is or where he comes from (though he must be somehow connected to Greece). He seems to arrive from nowhere. And like Durden, he arrives not as a whisper but as a thunderstorm. Yet unlike Durden, Pseudo-Dionysius doesn't end up a villain but remains a central sage and a saint for both the Eastern and Western churches (at least until the Reformation and Luther—I'll return to this soon). Pseudo-Dionysius's thought impacted Gregory Palamas in the East as much as Gregory the Great in the West. Pseudo-Dionysius is praised as often by Eastern theologians as Western theologians (something not even Augustine could accomplish!). He is the most important Christian thinker no one has really heard of. This important Christian leader remains in the shadows, his identity obscured in those shadows, confused as much as inspired. And in the shadows is where Denys remains.

In the shadows is how Denys wants it. The "Dionysius" in Pseudo-Dionysius is the name that this author gives himself. The author of this new mysticism asserts that he is Dionysius the Areopagite, whom Paul himself converted when Paul visited Athens (Acts 17:34). This mystical writer puts together the Pauline theology of the cross and Neoplatonism. Dionysius the Areopagite is the perfect pseudonym. It signals that this author is aware that he is writing something new, a chemist combining thoughts and perspectives. But he wants this new formula to be received not as a novel creation of his own imagination but as a perspective bound in the tradition of Paul. The author calls himself Dionysius the Areopagite not to deceive the reader but to claim that his mysticism rests on Neoplatonist thought (that's what's new about it) and on Paul's theology of the cross. The author is first and foremost a student of Paul, but he is also a citizen of Athens.

Eventually it became clear that Dionysius the mystical writer could not really be the Dionysius the Areopagite of Acts 17:34. The earliest manuscripts of this new mysticism were found in Syria in the sixth century. The dates didn't match up. It would take until the Renaissance, when people started caring about dates and authorship (and the work of a humanist from Florence named Lorenzo Valla), for this to become clear. For hundreds of years before that, people knew. But it just didn't matter. Luminaries such as Thomas Aquinas, Nicholas of Cusa, and Peter Abelard knew that the Dionysius of the mystical writings was not *the* Dionysius of Acts—it was all literary flare. They knew the name was a fan fiction throwback. But that just added to the inspired mystical perspective of the monk who called himself Dionysius the Areopagite. People like Aquinas, Abelard, and Nicholas weren't concerned—not like those in the Renaissance and in modernity would be—with shining a light in the shadows of every mystery.[2]

And the shadows of Denys's mystery get much thicker and longer.

---

2. Jaroslav Pelikan discusses this history of Denys's identity further in *The Christian Tradition: A History of the Development of Doctrine*, vol. 1, *The Emergence of the Catholic Tradition (100–600)* (Chicago: University of Chicago Press, 1971), 344–45.

A Paris Beheading

The shadows are so long that they stretch to Paris. Denys burrowed his way so deeply into the imagination of the Eastern and Western church that the great Maximus the Confessor in the East wrote about him with veneration as early as the seventh century. And as far west as Paris, it was claimed that in the third century, when Paris was young and small, Dionysius the Areopagite arrived from the East and became the city's first bishop. The French were responsible for shortening Dionysius the Areopagite's name to Denys. But as with Tyler Durden, a bad head wound was in Denys's future.

The story from Paris goes that Denys converted so many to the faith of Jesus Christ that the pagan priests who dominated little Paris compelled the Roman governor to arrest him. Denys was taken to the highest hill in Paris and beheaded. Not that different from Tyler Durden at the end of *Fight Club*. Both the film and the story of the Parisian Denys have a lot of talking after a severe head wound. Ed Norton's character shoots himself in the head to rid himself of Durden, still talking to his girlfriend while having a bullet in his skull. The bullet in the skull is somehow a happy ending as the lovers embrace. Denys's story, too, is made for Hollywood.

It's claimed that after Denys's head was cut off, he stood, picked it up, and walked down the hill. Denys's head, detached from his body—à la *Beetlejuice*—preached the whole way. Each place that the head-in-hand Denys preached was marked and venerated for generations by the French. The place where Denys finally fell and died turned into the most holy of Parisian sights. Denys's body was buried in a crypt built on the site of his headless death. The Basilica of Saint-Denis was erected upon the crypt. It became the place where all the kings of France would be buried. When the great Gothic cathedral builder Abbott Suger renovated and rebuilt Saint-Denis in the twelfth century, he moved Denys's bones from the crypt to the altar. Denys has been the patron saint of Paris ever since.[3]

---

3. Paul Rorem, who is to my mind the foremost interpreter of Denys, adds depth and dimension to this, saying, "While most mystics largely ignored the role of the symbolic veils in the Dionysian synthesis, other authors put it to good use within their own agenda, notably Abbot Suger of St. Denys. Suger's account of the new church at the (now Parisian) abbey of St. Denys quite directly involved the writings of the abbey's patron saint and supposed founder, our own Dionysius. When the Carolingian era sealed the mistaken identification of Denis the martyred Apostle to France with Dionysius the biblical convert from Athens, the Pseudo-Areopagite's writings entered French history with an authority their author never dreamed. Suger's primary authority for the lifting effect of the building's luminous beauty was the Dionysian tradition. Ironically, any discussion of

It's now believed that there is no way that Pseudo-Dionysius the Areopagite of the mystical writings is either the same Dionysius the Areopagite of Acts or the same Dionysius the Areopagite of the Paris beheading and headless preaching. But Pseudo-Dionysius the Areopagite's mystical writings of the late sixth and early seventh centuries made their way to Paris, and the French were sure that this author was one and the same with their beheaded bishop. They embraced the mystical writings as the words of their venerated Saint Denys. Pseudo-Dionysius the Areopagite of the mystical writings may be the first real man of mystery. His writing is so moving, his leadership into the mystical so trusted, that his words inspired mystical thoughts and encounters across the East and West. Denys's impact was so deep and broad that his person was spotted in Athens, Paris, and beyond. From the sixth to the sixteenth century Denys was uniquely and almost universally loved and lauded.

That is, until Luther.

Luther's Hate and the Other Mystics

Luther asserted—as only Luther could—that Denys was a dangerous dud. As with everything with Luther, it was personal. The backstory is that at first, like all late-medieval theologians, Luther liked Denys, well enough at least.[4]

---

the origins of Gothic architecture, the most concrete and visible legacy of the medieval church, must include the writings of Pseudo-Dionysius, perhaps the most evasive and shadowy figure of the early church." Rorem, *Biblical and Liturgical Symbols within the Pseudo-Dionysian Synthesis* (Toronto: Pontifical Institute of Mediaeval Studies, 1984), 145.

Paul Sigmund adds, "In the eighth and ninth centuries the French kings possessed Greek manuscripts of Dionysius' works sent by the pope and by the Byzantine emperor. A faulty translation completed between 832 and 835 by Hilduin, the Abbot of St. Denis, the famous monastery near Paris supposed to have been founded by Dionysius (St. Denis in Latin is Sanctus Dionysius), was superseded by that of John Scotus Eriugena, who published translations and commentaries of the works of Dionysius around 858. Between 862 and 866, Eriugena also wrote a philosophical work, *On the Division of Nature*, which was a development of some of the ideas which he had found in Dionysius." Sigmund, *Nicholas of Cusa and Medieval Political Thought* (Cambridge, MA: Harvard University Press, 1963), 52.

4. Heiko Oberman says, "In the case of Pseudo-Dionysius we have the very positive statement by Luther in 1514 that the *via negativa* is the most perfect. 'Hence we find with Dionysius often the word 'hyper,' because one should transcend all thought and enter darkness.' Luther seizes here upon an aspect of the theology of Dionysius which in the *Disputation against Scholastic Theology* in 1517 will be formulated as 'the whole of Aristotle relates to theology as shadow to light.'" Oberman, *The Dawn of the Reformation* (Grand Rapids: Eerdmans, 1992), 132. Oberman continues, "In 1514 it is already clear that 'darkness' . . . shares in the double meaning of *abscondere* and *absconditus*: not only apart from faith is God obscured in our speculations, but even in faith the faithful live 'in umbraculo,' in God's protective custody, as

Denys had a massive impact on Meister Eckhart. Also, as we've said, one of Luther's favorite preachers was Eckhart's student, the mystic Johannes Tauler. Luther's theology of course did not have its origins in mysticism, but mysticism colored his reading of the Psalms and Pauline epistles (particularly Romans).[5] The concreteness of both Paul's experience with the risen Christ and the psalmist's cries to God led Luther to construct his theology far away from speculation and therefore always near the life, death, and resurrection of Jesus Christ. For Luther, faith and theology were in Jesus Christ alone. It all starts and ends with Jesus Christ. The whole of faith and theology must pass through Jesus Christ.

The problem with mysticism, Luther contended, was that it was not centered on this christological reality,[6] particularly Denys's Neoplatonism. While giving a commendable stance on the first article of the creedal assertions (about God the Father), Denys says little about the second article (Jesus the

---

friends of God on earth. If one turns for comparison to a passage from the hand of such a true disciple of Pseudo-Dionysius as Dionysius the Carthusian (1471), where he discusses the *unio mystica* in terms of the most intimate sons of God . . . elevated halfway between the blessed and the average believer and through love and rapture absorbed in the ocean of God's infinity, one sees immediately that it would be misleading to overlook the '*sic et non*' character of this and other asides Luther makes to Dionysius in the early years. When from 1519–1520 onward Luther attacks 'Dionysian speculations' there is no reason to base on this finding a theory of development, let alone of reversal. Rather, he now associates the name of Dionysius with a theological position which had never been his own, a phenomenon perhaps not unrelated to the fact that his earliest opponents had started immediately to make use of Pseudo-Dionysius to defend the validity of the papal hierarchy" (133).

5. Steven Ozment adds texture to this: "Was mysticism a more congenial medieval source of Luther's theology than scholasticism? During the important formative years 1516–18, he had only the highest praise for the German mystical tradition. In a letter to his friend Georg Spalatin he described Johannes Tauler's sermons as 'pure and solid theology' and professed to know no contemporary work in either Latin or German more beneficial and in closer agreement with the Gospels. When he defended the ninety-five theses in 1518, he confessed to having found more good theology in Tauler than in all the scholastic theologians combined. In that same year he published the full text of the *German Theology*, declaring that only the Bible and St. Augustine had taught him more about God, Christ, man, and all things." Ozment, *The Age of Reform, 1250–1550: An Intellectual and Religious History of Late Medieval and Reformation Europe* (New Haven: Yale University Press, 1980), 239.

6. Oliver Davies adds, "Yet, even though there was much in the work of the Rhineland mystics which appealed to Luther, including their German solidity (as distinct from the corrupting influence of alien Rome), their stress on the primacy of intent rather than action in the moral sphere, and their central focus on authentic, inner piety, they also contained elements which Luther found unwelcome. His criticism was that they were primarily God-centred rather than Christ-centred and seemed to him to be lacking in a theology of the cross. Their concern with *Deus nudus* ('God in himself') served to distract from the engagement of the individual soul with the saving act of Christ." Davies, *The Rhineland Mystics: An Anthology* (Eugene, OR: Wipf & Stock, 1989), 22.

Son) and doesn't embed his thought in the life and death of Christ as Luther sees necessary.[7] Because of Denys's impact, this lack of christological grounding is true of most of the mystics between the sixth and seventeenth centuries. Eckhart's Christology is muted in his own mysticism. The early Luther affirms Denys's attention to darkness, impossibility, and negativity (a theme we'll unpack soon, and we will use Denys's thought here to make a case for the Beyonder pathway of confession and surrender). The darkness, impossibility, and negativity central in Denys, are affirmed by Luther—it all connects to the Psalms for Luther. But it's ultimately done with too much Neoplatonism for Luther's taste.[8]

Erich Vogelsang, in an important article on Luther and mysticism in 1936, explains that we can place most of the premodern mystics into three categories.[9] We have the Dionysius school, the Latin school, and the German school. Luther appreciates the focus on darkness and negativity in the Dionysius

7. Piotr Malysz says, "Consequently when one takes the one-sidedness of Luther's interpretation into account and moves beyond the few negative references to Dionysius, it may be possible to uncover in the reformer's writings ideas that not only are suggestive of those of Dionysius but may also be viewed as Luther's contribution to a more Christocentric interpretation of the Dionysian heritage." Malysz, "Luther and Dionysius: Beyond Mere Negations," in *Re-thinking Dionysius the Areopagite*, ed. Sarah Coakley and Charles Stang (Malden, MA: Wiley-Blackwell, 2009), 151.

8. "The point is, however, that true negative theology is 'theology of the cross' and . . . its corresponding experience is the crying and groaning of the soul, the *'gemitus inenarrabiles'* (Rom. 8:26)." Oberman, *Dawn of the Reformation*, 143.

9. Heiko Oberman explains the importance of the article, saying, "In addition to the phenomenological and dogmatic solutions, there is still a third option, namely, the historical-genetic approach. Again in the year 1936 Erich Vogelsang made a significant contribution by no longer operating with the general and usually vague concept of mysticism. After first enumerating the mystical authors said to be known to Luther—Dionysius Areopagita, Hugh and Richard of St. Victor, Bernard, Bonaventure, Gerson, Brigit of Sweden, Tauler, and 'the Frankfurter'—Vogelsang distinguished between 'Dionysian mysticism' (*areopagistische Mystik*), 'Latin mysticism' (*romanische Mystik*), and 'German mysticism' (*Deutsche Mystik*). With this more differentiated view of mysticism, Vogelsang could give a more refined answer to our question: (1) From 1516 onward Luther renders the clear verdict of 'No' to 'Dionysian mysticism' as a speculative bypassing of the incarnate and crucified Christ; (2) *re* 'Latin mysticism' both a 'Yes' to its emphasis on the earthly Christ and on mysticism as experience rather than doctrine, and a 'No' to its bypassing spiritual *Anfechtung*, to its erotic marriage mysticism, and to its ultimate goal of ecstatic union with the uncreated word; (3) an enthusiastic 'Yes' characterizes Luther's evaluation of the third type of mysticism, 'German mysticism,' in which Luther found what he hailed in 'Latin mysticism,' but beyond that a spiritual understanding of purgatory as self-despair characteristic of the Christian life, and the idea of the *resignatio ad infernum*, both presented in his German mother tongue and representative of a nearly forgotten, submerged, genuinely German theological tradition." Oberman, *Dawn of the Reformation*, 130, citing Erich Vogelsang, "Luther und die Mystik," *Luther-Jb* 19 (1937): 32–54.

school but rebuffs the Neoplatonism. Luther rejects everything about the Latin school (made up of the likes of Ignatius and Teresa of Ávila, to name just two). Luther finds their assumption that there is some kind of inner spark in the human soul that can be ignited by practice and effort, giving direct availability to God, very problematic. The Latin school's anthropology is far too high for Luther. Luther denies completely the contention that humanity possesses its own inner equipment to commune with God. To put it in the words we've been using throughout this project, the Latin school assumes the soul is magnificent. The Latin school, even more than the Dionysius school, has little incarnational impulse. Because of its high anthropology, it believes that the *vita contemplativa* can save. It assumes that human contemplation, even human religious practices, are able to influence God's action. This Luther and all the Reformers deny completely.

The German school is different. Like the Latin school, the German school believes that the soul (the person) can participate deeply in the life of God (Luther believes this too). They equally hold that the person can find the deepest of unions with God, experiencing transformation (there are deep echoes of *theosis* here that are central to all the Eastern schools of mysticism). Yet for German mysticism, the shape of this participation, the very ground where this union with the life of God happens, is not through our inner magnificent spark but in our empty impossibility. The soul for the German school is *not* an environment de facto ready to receive the spark of God. The soul is not dry kindling ready to burst into flame; rather, the self is wet and worn ground. This union with the divine is bound in the self's own abilities not to fill itself with contemplations and rites but to empty the self by prayer and confession, surrendering to the nothingness, to the impossibility that the self possesses any spark to light its union with God. The union comes as God is met really and truly in impossibility, on wet ground. God alone brings the heat of union from within the nothingness of the self. Only through the embrace of nothingness can we find our souls in union with the divine being who inhabits nothingness.

Not surprisingly, Luther affirms the German school—which we've called the Rhineland mystics. In many ways, Luther learns the importance of a low anthropology from these German mystics. Denys's focus on darkness and negativity is placed right into the self by the German mystics. The negativity and nothingness become not just a metaphysical assertion but an existential one as well. Darkness, nothingness, and negativity become the way to conceive

of how God encounters us and makes a life within us. Luther believes that
this focus on the human being's impossibility as the place of God's arriving
predates him in the German mysticism of the Rhineland. Luther tells his papal
accusers that his theology is not the raging fancy of a madman but rather is
in direct company with the German mystics of the Rhineland.

Luther's appreciation for the Rhineland/German mystics should have given
him more patience for Denys. But it didn't, because things got personal. During Luther's conflicts with Rome, the pope's theologians tried to use Pseudo-
Dionysius to put the backwater German professor and preacher in his place.
The pope's theologians assumed that Denys was an authority all theologians
had to respect. But they didn't yet know the sharp-minded and bombastic will
of Luther. The pope's theologians used Denys's *Celestial Hierarchy*—a piece
that draws deeply from Neoplatonism to articulate the spiritual hierarchy
of the universe—to point out that Luther's opposition to the pope, and his
cardinals, disrespected the very order of the heavens. The pope's theologians
claimed that Luther was not obeying the laws of the (spiritual) universe that
the great mystic Denys had named. This they figured was checkmate. Not even
Luther would oppose Denys. They had used Denys perfectly, they thought,
to paint Luther into a corner. But no one (no one!) puts Marty in a corner.

With impassioned frustration, Luther responded by swinging not only at
the pope's theologians but at Denys too. Luther's white-hot anger led him,
like a spouse who regrets their words after an argument with a partner, to
make claims that a cooler head might not have made. Now with those claims
out, Luther (like that spouse) needed to stand behind them, even coming to
believe them more than he did when he first uttered them. Luther doubles
down and rejects Denys completely. Denys's important words on darkness
and negativity get lost (and denied) in Luther's heated conflict. To tweak our
analogy, Denys became like a friend of a couple after they divorce. Inside
the heated conflict of a couple's breakup, all friendships are divided. You're
moved onto one or the other side of the splitting couple. Denys was placed
on the side of the pope in the Reformation divorce proceedings. This made
Denys, by default, Luther's adversary.

Now that there have been five hundred years of water under the bridge,
it's worth reengaging Denys, even after our conversations with Luther (the
Rhineland mystics being our connecting point). Denys, as the founder of
apophatic mysticism, can help us address Han's critique of smooth positivity
and the necessity of negativity for otherness. Turning to Denys can help us see

the depth, texture, and ancient grounding of the Beyonder pathway of confession and surrender and its particular shape of transformation. Denys helps us make a further case for why the pastor's imagination of transformation and spirituality should take the shape of the Beyonder pathway of surrender and confession. Ultimately, Denys will help us see why surrender and confession move our attention onto an inbreaking transcendence of an arriving God.

Negativity

In *Fight Club*, Tyler Durden knows the way of transformation, the route to recover our spirit. The movie is a late 1990s hit and remains a cult classic because it presents a medicine for our spiritual disease of neoliberalism and the heavy malaise of immanence (something almost all of our new spiritualities and mystical memoirists are seeking). Durden, the man of shadows who appears from nowhere, is sure that this way of transformation is a negative way. It is a way that rejects the smooth obsessions of consumer positivity. It violently looks to smash positivity, blowing up all the institutions that sell and perpetuate it. Durden would hate Koons's smooth artwork as much as Han does. Durden is sure that the only way forward is to bruise and bloody our own smooth faces, making them rough and scarred. For Durden, the way to free the soul is to strip away the positivity by learning to take a punch—right to the face. You're healed from the disease, opened to transcendence, by embracing pain, spitting out blood (and maybe a few teeth). Only in the thrill of the fight, in bleeding, can you discover again that you're alive. *Fight Club* is its own kind of masochistic embrace of negativity. It's unique in that way. But its full-on embrace of bloody negativity has kept fight clubs from moving from the silver screen to the streets (at least in the same way that CrossFit has).[10]

10. There is much more to say about this. Byung-Chul Han spends a lot of time discussing self-mutilation. See *The Expulsion of the Other: Society, Perception and Communication Today*, trans. Wieland Hoban (London: Polity, 2020), 20–29. He shows how this masochism is bound inside our obsessions with smooth positivity. Real fight clubs are similar. They arrive because of our smooth positivity. Han continues, "The human being has lost a narrative protection, and thus also the ability to alleviate pain symbolically. Without this protection, we are at the mercy of a naked body deprived of meaning and language." Han, *The Palliative Society*, trans. Daniel Steuer (London: Polity, 2021), 20. Getting to a sharp point, Han concludes, "There is a relationship between the 'Mission Happiness' of positive psychology and the promise that one can live a life of permanent drug-induced well-being. The US opioid crisis is emblematic in this context" (3).

Yet, in the end Durden's mysticism of the secret sect of bleeding men can be of little help to us (it's still a great movie, mind you!). The mysticism Durden offers is ultimately a Counter-Enlightenment mysticism of heroic action (a radicalized form of the exercise lane). Labeling it as such helps us recognize that it's bound to a transcendence 1 (T1).[11] Therefore the self doesn't so much confess as bleed. Bleeding is the self's way of recovering its own magnificence. Denys's negativity takes a much different shape. His negativity is directed toward and attentive to what is beyond. Denys, unlike Durden, is a Beyonder.

The kind of negativity that Denys wants us to enter is not the pain of a bloody nose but the confession that there is nothing in the self that can provide what the self so desperately seeks. The negativity that Denys builds his mysticism around also has its sources in the self, but in a much different way. The mysticism that Denys molds gives ultimate attention *not* to the self but to what is beyond the self. Denys's negativity is a direct release from the divinizing of the self. Denys's negativity keeps the self from any apotheosizing illusions.

Denys is the founder of what's called *apophatic theology*. This approach to theology grows directly (is inseparable) from the practice of mysticism. It is first a form of mysticism and only secondarily a theology. Denys's apophatic theology rests squarely on a mysticism of confessed negativity, therefore directly embracing negativity. This mysticism asserts that the only way into transformation, brought about through union with the true God, is by way of negativity. We must surrender to this form of negativity, confessing our impossibility, to be ushered into a mystical encounter with the God who is truly God.

Denys asserts that the self is opened to an encounter with what is radically outside the self through the confession of negativity. Negativity is the embrace of a passivity (moving into a life of reception, as Luther taught us). Negativity is the way to encounter the inbreaking (the true otherness) of the God of Israel. Negativity opens the self to an encounter with the true otherness of God.[12] The mysticism that Denys develops starts and ends in negativity, being infused all the way through with it. Denys's mysticism (which sets the terms

11. It is interesting that Norton's character starts on the path of Counter-Enlightenment mysticism by first following the beaconing of T3 and embracing the support group. He faces negativity, feeling alive, by taking on the practice of dying, by going to cancer support groups. This too is a negative path, but transcendence is bound only within the self (again T2).

12. Hans Urs von Balthasar, a big fan of Denys, discusses the negative much further in *The Glory of the Lord: A Theological Aesthetics* (San Francisco: Ignatius, 1986), 370–75.

for all Christian mysticism in the East and West for a thousand years) is the full-on embrace of negation. This negation is for the sake not of masochism or heroic rebirth (no Tyler Durdens needed) but of encounter with the true otherness of God.

Denys's mysticism rejects all forms of the smooth. The Christian life, Denys believes, can never be smooth. Only idols are smooth. The crucified Christ is never smooth. The route for the human spirit to participate in union with the Spirit of the true and wholly other God is through negation. This route must be through negation because this God is *not* the same as us. Rather, this God is completely other than us. Christian mysticism from the sixth century onward (even back to Anthony in the desert in the third century)—as opposed to our late-modern mysticism and spiritualities—rejects the smooth. There is no smooth way to encounter the God of Israel, for the smooth makes what is other than us the same as us (again, an idol). This God cannot be the same as us or anything in the world. This God is fully and completely other. This otherness, Denys believes, can only be reached by negativity and negation. Christian mysticism has believed, in one way or another, that our transformation through an encounter with the living God can only come through some kind of surrender to the negative for the sake of an encounter with true otherness (as Han has shown, this is not something late-modern mysticism without God can embrace[13]—not without the demonic turn to violence and dehumanization that seeks not union with the triune God but evil).[14]

The Shape of Negativity

Now that we've come this far with Denys, seeing the centrality of negativity, we need to get more specific. For Denys, negativity is the confession that the self—which so needs to encounter what is beyond and other—has *no* (zero) capacity from within the self to do so. The self that is so addicted to the

13. Han affirms the Christian story, feeling that its extraction from our social world has made pain pointless, malforming us in relation to pain itself. He says, "The Christian narrative gives pain a language. It also transforms [Mary's] body into a stage. Pain deepens the relationship with God. It creates intimacy, intensity. It is even an erotic process." Han, *Palliative Society*, 21.

14. Evil, too, is dependent on negativity, but it seeks a dehumanizing destruction as its *telos*. It is not an embraced negativity but rather a hopeless drowning in evil. The negativity of Christian mysticism has embraced a negativity that finds the arriving of the ministering God who breaks all evil by bearing negativity, giving life (not the smooth) to all creation. Evil wants no confession of negativity, it wants no pleading for God's act, it wants only destruction instead of life out of death.

smooth and the same cannot find any way inside itself to reach for otherness and therefore find the transformation needed. This transformation is
too other, too beyond. A spirituality that is more than an opiate to the self's
(guilty) performance will need to confess that the self is void of what it most
longs for. The embrace of negativity is the confession that the self has no
ability (no power of piety, potency, or intellect, nothing) to know this God
who is truly and completely beyond and other. The negativity is the surrender
and confession that the self cannot know what it so deeply seeks.

Denys is a radical Beyonder. He believes that there is something beyond
human flourishing and beyond death, and he holds that God is beyond all
knowing, surpassing all understanding.[15] Because God is beyond all knowing
and understanding, the self cannot, in any way, directly comprehend God
(Denys is as skeptical of speculation as Luther is). Denys asserts that if God
were able to be known by human minds, God would not be God.[16] If human
minds (if the self's own magnificence) could comprehend God, then God
would be just another smooth object or phenomenon in the world. But God is
beyond this world, as this world's maker. This God is the creator of this world
and not just another thing or creature (even a mysterious one) bound in it.[17]

15. Here Denys is moving into a metaphysical assertion. It's impossible not to do so in
some way. Denys does not hesitate to make metaphysical assertions (as do late-modern theologians living inside an immanent frame, myself included). Denys is freely running into this
metaphysical space because of the influence of Neoplatonism. This influence has opened him
to critiques by those who believe the only credible way to speak of God inside an immanent
frame is to attend only to the acting God of Israel, rejecting Athens for Jerusalem. In many ways
this is what Luther does, and in the twentieth century it becomes a more central practice due
to Luther's influence, fully sprouting in the dialectical or crisis theology of the early twentieth
century. I follow this crisis theology in many ways. I tend to stay away from metaphysics (my
practical theological focus encourages that), but I'm not allergic to the metaphysical in the way
that other theologians impacted by Karl Barth are.

16. Vladimir Kharlamov adds, "There is nothing really negative about negative theology.
Divine un-knowability does not imply agnosticism or refusal to know God. Actual union with
God is simply above any conceptual activity. The *via negativa* in Dionysius represents the
epistemology of faith that guides human beings to experience and acknowledge the existence
of the One who is beyond human understanding. It is negative in the sense that we can not
find appropriate terminology to adequately describe our experience of God." Kharlamov, *The
Beauty of the Unity and the Harmony of the Whole: The Concept of Theosis in the Theology
of Pseudo-Dionysius the Areopagite* (Eugene, OR: Wipf & Stock, 2009), 199.

17. Ozment adds, "Dionysian mysticism is especially distinguished by its emphasis on God's
transcendence of reason. No other medieval theologian stressed the hiddenness of God, even as
revealed in Scripture, more than Dionysius. He made a famous distinction between affirmative and
negative ways to God, the *via affirmativa* and the *via negativa*." Ozment, *Age of Reform*, 118. Ozment continues, "The affirmative way thus opens onto the negative way, which is the mystical way,
so that the reality of God can be reached beyond his names. Dionysius urged man to 'go beyond all

Denys's point is that holding to a transcendence 3 (God is truly other and is encountered only through God's own inbreaking) demands that we embrace negativity. The shape of the negativity is the confession that we cannot know and comprehend this God. A transcendence without negativity and negation will be a transcendence without otherness. It will be hollowed out to fit only the magnificence of the self, not God (or the beauty of any kind of otherness). It will be hollowed out of its divine otherness so that transcendence must be squeezed to fit inside the self's own feelings (T2) or actions (T1)—losing otherness.

Surrendering to negativity leads us to confess that we cannot know this God. This confession of our inability to comprehend this God allows the self to be open to the inbreaking transcendence of a living God. It makes us aware that the only God we can know is the God who comes to us, who encounters us, meeting us in negativity (in the cross, to reunite Denys and Luther). Through the negativity of the self's inability (un-magnificence), we find ourselves in union with God. When Leslie Jamison and Mary Karr, in their addiction memoirs, give themselves over to prayer—confessing that they don't know what they're doing, surrendering to the fact that they don't even know how prayer works, or whether they even believe it—they find an encounter that heals and claims. It comes not around or outside but right inside the negativity of confessed impossibility.

But what do we do with this negativity? What do we do with this confession that we cannot comprehend God? American Protestantism has often succumbed to the temptation to smooth this negativity out, denying it completely. The temptation is to rebrand the incomprehensibility of God's great otherness in platitudes that turn God into a smooth, soft object, like a stress ball. It takes little time to spot this avoidance of negativity and incomprehensibility in the worship songs, stickers, devotion books, and T-shirts of American cultural Christianity.[18] It's no wonder that cultural Christianity's zenith followed Norman Vincent Peale's preaching on the power of positive thinking, which produced the prosperity gospel and eliminated the stark otherness of God (and in turn God's beauty).[19]

---

mind and reason,' denying every name and description of God, becoming 'totally dumb,' so that, in such ignorance and unknowing, he might know him who is unutterable and nameless" (119).

18. This apophatic focus on negativity guards against cultural Christianity. Smooth religion can never love this return to the theology of the cross.

19. For more on this, see Kate Bowler, *Blessed: A History of the American Prosperity Gospel* (New York: Oxford University Press, 2018). Bowler does not, however, return to the *via negativa*, as I am doing here.

The only way forward inside the confession of incomprehensibility is to fully embrace negativity. We can speak of this God of complete otherness, moved to comprehend God's actions and being, only by passing through negation. Only by confession can we have no positive words to say about this God, because we cannot comprehend this God. Therefore, we can only say what this God is *not*. Denys's apophatic teaching speaks of God by speaking in the negative (like a film negative), speaking of what God is not. We do theology in the mystical act of confessing what God is not. We confess that we are not the kind of creatures who can possess God but rather must stop and be attentive to God's coming to us.

Those in the Western tradition—who were inspired by Denys—have called this approach the *via negativa*, the negative way. Luther's own theology of the cross is a *via negativa*. It's a reworking of the *via negativa* in relation to Jesus's own life and death and the cries of the psalmist. Luther puts together the apophatic with the lived reality of an encounter with the God of life inside the cries of our human deaths and losses. Denys teaches us that we must follow the negative path to comprehend this God, to be able to say anything at all about this God who is other. Luther shows us that this negativity stretches deeply into our being, into the realities of our own deaths. The negative path leads not only into a way of comprehending the otherness of God but of encountering the otherness of God who draws near to us to minister life to our deaths. The *via negativa* is not just a way of thinking but a way of living in union with God's own ministering being.[20] The *via negativa* is a way of thinking and living for those grounded in the *vita passiva*.

Beauty of Otherness

It seems paradoxical, but Han has prepared us to recognize that negativity is the way to witness true beauty. Denys considers this kind of negativity to be beautiful. For it is a union with unpossessable otherness. This negativity

---

20. Louis Dupré says with insight, "If consistently maintained, such extreme negations would result in a divine darkness that excludes any kind of divine revelation. But for Christian mystics the negation of divine names has been a method of spiritual ascent more than a theoretical principle. Negative theology has always recognized that God is manifest, even though none of our attributes adequately describe Him. In the end the dark of unknowing turns into the light of divine self-manifestation. What distinguishes its spiritual ascent is that the divine unity constitutes a point of ultimate rest." Dupré, *The Deeper Life: An Introduction to Christian Mysticism* (New York: Crossroad, 1981), 32.

experiences knowledge out of ignorance, life coming directly out of death, renewing and binding us to the very being of God. To push Denys in the direction of Luther, it is in the negativity of the cross that we are hidden with Christ in God (Col. 3:3), given the full union of God's life through the resurrection. Han is enough of a throwback mystic to know that beauty is dependent on otherness. And the route to otherness cannot be traversed outside negativity. But Han doesn't seem to want to embrace the Beyonder pathway (he seems satisfied to stay in a nihilistic place, resembling the philosophy of Tyler Durden).

Denys, on the other hand, gives all his attention only to the Beyonder pathway, writing his mysticism to get us on this path of negativity for the sake of catching a glimpse of God's complete and beautiful otherness. Denys begins his *Mystical Theology* with a prayer that is beautifully poetic as it encompasses the apophatic way of negating every smooth positive statement made by the prayer with a negative one. He reminds us that when we pray, we seek communion with the otherness of God. Denys Turner, in his book *The Darkness of God*, calls this move for the positive being met immediately by the negative the "self-subverting utterance." Denys is directly showing us in prayer how the self is reminded that it is not magnificent, that it needs what is outside it (even outside its comprehension) to find transformation. The self is not the kind of creature that possesses the genius to know this truly other God. The self-subverting utterance works by "first say[ing] something and then, in the same image, unsay[ing] it."[21]

For example, in the prayer that begins the *Mystical Theology*, Denys says, when describing God's Word, that it is "brilliant darkness." He calls the "Word" itself a "hidden silence." It is inside such a dialectic that we are to seek for God, finding words to speak of God's coming to us. It is inside our own experience of death and loss that we are to find the God who gives life. Denys continues with this subverting talk all the way through his *Mystical Theology*. In the final chapter, Denys calls God the "Cause of all": "Darkness and light." God *is none of these*. God then is both darkness and light. God is a luminous darkness and a dark brilliance. God is neither darkness nor light.[22] This paradoxical way of speaking and being is the way the self comes out

21. Denys Turner, *The Darkness of God: Negativity in Christian Mysticism* (Cambridge: Cambridge University Press, 1995), 21.

22. Pseudo-Dionysius, *The Mystical Theology*, in *Pseudo-Dionysius: The Complete Works* (New York: Paulist Press, 1987), 135, 142.

of itself to encounter the God who is God.[23] Every positive statement about
God must be met by a negative. God is luminous darkness, dark brilliance;
we cannot comprehend what God is.[24] What we must surrender to, what we
must find in our confession, is that we are not God and that we need this God
who is beyond us to come and minister to us to save us. God gives us God's
own life that we can never possess but only stand inside as a beautiful gift,
receiving it and living a life of reception in the world.

What Denys believes happens after we negate all our statements about God,
praying to the God who is brilliant darkness, to the God who is neither darkness
nor light, is that we encounter God's otherness. It is inside the negation of negation that we encounter the living God. By the negation of negation, we glimpse
what we can't glimpse, that God is God and beyond all. Life itself comes from
beyond us. And yet the beyond comes so near to us as to minister and love us.
In this prayer, in this encounter with God's otherness, we are rendered silent.
We silently rest in God's presence. We passively receive God's gift of beauty
through God's inbreaking and coming to us in silence—most often as silence.

And this is enough. We are invited to just be. To put away all performance
and find our transformation in union with God as a gift, as welcome silence.
We are freed from performance to just be silent before God's beauty, receiving
our humanity as we are called to receive others as ministers in the world. In
response to God's beauty we see the beauty of the world and recognize the
gift that we are beautifully alive, that God moves in the world, that God is
beyond. It is all a gift. We confess this. We surrender to its beauty as pure life.[25]

---

23. In the Areopagite's own words, "The divine darkness is that 'unapproachable light'
where God is said to live. And if it is invisible because of a superabundant clarity, if it cannot
be approached because of the outpouring of its transcendent gift of light, yet it is here that is
found everyone worthy to know God and to look upon him. And such a one, precisely because
he neither sees him nor knows him, truly arrives at that which is beyond all seeing and all knowledge. Knowing exactly this, that he is beyond everything perceived and conceived, he cries out
with the prophet, 'Knowledge of you is too wonderful for me; it is high, I cannot attain it.'"
Pseudo-Dionysius: The Complete Works (New York: Paulist Press, 1987), 265.

24. Sarah Coakley says, "Darkness as the condition of revelatory presence is, it emerges,
importantly different from darkness as mere absence or 'deferral.'" Coakley, *God, Sexuality, and
the Self: An Essay 'On the Trinity'* (London: Cambridge University Press, 2013), 23. Vladimir
Kharlamov adds, "Divine darkness is the way to know God through unknowing. The apophatic
way is the most preferable and desirable consequence of the human search for God. It is the
logical climactic point of any affirmatively stated knowledge about God and eventually leads to
the explicit affirmation of what God is not. It is a darkness that is 'more radiant than light.'"
Kharlamov, *Beauty*, 198.

25. Charles Stang states, in relation to Denys, the point I've been trying to make all along.
He says, "Dionysius insists that the self that suffers this 'unknowing,' who is united to the

Moving Forward to the End

There is one final concern we must wrestle with before completing this project. The first half of this project was descriptive. It culminated in our mapping of our cultural (even secular) mysticisms. We saw why spiritualities have arisen, and we've described and related them to one another.

In chapter 8, we turned from description to normative assertions. While the E.Hum and CE mysticisms of inner genius and heroic action are commendable in one sense, they are tragic in another. In dialogue with Byung-Chul Han, we've exposed the problems with these secular mysticisms—particularly their inability to embrace negativity, hiddenness, and a life beyond (hyper)activity. In contrast, a mysticism that attends to the act and being of God, a Beyonder mysticism, is bound in a low anthropology of the self's need. It is a mysticism built directly within negativity and hiddenness. Being built this way, it releases us from activity. Therefore, a Beyonder mysticism cannot be done without some confession of a living God.

In chapters 8 and 9 we've moved into this normative work through retrieval, first with Luther and the Rhineland Mystics, then with Pseudo-Dionysius the Areopagite. Luther helped us understand the shape of a low anthropology that confesses the self's un-magnificence. Luther led us to see how this low anthropology connects with the hiddenness of the cross, which frees us from a life of (hyper)activity. Pseudo-Dionysius (Denys) assisted us in recognizing the importance of negativity. An apophatic mysticism that embraces negativity is essential in forming us as Beyonders.

But now we need to take one final step. This last step will both safeguard us from misunderstanding and further drive this retrieval of mysticism into the practice of ministry. To make a call for a Beyonder mysticism seems to risk losing the world and the importance of its redemption. Some have read Denys particularly to be unconcerned for the everydayness that Protestantism upholds as essential. It is fair to ask whether any type of mysticism would

---

unknown God, must also become unknown, that is, suffer 'an absolute abandonment of the self and everything, shedding all and freed from all.' Thus his apophatic theology assumes what I am calling an 'apophatic anthropology,' wherein the self is progressively unsaid, or, to use another favorite term of this author, 'cleared away.' . . . The way of negation is then a practice of transforming that self so that it can best solicit union with the unknown God. Apophasis is, for Dionysius, a sort of asceticism, an exercise of freeing the self as much as God from the names and categories that prevent it from being divine." Stang, "Dionysius, Paul and the Significance of the Pseudonym," in Coakley and Stang, *Re-thinking Dionysius the Areopagite*, 16.

take us out of the world. Wouldn't a Beyonder mysticism be a double risk of such escape?

I don't believe so.

To show why, we need to meet a strange boy and explore what happened to him on July 7, 1913.

10

•———————•

When a Late-Night Talk Leads
to Deconversion

Or, How We Keep from Hating the World

In summer 2021 our timing was impeccable. Europe opened just hours before our flight. We were in Paris when curfews ended. There were still restrictions, but the borders were open.

Our timing isn't as perfect in March 2022.

The Omicron spike is tumbling and all restrictions across the Western world are evaporating, but we miss the lifting of Hawaii's restrictions by two days. Two days after we arrive, Hawaii will remove all entrance requirements. But two days earlier, we still need to fill out forms and receive a wristband to board our flight. But it's all worth it! I'd fill out a hundred forms to fly to Hawaii.

It's been three years since our trip to Kona on the Big Island, which planted the earliest seeds to this book. It's been three years since I carried Tara Westover's memoir *Educated* in my backpack, reading it next to the Pacific Ocean right outside the back door of our Airbnb. This time our destination is Kauai, with our Airbnb in Princeville. We've been to Kauai one time before. Nine years earlier, when Maisy was five and Owen was eight. Nine years ago, it took two days for us to realize we'd made a mistake. Of course, it's never a mistake to be on any of the Hawaiian islands. But we hadn't realized that Kauai is the country. It's rural. It's for adventure. Kauai is for hiking, kayaking, and swimming in hidden waterfalls. It's not ideal for little kids. But now in 2022, without little kids, we're back, ready for the adventure, with hiking shoes and snorkel gear at the ready. We're eager to hike those mountains, traverse their muddy paths to hidden beaches, find raging waterfalls, and jump into the Queen's Bath.

It's hard to hate the world—wanting to escape it for something else—when you're in Kauai. The world feels like a pure welcome. The ocean air, soothing breezes, and stunning vistas in all directions make an aversion to the world nearly impossible. But both of my children have managed to pull it off.

After we get our rental car and load it with groceries, we head north up the island to the Airbnb. It's dark and getting late, especially late for our jet-lagged bodies; it is the middle of night. We've been traveling over fifteen hours. As I did three years ago on the Big Island, I roll down my window of the rental car, letting the warm Hawaiian air massage my face as we drive. I do this mostly as pure enjoyment, but also as a strategy to stay awake and to avoid the smell of automotive air freshener. The rushing air keeps me alert, getting us safely up north.

Nine years ago, we stayed on the south end of the island. As we pass the exit for that road, I think again about my most vivid memory of that trip. It happened not long after we realized that Kauai was for adventure and that we were in no position for adventure. Owen was eight, and things had been tense for days. Fights or the threat of fights were present constantly. Owen was a strong-willed child, always with deep thoughts. I knew from the time he was five that he was a little existentialist.[1] Questions of death, limits, yearning, and stuckness circled his thoughts. Every night of that trip, as is a Hawaiian tradition, we, along with everyone else staying at our resort, walked to a rocky beach to watch the sunset. There is something mystical, a sense of the beauty of time and the gift of being alive, about watching the sun wave goodbye to the day as it sinks into the sea. The people gather to watch the sun's departure in silence, often breaking the silence with claps of joy and gratitude as the sun splashes and slowly sinks into a wash of orange and sparkling blues of sky and sea.

That night as we sat in utter beauty feeling the world saying "happy good night" to us all, my eight-year-old leaned over to me, his face still painted with the frustration of an earlier argument, but his eyes also glowing with

1. For proof, see my stories in a book called *The Promise of Despair* (Nashville: Abingdon, 2010).

the reflection of the sunset. He said to me, "The world is just impossible. Do you know what I mean? It's just impossible." His head was shaking like a weathered sage who's lost faith.

I did know what he meant. I too possess that existential gene, so I knew just what he was feeling. Even against the backdrop of this beauty, even in this moment, his own being yearned for redemption he couldn't name. The world at its most beautiful couldn't produce this redemption within itself. I told him I understood, but I also told him to look around, to embrace the world, to try to be here even in his frustration to love the world, to breathe in the gift of being alive. He was too frustrated. Too caught in his yearning. Owen could only respond with, "It's just impossible, the world is impossible," repeating it to himself. As he looked out at the orange and blue wash, he said one more time, "It's an impossible world."

Back in Kauai nine years later, he's seventeen, and while still an existentialist, he is a delight to travel with. We finally get to the Airbnb on the northern end of the island. It's not right on the water but tucked up on the cliffs. But the pool is a stone's throw away. We type in the code and enter the Airbnb. It's nice, recently renovated. We go straight for the beds. But this time as the lights go out on a long day, it's fourteen-year-old Maisy's turn to kick against the world. She's tired, discombobulated, and unhappy to be sleeping on the couch (we find an air mattress the next day). It all brings on a panic. She needs sleep but can't rest her mind. She, too, is feeling a deep sense that the world is filled with contradictions that she, in her tired state, cannot bear. Her mind is spinning with sadness and fear. She's in Hawaii, but the planet is dying, war is raging, some of her friends are in crisis, and school, even now four thousand miles away, still sucks. She, too, is sure that the world is impossible. She, too, in her sleep deprivation, is sure that the world cannot create its own redemption. She's not sure the world is worth her love.

Ironically, the only way she can break the circle of panic is by placing her feet in the grass, breathing in the cool air, and touching some plants. She and Kara slip into the night to walk under the stars. It grounds her again. She returns. Her body back in a place, her mind smoothed, sleep can now come. But as she slides into sleep, she knows, like Owen nine years ago, that the world is long from redeemed. Therefore, she's not sure the world is worth loving.

Maisy is not alone. A common critique of mysticism in any form is that it seeks to escape the world. The critique is that mysticism upholds the ecstatic over the ordinary, the metaphysical over the physical. It seeks another place or state over (even against) this world. It is believed that mysticism ultimately wants union between the soul and the divine being more than it wants the redemption of the world. Even a flat reading of Luther is open to this critique. It might not be completely true or fair, but still the assumption remains, and for some good reasons (which I'll touch on soon). To cut this critique off at the knees and connect my attention to mysticism in this project with the revelation-based theology I've been working in the other volumes of this series, we'll turn to the most important and yet overlooked theologian of the twentieth century as a way of concluding this project (and series): Franz Rosenzweig. Rosenzweig's transformation is one that ushers him deeply into the world.

The Backstory and All the Confused Lore

As a young man, Franz Rosenzweig was wired much like Owen and Maisy in those Hawaiian moments. He wasn't sure the world was worth loving. But Rosenzweig's story, and the theology that follows it, is all about conversions (making him the perfect figure to conclude this project with). As we said in chapter 4, Rosenzweig is the *ba'al teshuvah*, the master of turning, the one who believes again. He had turned away from Judaism but eventually turned back. He found a way to believe again. The question is, When did his conversion happen and what was this conversion from and to? As we'll see, the common lore of Rosenzweig's conversion may be wrong.

What we do know—and I touched on this at the end of chapter 4—is that Rosenzweig was born into an assimilated Jewish family. Rosenzweig's background is much different from that of his collaborator and friend Martin Buber. Buber was raised by a grandfather who brought him into the heart of Judaism, bathing little Buber in the Torah, Talmud, and the Hasidic mystical writings. It was not the same for Rosenzweig. Inside the bourgeois ethos of Kassel, Germany, Rosenzweig watched his older cousins' assimilation go so far that they converted to Christianity. Rudolf Ehrenberg, who plays an important part in this story, was one of those cousins. Yet, in Rosenzweig's mind, his cousin's turn to Christianity wasn't so much a conversion as a natural step. It wasn't a mindless step; it seemed natural inside their assimilation. Rosenzweig decided that this step of assimilation was the best option for him also. In the early days of the twentieth century, it seemed natural to leave his Judaism behind and become a Christian. But right when Rosenzweig was about to take this step, he turned back.

What we do know is that Rosenzweig believed that if he was going to take this step into Christianity, he would do it more deliberately than his cousins did. He believed that the most prudent way to convert to Christianity was to convert not as a pagan but as a Jew, like the apostles before him.

This is where the lore begins.

We know that Rosenzweig stated that he'd go to one more Yom Kippur service as preparation for his conversion. It would be a kind of last rite, a goodbye, to his Judaism. Of course, Rosenzweig never left, turning back instead to embrace his Judaism more firmly than ever. The lore is that Rosenzweig was so moved by the Yom Kippur service, really participating in it for the first time, that, like a reverse Saul of Tarsus, he felt the scales fall from his eyes and realized that Judaism was what he had been seeking all along. The lore is crystal clear: it was the power of Jewish practice—for the first time really and truly attended to—that turned Rosenzweig back and stopped him from leaving.[2]

The problem is that Rosenzweig never says this. Never once does Rosenzweig credit his return (his unconversion), which he talked about quite a bit, to the experience of the Yom Kippur service. It just fits so nicely in the tale that any late-modern rabbi or pastor wants to tell. Here is a smart young Rosenzweig, who's never really paid much attention to the practices, chants, and liturgies of his religious worship service. But at the precipice of leaving his religion, he enters a synagogue in Berlin and focuses in, really and truly for the first time paying attention. He pays attention in order to say goodbye to his religion, but once he really focuses in, he can't say goodbye. It's just too true and powerful. Having tried on his religion, he realizes he can't leave it. Instead, he gets into it. "And you know what?" the lore says, "It changes him! It brought him back to his religion. See, all we have to do is get people to really focus on our worship services and then they'll stay." The religious stickiness is already present in the shape of our worship and rites. You just need people to pay attention and focus. Rosenzweig shows—the sharpest point of the lore asserts—that people only leave because they haven't *really* tried our religion.

2. Paul Mendes-Flohr perpetuates this lore in his introduction to *The Philosophy of Franz Rosenzweig* (Hanover: University Press of New England, 1988). Nahum Glatzer provides another example, saying, "He was stopped on his way and called back into Judaism. This event came about with that suddenness and in that spirit of absolute finality reported in great conversions. Rosenzweig's biography indicates that it happened during the service of the Day of Atonement, 1913." Glatzer, *Franz Rosenzweig: His Life and Thought* (Indianapolis: Hackett, 1998), xvii.

But there is a big problem with this lore. If the lore is correct, if Rosenzweig turns back because he finally tried his religion enough to get it, why doesn't he say so? Not once does Rosenzweig claim what the lore claims. Not once does Rosenzweig say that the Yom Kippur service was ground zero to his conversion. He, no doubt, turns or converts back to his Judaism, but he never locates this directly happening because of the service. The Yom Kippur service was attended by him and it was important to him, but Rosenzweig never names it as the place of (or reason for) his conversion.

Jewish religious studies professor Benjamin Pollock, in his important book *Franz Rosenzweig's Conversions: World Denial and World Redemption*, believes the lore cannot hold. He argues convincingly that Rosenzweig never names the Yom Kippur service as ground zero for his conversion, because it wasn't. The Yom Kippur service was neither the point nor the place of Rosenzweig's turning. Pollock contends (and I'm convinced by him) that it wasn't in the synagogue that Rosenzweig reclaimed his Judaism but in the Leipzig home of his cousin Rudolf Ehrenberg's parents.

On July 7, 1913, twenty-six-year-old Rosenzweig participated in an all-night conversation with his cousins Eugen Rosenstock and Rudolf Ehrenberg. Pollock states, "Rosenzweig would look back on this *Leipziger Nachtgespräch* (Leipzig night conversation) as the transformative event of his life."[3] It's from this all-night conversation that Rosenzweig does his turning, becoming the *ba'al teshuvah*. This July night was so significant that it took months for him to really understand it. But he names it multiple times as the event that changed him, placing him on a new path. It took time to find the language to articulate what he came to see and encounter in that late-night conversation. It took right up to the time of the Yom Kippur service in early October. Pollock's point is that the Yom Kippur service is not the beginning of or even the impetus for Rosenzweig's transformation; it is the bookend. The Yom Kippur service is the final resolution of what started during the *Nachtgespräch*. The Yom Kippur service is the denouement (as the French would say) of his transformation.[4]

3. Pollock, *Franz Rosenzweig's Conversions: World Denial and World Redemption* (Bloomington: Indiana University Press, 2014), 1.

4. Pollock says, "According to Rosenzweig's mother's account, Rosenzweig had traveled from Kassel to Berlin, between Rosh Hashanah and Yom Kippur that year. Rosenzweig provides as the decisive date for his decision to remain a Jew the day of his arrival in Berlin. Horwitz concludes, 'He must have found the solution before Yom Kippur, which is not mentioned in the letter to Rudolf Ehrenberg.' Horwitz goes on to suggest that a visit to a synagogue on Yom

It was something else other than Rosenzweig's realization of the significance of worship, rite, and liturgy (really trying them) that transformed him. In reflection, Rosenzweig himself says that the *Nachtgespräch* transformed him by awakening him to the world.[5] The *Nachtgespräch* profoundly invited him to love the world, to see the utter centrality of the world and its redemption. Rosenzweig's transformation was in the world, it was directly connected with coming to see that the world itself must be affirmed, embraced, and loved. Rosenzweig's conversion is important for us because it can teach us how an embrace of the mystical pathway of confession and surrender can remain committed to (and deeply in love with) the world, attending to the everyday, focused on revelation and the world's redemption as the place of union with the divine. There is always danger, when crowing against late modernity with Han or following the negative mystical steps of Denys, of turning from the world (Rosenzweig himself worries that mystics turn from the world in a kind of Gnosticism). Yet, mining Rosenzweig's conversation at the *Leipziger Nachtgespräch* may help keep our feet and hearts turned toward the world, keeping our mystical longings in the world as we attend to the concrete place of confession with and for our neighbor.

The All-Nighter

In the early evening of July 7, 1913, Rosenzweig strutted with confident assuredness as he reached the door of his cousin Rudolf Ehrenberg's parents' home. Rosenzweig's gait was the common strut of a young man puffed with self-assuredness. Rosenzweig had little doubt of the recent position he'd come to and the decisions that would soon come from this position. He was ready to convert to Christianity. In a sense he already had. He would formally convert after Yom Kippur, but intellectually he'd already made the move. On this July night of confident strutting, it was unimaginable that in a short fifteen years this confident young man of privilege would see the hells of war and disease. The young man with this easy stroll and eagerness to convert to Christianity

---

Kippur may indeed have confirmed for Rosenzweig the decision he had made. But it could not have made it for him." Pollock, *Franz Rosenzweig's Conversions*, 118, quoting Rivka Horwitz, "Warum liess Rosenzweig sich nicht taufen?," in *Der Philosoph Franz Rosenzweig (1886–1929)*, ed. Wolfdietrich Schmied-Kowarzik (Freiburg: Alber, 1988), 79–96.

5. For a long and detailed discussion of this point, see the introduction to Benjamin Pollock, *Franz Rosenzweig's Conversion* (Bloomington: Indiana University Press, 2014). Pollock's whole book argues this point.

would soon be overtaken by paralysis, would die, and would be remembered as the greatest Jewish theologian of the twentieth century. As Rosenzweig rang the Ehrenberg doorbell, these happenings were all out in the unforeseeable future. As his steady and strong finger pressed the bell, it was unfathomable that in his near future he'd be unable to move his fingers, let alone leave his bed. Soon there would be no bounce in his step, no strength in his hands, no ability to move his own body at all. But on this night in 1913, with war and disease unforeseen, Rosenzweig was cocksure, convinced he'd made the right decision to leave his Judaism behind and embrace a kind of Christianity of intellectual depth.

We know what happened over the next hours that stretch into the morning from a letter that Rosenzweig wrote to Rudolf Ehrenberg on October 31, 1913, and then another written in 1917, during the war. These letters speak in detail about this night. They say nothing about the Yom Kippur service. Rosenzweig claims that this night transformed him. This is the event of his turning back.

The Conversation Begins

As Rosenzweig entered the parlor of the house, there were no plans for a deep conversation to commence, let alone for such a conversation to last until dawn. According to both Rosenzweig and Rosenstock, it all started with an impromptu conversation about a novel called *Antikrist mirakler* (The miracles of the antichrist) by Selma Lagerlöf.

The novel explores the tensions between Christianity and the socialism that had arisen in Italy. The novel particularly examines the spiritual state of the world. What is the place of redemption for the world? Should we concern ourselves with miracles of such redemption, or should the mystical take us out of the world? Is the world redeemable at all? And will it be God's actions in the world or our own actions that redeem the world? What are we to think about the world? Ultimately, Pollock contends that the questions that sat between these three cousins as they discussed the novel were whether a relation to God came as redemption *from* the world or redemption *in* the world.

The confident young Rosenzweig of this July night was assured that it was the first. It was redemption *from* the world. This was the Christianity he was converting to, the Christianity he'd been studying. It was a world-denying theology that Rosenzweig held. The Christianity that Rosenzweig was readying himself to convert to, in his own words, was a Marcionite Christianity. This version of Christianity believed that it was only in the kingdom not of this world, a kingdom that did not love this world, that the soul could be saved from this world. Rosenzweig didn't use the name "Marcion" on his July night, but in his letter reflecting on the *Leipziger Nachtgespräch* years later, that is exactly what Rosenzweig called the theology he carried into the Ehrenberg parlor.

A Marcionite Theology

"Marcion" refers to Marcion of Sinope, the first-century heretic who believed that the God who created the world (the God of the Hebrews) was an inferior, even evil, God. This lesser God of the Hebrews created this awful world and governed it by anger and punishment. Therefore, there was little to nothing to love about this world because there was no love in this world. How could there be? The creator of this world was vindictive and harsh, giving us a vicious and detestable world. But Jesus Christ, according to Marcion, was not part of this world. He was *not* the son of such an awful Hebrew God who created this terrible world. Rather, Jesus conquered this world to lead us out of this world and away from this Hebrew God of creation. Jesus gives us a kingdom not of this world and completely against this world. Because this kingdom is not of this world, the creator God of the Hebrews cannot reach this other world, making for a true salvation. Marcion reiterated that the vindictive God of the Hebrews cannot reach beyond this world because this version of the Hebrew God is the creator of this yucky world. Mysticism, in a Marcion tone, becomes a way to escape this world while still being bound in it. Therefore, Marcion contended that there was no redemption at all for this world. The core commitment of Marcionism, according to the great church historian Adolf von Harnack—the foremost expert on the subject of Marcion—was to abandon "the belief that the God of creation is also the God of redemption."[6] They were two different Gods. The God of redemption, represented in Jesus Christ, stood over and against the Hebrew God of creation. The redemption that would come from this God of Jesus Christ was not for this world; it was a redemption intended for souls who could escape and abandon the world forever.

6. Harnack, *Lehrbuch der Dogmengeschichte* (Freiburg: Mohr-Siebeck, 1886), 1:212, quoted in Pollock, *Franz Rosenzweig's Conversions*, 19.

A question quickly arises: Why would the self-assured young Rosenzweig be interested in such thoughts? Harnack explains, and Pollock highlights, that what made Marcion unique among Gnostics of the first century was that Marcion believed salvation did not come from a process of *knowledge* (gnosis) but by *faith*. This made Marcion appealing to nineteenth-century German Protestant theologians. In that time, Germany, being the land of Luther and influenced by his focus on faith, met the impact of philosophical idealism at a time when confidence, even love, for the world had been waning. The bourgeois cultural rise of the nineteenth century led the likes of Arthur Schopenhauer, Richard Wagner, and Nietzsche (not to mention Karl Marx and Friedrich Engels) to speak boldly of their disdain for the bourgeoisie of the world. Protestant theology after Schopenhauer and Nietzsche, in the context of looking at the world through the lens of faith, fostering a hatred of the bourgeois, and being suspicious of orthodoxy, gave Marcion a comeback (not to mention that just below the surface boiled deep-seated anti-Semitism that would explode in the twentieth century). Harnack himself started to take a shine to old Marcion. Stripping off the patina of church orthodoxy led Harnack to wonder whether Marcion had something to say to the modern world. Maybe the poor guy had gotten a bad rap long ago.

Pollock goes further in explaining this nineteenth-century appeal to Marcion. Pollock says the appeal was due to "Luther's repudiation of Church institutions . . . , his Pauline opposition of gospel to law and his theological insistence on the tensions between the hidden and revealed God; Schleiermacher's grounding of Christianity in personal faith experience; [and even] Karl Barth's early insistence on the impossibility of speaking of the transcendent God in terms borrowed from the worldly."[7]

These foci weren't necessarily Marcionite, but particularly the Lutheran commitments moved late-nineteenth-century German Protestant theology in that direction. Pollock's words are important for us. Pollock is clear that interpretations of Luther, and even the early Barth, opened the gate to a *possible* denial of the world.[8] Pollock may be overstating the point, but it's a warning we must heed. Luther has been central in our articulation of the mystical pathway

---

7. Pollock, *Franz Rosenzweig's Conversions*, 19.

8. This assertion cannot be made about the late Barth. It really can't be made about Luther either. But I agree with Pollock that some interpretations may have pushed in this direction (more on the Luther side than the Barth side). Barth's *Church Dogmatics* is completely world-affirming, even more world-affirming than it is church-affirming. See, for instance, Barth, *Church Dogmatics* IV/3, trans. Geoffrey Bromiley, ed. T. F. Torrance (Edinburgh: T&T Clark, 1961), 762–95.

of confession and surrender, and so has Denys. Karl Barth's early theology has more than a tangential connection, at least in emphasis, to the negative (apophatic) dispositions of Denys.[9] In turn, our view of transformation inside a Beyonder pathway must stay in (be committed to) the world, seeking transformation in the everyday through revelation. It must always affirm the world—its confession and surrender is a world affirmation. This makes it important that we balance Luther's passivity, the low Rhineland mystical anthropology, Denys's negative theology of God's complete otherness, and the overall confession of the un-magnificence of the self with Rosenzweig's (eventual) affirmation of the redemption and goodness of the world. We must embrace the creator God of Israel, who arrives, speaking in the world (revelation) as the Father of Jesus Christ—not just in the soul of the self.

But we've now gotten ahead of ourselves.

Rosenstock and the Cross

Back on July 7, 1913, Rosenzweig and Rosenstock found themselves on different sides as they discussed *Antikrist mirakler*. Rosenzweig asserted that any redemption comes from escaping the world. Rosenzweig, drawing from the new Marcionites, denied the world. Rosenstock, himself a convert to Christianity, could not deny the world. Rosenstock affirmed that God's redemption was not from the world but for and in the world. They discussed this point until daybreak.[10]

Both Rosenzweig and Rosenstock centered their theology on revelation—though in different ways as the conversation began. God acted in the world; God arrived in history—they both held to something Hebrew in their Christian theologies. But the difference was massive (large enough to keep them talking until dawn). Rosenstock believed that this revelation is for the world. Whatever transformational experience the encounter with revelation has—whatever union is produced by the event of revelation—it calls us deeper into the world to love the world. Encounter and union with the being of God moves us to live with and for the world. Revelation is inseparable from mission (as we'll see, Rosenzweig will help us connect mysticism, transformation, and

9. See Timothy Stanley, *Protestant Metaphysics after Karl Barth and Martin Heidegger* (Eugene, OR: Cascade Books, 2010), 185–200.

10. On Rosenzweig's relationship to Rosenstock, see Mendes-Flohr, *Philosophy of Franz Rosenzweig*, 4–10; and Ernst Akiva Simon, "Rosenzweig: Recollections of a Disciple," in Mendes-Flohr, *Philosophy of Franz Rosenzweig*, 209–11.

mission). However, on July 7, 1913, Rosenzweig believed the opposite. Rosenzweig, like Rosenstock, centered things on a kind of revelation but contended
that revelation is not for the world but instead to rescue us from the world.
God's revelation leads us out of the world, not deeper into it. Revelation is
an exit out of the world.

Yet, with every hour of the night bleeding away, Rosenzweig's position
eroded. By breakfast Rosenstock had convinced Rosenzweig that the world
was to be loved. He had convinced him that revelation is an encounter that
puts us back into the world. To put this in the language we've used throughout
this project, Rosenzweig came to see that a Beyonder mysticism of encounter
with God's revelation does not take us out of the world but moves us deeper
into it. The confession that "at once I knew I was not magnificent" takes us
deeper into the world to minister to the world as God leads us. It moves us to
participate in the world's redemption through its own confessions.

Interestingly, a theology of the cross was ultimately what knocked down
the wall between Rosenzweig's and Rosenstock's positions. For Rosenstock
the cross "was . . . the event [that] holds the key to grasping *history* as a
single redemptive course."[11] The cross is the place where we see God's utter
commitment to the world. The cross reveals that in and through confession
and surrender, history is turned (transformed) and a new way of being in the
world is inaugurated.[12]

This new way of being, Rosenstock believed, is concretely the encounter
of persons in I-You relationships. Revelation and redemption come into the
world inside the everyday encounters in which we call each other by name. The
I-You relationship is a mystical encounter that has its shape in the friendship
of a ministry of confession (naming our impossibilities, opening ourselves to
receive the gift of ministry) and surrender (being with and for each other for
no instrumental purpose, just being bound in relationship, *giving* ministry
to one another).

---

11. Pollock, *Franz Rosenzweig's Conversions*, 66.

12. Pollock continues, "Part and parcel of Rosenstock's later understanding of the orient-
ing power of the Cross was his view that the event symbolized by the Cross holds the key to
grasping history as a single redemptive course, and that the very fact of our shared reckon-
ing of time from that event reveals the way we participate in this single historical course in
concrete, often tacit fashion. But it is at once in the intimate confines of interpersonal speech,
according to Rosenstock, that our orientation in history happens. Rosenstock suggests that
when two people enter into an 'I-You' relation, when they call each other by name, they
both orient themselves within, and help forge actual history." Pollock, *Franz Rosenzweig's
Conversions*, 67.

Into the wee hours of the night, Rosenstock asserted that the cross is *not* a world-denying event but the most world-affirming event to be imagined. To give Rosenstock my own theological language, the cross is the place of the union of God with the world. It is the place where I-You relations become mystical (*Stellvertretung*—or place-sharing—on which both Luther and Bonhoeffer center their theologies, becomes mystical, participating directly in the act and being of God from the place of the cross and the *Stellvertretung*'s ability to concretely bind persons to persons).[13] The cross calls us to embrace the passivity of receiving the name of another who ministers to us, to whom we are also called to minister. The cross is the ultimate act that reveals that God's own being is shaped as the giving and receiving of ministry in and for the world.

On the cross the Second Person of the Trinity *receives* the ministry of the Father, as the Father gives ministry to the Son—all happening in the darkest corner of the world. Through the cross the Son ministers, by the Spirit, to the world. The Son pours out the Spirit of the Son's union with the Father into the world for the sake of the world—to love the world by naming it inside the I-You relation which has no ends but to be with and for.[14] The cross—seen in this cosmic way—is the ultimate picture of world affirmation! The world is pulled into the very being of God through the act of the cross. Redemption is in and for the world, for the cross is God's unveiling deeply in the world. The cross and the incarnation reveal that God loves the world because God loves the world. Period. God gives God's life of resurrection to the world. God moves in the world to be in relationship with the world, to be friends forever (through resurrection) with the world. The world is the object of God's love. The reality that God acts in the world by addressing others by name—the I-You relation of God to humanity and humanity to humanity—reveals that God chooses to love the world not as an object but inside relationships of pure subjects. God embraces the world through I-You relations, by speaking and naming.[15]

13. This assertion that *Stellvertretung* is mystical is more *my* assertion. The heart of this project is to make that case. My contribution to this theology that is personalistic at its core is to connect it mystically to the practice of ministry—to have a view of ministry that is inseparable from the revelation of God's act and being.

14. Keen readers will see that I'm affirming the *Filioque* here. I do lean in this direction doctrinally, but not without sympathy, hesitation, and some desire to embrace the East over the West.

15. This is the heart of Rosenstock's assertions, but it is more my theological construction than his.

Rosenstock tells Rosenzweig that history itself is formed inside the event of such I-You relationships.[16] To again give Rosenstock my theological language, it is this movement into an encounter with the other person in I-You relations of ministry that the mystical and the worldly unite—that we become Beyonders in the everyday, mystics of the concrete, keeping mysticism from becoming a world-hating Gnosticism (which the post–July 1913 Rosenzweig fears).[17] The cross calls me to my neighbor, to see my neighbor as a gift inside passivity, to join their negativity as confession, and surrender to the otherness of their beautiful humanity in the world. The Beyonder disposition of this mystical pathway keeps us in the world, not through heroism or the genius of the self but by the call of the suffering and beauty of the name of our neighbor.[18] I remain in and for the world by the call of the event of ministry. Here mysticism and mission are bound together, becoming one reality, inside God's own ministry and our call to join God's ministry in and through *Stellvertretung* (inside I-You relations). Ministry imagined this way keeps mysticism in the world. It fuses world-embracing with a mystical longing of transformation for the world.

The locale of a mystical encounter with the living God is in and through the receiving and giving of ministry to another. Inside relationships of I-You we share in each other's personhood in beauty and negativity. This is how the soul (the self) and the world become united and not divided in opposition. In his letter, Rosenzweig, making sense of his conversion during the *Leipziger Nachtgespräch*, "points to Rosenstock's long-standing insistence that speech has the power to mediate between soul and world. This means that interpersonal relations of love, rather than forcing the soul to choose

16. Here I'm giving Rosenstock some of my own language. He doesn't use the term "ministry," but this is central to my own project.

17. Pollock explains this fear: "The mystic's desire to preserve the purity of her relation to God is thus a threat to the advance of redemption. The mystic exhibits a one-sided response to the problem of self and world; she identifies wholly with the self in relation to God and denies the world, thereby hindering the process through which self and world are reconciled." Pollock, *Franz Rosenzweig's Conversions*, 172.

18. Placing our feet back in the twenty-first century and inside Christian theology, Rowan Williams says, "The neighbor is our life; to bring connectedness with God to the neighbor is bound up with our own connection with God. The neighbor is our death, communicating to us the death sentence on our attempts to settle who we are in our own terms and to cling to what we reckon as our achievements. 'Death is at work in us and life in you,' as Saint Paul says (2 Cor. 4:12), anticipating . . . the desert. He is writing about how the apostle's suffering and struggle make the life of Christ visible in such a way that others are revived in hope." Williams, *Where God Happens: Discovering Christ in One Another* (Boston: New Seeds, 2007), 35.

between God and others in the world, in fact unite God, world, and the soul within a common history." Pollock continues, "One may suggest, therefore, that the new sense of 'Christian world-activity' which permitted Rosenzweig to take the world seriously once again after the *Leipziger Nachtgespräch*, may have been a sense of just this task of building up a world community out of interpersonal relations of love, inspired by the revelatory 'Word.'"[19]

The Conversion of the Unconversion

Rosenzweig left the house of Ehrenberg's parents converted. He left convinced that the world was to be affirmed and loved. He saw clearly that redemption was *for* the world, not *from* it. He now realized that Christianity (the cross and resurrection) was to take us deeper into the world. Rosenzweig left convinced that the Marcionite theology he'd come with needed to be abandoned completely.

But this is where things get interesting. This is where Rosenzweig becomes the *ba'al teshuvah*, the "master of turning." This is where Rosenzweig breaks his own ground, stepping beyond Rosenstock.

Between July and October, as Rosenzweig did the work of abandoning this Marcionite theology, leaning into a Christianity that saw the cross and the I-You relations as the place of both revelation and redemption of the world, he realized there was no reason to convert. He saw that Judaism served an essential purpose in the redemption of the world. Christianity is moved by its mission of redemption. This mission *should be* noninstrumental, having no other ends than sharing in the lives of others. It is a mission that affirms the world as the place where God ministers to the world inside I-You relationships. Mission is neither imperial (Constantinian) nor bound in market growth; it is personal, bound in relationships of persons in confession and surrender.

Rosenzweig saw that Christianity is fundamentally missional. It seeks to participate directly in the redemption of the world. But this missional impulse can easily become Marcionite. Either it can become Marcionite in the cadence of the late-nineteenth-century hate for the (bourgeois) world and therefore adopt a mission to convert people out of the world, or this Marcionite missional theology can have the cadence of the early twenty-first century. It can see the world as an inert market that can be objectified, contending that all

19. Pollock, *Franz Rosenzweig's Conversions*, 67.

relationships in the world are for the sake of parlaying them into resources and relevance (into objects, smashing the mystical, making transformation a flat reality of growth). Mission becomes a hard or soft church-growth strategy.

Rosenzweig believes this necessary missional impulse of Christianity is ever tenuous. As a matter of fact, Christianity often fails in its mission, confusing its mission of redemption, choosing domination over ministry. The call to participate in the redemption of the world easily slides into triumphalist hatred of the world or obliteration of the I-You relationship (the flattening of the personalist quality of the world). Christianity can easily ignore that it is God who is minister, and God wants union for the sake of union. That redemption comes through a confession and surrender to the otherness we encounter in the world. The cross is our way of being in the world and being for the world.

As a matter of fact, Rosenzweig came to see that when Christianity loses its connection to Judaism, it falls directly into this world denial and world hatred. (This is a prophetic insight that the Nazification of Germany ten years after Rosenzweig's death will confirm.[20]) Rosenzweig came to see that it is Judaism's responsibility to remind Christianity—to demand of Christianity—that it must stay in the world, avoid all forms of Gnosticism, and remain committed to the world.[21] Judaism is to remind Christianity that God acts in the world to save the world. Judaism is to remind Christianity that we share in God's being through personal names in the world. Judaism demands that Christianity abandon its triumphalism and remember that God enters the world to minister to Israel in Egypt. That Israel's own confession and surrender is heard by God.[22] That the God of Israel acts in the world for the sake of the world's redemption. God does this saving of Israel through the I-You, by

20. For a similar argument in relation to Judaism and race/colonization, see Willie James Jennings, *The Christian Imagination: Theology and the Origins of Race* (New Haven: Yale University Press, 2010). Jennings draws on T. F. Torrance here to make this point. Torrance's book *The Mediation of Christ* (Colorado Springs: Helmers & Howard, 1992) is central to Jennings's overall project.

21. This is Rosenzweig's exact point. I am not adding anything to his voice. He thinks Judaism's mission is to keep Christianity from triumphalism. He thinks Christianity's mission is to spread the good news to the whole world. These are fundamentally interconnected and yet distinct realities for him.

22. Pollock says, "By October 1913, however, Rosenzweig had arrived at a critical conclusion. This historical reconciliation of soul and world—the only viable alternative, to Rosenzweig's mind, to Marcionism—although carried out actively by those of the Christian faith, could not be realized unless the Jew remained a Jew. For without the Jewish insistence that redemption is the fulfillment of the creation of the world—and not the escape from it—without the Jewish

giving Israel (Moses) God's name, being their God in the world, calling them to bless the world. Christianity's mission is to witness to this redemption, to participate in God's action of revelation, but never outside or elsewhere than the I-You. Never in a way that makes the world, or the persons in it, into objects of possession. Mission can never destroy or ignore names. Judaism keeps Christianity in the world, seeking encounters with the being of God not through Christianity's heroism or inner genius but through Christianity's confession that God is redeeming the world right at the place of our un-magnificence—in the cross, out of Egypt. Judaism reminds Christianity that it must uphold the I-You as witness and participation in the mystical and eventful encounter with this God in the world of our concrete relationships.[23]

At the Yom Kippur service in October, Rosenzweig turned back to Judaism because he saw its essential place in the redemption of the world. He saw the necessity of Judaism in calling Christianity back to love the world and encounter God through the I-You. The Yom Kippur service was *not* Rosenzweig's conversion but his confirmation that Judaism was essential to the world's salvation.

A short ten months after the Yom Kippur service of confirmation, the (demonic) spirits of August would pull the world into a hell it had never seen before. The world's salvation seemed as far away as could be from the bloody front of World War I. The bleeding trenches were a hell like no other. And Rosenzweig had a front-row seat to it all.[24]

The Star of Redemption

There was no longer an easy strut to the young Rosenzweig. There was no calm confidence. There were no longer nights like the one in his cousin's house. There was no ease to any of it. No comforting quiet, no stillness to

---

insistence that redemption has not yet come, but is still to be realized, no such historical reconciliation of soul and world would be achieved." Pollock, *Franz Rosenzweig's Conversions*, 114.

23. Pollock continues, "In Rosenzweig's letter to Ehrenberg of October 31, 1913, Rosenzweig asserts that the danger that threatens to cause the Christian to forget her task in the world lies in the fact that she is 'sent to all,' and thus might 'lose herself in the universal.' But in a number of later formulations, the explanation Rosenzweig offers suggests that the existence of the Jew serves the vital function of ensuring that Christianity not fall into those Gnostic tendencies from which, apparently, it is never truly immune." Pollock, *Franz Rosenzweig's Conversions*, 109.

24. Paul Mendes-Flohr reminds us that Rosenzweig wrote while fighting on "the Macedonian front, where he served in an antiaircraft unit." Mendes-Flohr, *Philosophy of Franz Rosenzweig*, 147.

fill your mind. The late nights in the trenches were filled with explosions, shouts, and cries of anguish. Rosenzweig was crushed by the torture and death all around him. By 1918 his body was ravaged by the sickness of the trenches. If the mortars and gases didn't get you in this godforsaken war, then infections and viruses would. In autumn of 1918 Rosenzweig lay sick in a hospital bed. In that bed he wrote notes on postcards, mailing them to his mother. His mother kept them in a shoebox in Kassel. When Rosenzweig returned home, those postcards were knitted together into his magnus opus, becoming one of the most important books of the twentieth century, *The Star of Redemption*.

The book, while very difficult, works out the theology that began in the July 7, 1913, conversation. The whole book—even after Rosenzweig had seen the unseeable—is about the importance of remaining in the world, embracing the world, yearning for the world's redemption.[25] It is odd how the peace of the nineteenth century made many hate the world, but the chaos and destruction of World War I (and World War II) turned many back to the world, seeking God not outside the world but directly in it. Han and Denys, thanks to their attention to negativity, would not be surprised. It's right here inside the (Western Christian) world at its most gruesome that Rosenzweig connects Christianity and Judaism. Christianity affirms the world by going into the world to minister to the world—this is its mission. Judaism reminds Christianity again and again that this God it follows into the world is an event of ministry who acts in the world through the naming act of I-You relations. Judaism prods Christianity to embrace the world, encountering the name of God in the world. (Naming God is something Denys longs for in his apophatic approach.) Judaism tells Christianity to seek God always inside the I-You relation.

25. Peter Eli Gordon expands, saying, "What is immediately striking about this notion of redemption is that it does not remove the individual from the world. Rather, it binds man and world more closely to each other but in a specific and self-sustaining fashion . . . so as to realize the 'permanence' of form that all life desires. It is crucial to notice, however, that such a permanence appears within, not beyond time. The terminological distinction underlying this idea of permanence—between existence and life—is one that occurs within the boundaries of temporality. Yet there is admittedly something odd about Rosenzweig's notion of time. The permanence that all life craves is always just arriving. Like Faust's striving, life's satisfaction is never entirely complete. In Rosenzweig's language, it always stands under the sign of the 'not yet' (*noch nicht*). Existence is therefore 'yet finite' and its emergence as wholly living being is always a process that is 'not yet finished.'" Gordon, *Rosenzweig and Heidegger: Between Judaism and German Philosophy* (Berkeley: University California Press, 2003), 194.

Lying in that hospital bed, Rosenzweig takes Rosenstock's theology from July 1913 into the deepest waters, pushing it into new directions. Rosenzweig admits that Rosenstock is his muse. The book Rosenzweig is writing on postcards is interested in connections that bring transformation. These connections have a kind of mystical quality to them (though Rosenzweig is not as directly interested in mysticism as Buber, who wrote his dissertation on Eckhart and had practiced Kabbalism since his childhood). Nevertheless, there is a kind of mystical quality to the connections that Rosenzweig sees (at least inside this project we can call them mystical).

In part 1 of *The Star of Redemption*, Rosenzweig discusses three kinds of being: God, world, and self. Rosenzweig thinks all three must be affirmed. To lose one is to lose the connections (the relations) that bind to the others. It is not possible to love the self without the world and God (something E.Hum and CE mysticisms try—their mysticism is a love for the magnificent self without God and inside a world flattened as a stage for performance). Nor is it possible, Rosenzweig believes, to love God and not the world and the self in it. Rosenzweig shows that to love God outside the world is to deny the God who acts in the world in and through I-You relations. The self must be seen not as a hero or genius but as a being bound in relations. The self is not constituted in its magnificent performances but by the self's I-You relations—we surrender to I-You relations; the I-You relation touches Spirit through the mutual confessions that open us to acts of giving and receiving ministry.[26] It is by being a friend, a brother, a sister, the one who has their being in and through relations with others in the concreteness of the (everyday) world, that we have being. The self cannot be magnificent in itself because the self is not a being solely or singularly constituted. The self has no name except inside relations—we all must surrender to our name. Our name is a testament to how fundamental relations are to us. We don't have a name solely as individuals; our name is a necessity of relations. Names come from and function for relationship.

The self realizes its un-magnificence not when it beats itself for its poor performance but when the self realizes that the self exists only inside of I-You relations. Receiving the gift (passively) of relationships, the self confesses its un-magnificence as a gift. But this confession of un-magnificence inside I-You relations means the self is never abandoned in its confession; instead, love to

26. For more on this, see Pollock, *Franz Rosenzweig's Conversions*, 151–53.

another is affirmed in the self's personhood. All three forms of being (God, world, and self) must remain connected. To overemphasize one to the detriment of the others (as our secular mysticisms do) is to lose the connections we yearn for that give us life and salvation, drawing us into transformation.

But the connections go deeper. In part 2, Rosenzweig articulates how God, world, and self are connected. Part 2 articulates the shape of these necessary relations. Rosenzweig discusses creation, revelation, and redemption. Creation, revelation, and redemption are connected in the same way that God, world, and self are connected. Creation and redemption are not in opposition to revelation, as Marcion claimed. Rather, they are held together when Christianity and Judaism are linked (when all secessionism is denied). In the same way, creation and redemption give coherence (and hermeneutical shape) to revelation.[27] Without creation and redemption, revelation is lost in a vague spiritualism—which again has happened in some of the lanes of E.Hum and CE mysticisms.

Inside these connections of creation and redemption the self encounters revelation, and in doing so, the self is revealed to itself. Recognizing the connections of creation and redemption leads the self to realize that it is a creature in need of salvation. The world is created and good, but it is also wrapped in an impossibility that keeps it from redeeming itself (there is always a longing for the eschatological). This realization gifts the self with its particularity, but this particularity demands confession. The self must confess that it needs a redemption from outside the self that nevertheless meets the self in the world as the revelation of God redeems the self in the world. Redemption comes when the self encounters an inbreaking transcendence in the world of I-You relations. This encounter leads the self to come outside of itself to receive and give ministry. This kind of I-You relation that connects God, world, and self with creation, revelation, and redemption is the Beyonder pathway of confession and surrender.

Rosenzweig draws these two relations of three (God, world, and self; creation, revelation, and redemption) in two triangles (yes, we're back to triangles). Rosenzweig overlays these triangles, articulating how these two

27. The cross, as Luther asserts, becomes the lens or hermeneutic of God's action in the world. The act to redeem us in the cross reveals the shape of revelation in the world. As Eberhard Jüngel has beautifully articulated, the cross is the response to the fall; it is bound to creation itself. It is the reinstating of creation's goodness. See Jüngel, *Justification: The Heart of the Christian Faith* (Edinburgh: T&T Clark, 2001), 111–15.

triangles connect with and feed each other. He connects the two triangles by flipping one of them on its head. They become a star. Rosenzweig calls this "the star of redemption." The star can be placed on top of the triangle we developed in chapters 5 and 6. The star is the shape of a Beyonder mystical pathway that stays in (and affirms) the world. It is the shape of transformation that attends completely to divine action.

The star becomes a way to imagine a Beyonder mystical pathway of confession and surrender that fully and completely is in and for the world—never abandoning the Protestant commitment to the everyday. The star is a way of recognizing that mysticism—our encounters with transformation—is inseparable from our everyday encounters of life and suffering inside the beauty of our I-You relations.

These I-You relations are mystical as they lead us to surrender to the fact that we are creatures in need of redemption who find this redemption in the revelation of God's own being in the life and death of Jesus Christ. This Jesus Christ calls us to confess our suffering and negativity to find him ministering new life to the world, to our own un-magnificent self. Receiving this ministry as a mystical encounter calls us *not* out of but into the world, to pray with the world as our mission of mysticism.[28]

28. Rosenzweig says beautifully, "To ask, to pray, is the most human of acts. Even man's silence may entreat; and mute nature acquires speech when it supplicates—as in the case of the silent eyes of an animal. Prayer awakens the man in man. A child demands with his first word. And the first word from him who awakens from the slumber of childhood is also a request, a

This transformation is in the shape of the cross. It is this cross-shaped transformation that pastors and ministers must seek to form their people into. This is the recovery of an inbreaking transcendence that invites the self not to perform but to receive the encounter of divine action and the blessings of I-You relations. The transformation we seek in late modernity draws us into the being of God. The mystical is in the world in the shape of Jesus Christ, who is in and for the world, calling us by name. This kind of transformation must shape the imaginations of pastors and ministry.

———————

We left for Hawaii with a heavy sadness—Maisy had been carrying a burden, but both Kara and I were as well. As we awoke the first morning in Kauai, we both wondered, "How could the world be without Jen in it?" This trip represented the end of something significant for our church.

Five months into the pandemic, in August 2020, Jen, a young mom in our congregation, was diagnosed with cancer. She had a young daughter she loved and adored. The shock of the illness was heavy and frightening for both her and her husband Brian. When Jen told Kara the diagnosis, she kept repeating, "I don't want to die. I don't want to die."

Every night over Zoom, Kara and Lisa (our associate pastor) did morning and evening prayer with Jen and Brian. It was the rhythm of our days for almost two years, Kara praying at 8 a.m. and then again at 7 p.m. Our whole family was shaped around the practice, but even more, around the confession and surrender of Jen's journey. Kara, in a real sense, shaped the whole congregation's life around praying for Jen, and for the many more that became sick and faced death over the course of the pandemic. Holding Jen in prayer, opening a space for her journey within each of our own journeys, knit our lives together as a church. We all surrendered and confessed our need, knowing our own un-magnificence, as we longed for and wrestled with the beyond. Every Sunday night at 7 p.m., the whole church was invited to log on to pray with and for Jen, but also to just come and confess our frail humanity and longing for something beyond.

It was almost two years of praying for Jen, of seeking the beyond with Jen, when word came that her fight was coming to an end. She was slipping

———————

prayer." Rosenzweig, *Understanding the Sick and the Healthy: A View of World, Man, and God* (Cambridge, MA: Harvard University Press, 1999), 98.

away. Just hours before we boarded our flight, Kara visited Jen in hospice, praying with her for the last time, saying goodbye as Jen slipped in and out of consciousness. Kara had promised Jen that the community, our church, would *not* allow Jen to go without our awareness, without our participation, without our prayer. We would be with her as she left this world and slid into the waiting arms of the God who was redeeming this world where mothers leave their five-year-olds and husbands lose their soulmates. The whole church was ready. When Jen's hour came we all, no matter where we were, would pause, breathe, grieve, and pray Jen into the beyond.

That time came on our first morning in Kauai. Our family received word that the time was coming soon. Jen was going. We made our way to a rocky, hidden beach. Standing in the shallow water, we stopped, held hands, looking into the majesty of the Pacific, and called on our God, in confession and surrender, to lead Jen beyond. We called God to redeem this world from this broken journey Jen and all of us were on, so that we might live forever and finally in God's goodness. All of us, in our church, at the same hour, lifted our broken hearts to God and confessed how deeply it hurt to lose Jen and how much we longed for the transformation that would bring life out of death. As we mixed our own prayers of grief and loss with a sense of releasing Jen from the bounds of this limited life into the eternal transcendent love of God, wherever we were, we were together a community in surrender and confession transformed as we sought the beyond. On that beach made by a million years of crashing surf, with Jen leaving, at once we knew we were not magnificent, and therefore we surrendered to the magnificence of the God of Israel.

INDEX